....

NAME

....

DATE OF BIRTH   **TIME OF BIRTH**

....

LOCATION OF BIRTH

....

MY SUN SIGN

....

MY MOON SIGN

....

MY RISING SIGN

COSMOPOLITAN

BEDSIDE ASTROLOGER

The Ultimate Guide to Your Star Power

BY AURORA TOWER WITH LAURA BROUNSTEIN

HEARSTBOOKS

NEW YORK

CONTENTS

CHAPTER 1

THE ZODIAC SIGNS

CHAPTER 2

ROMANCE & SEX

CHAPTER 3

HOW TO READ YOUR HOROSCOPE

FOREWORD

I LOVE TO CHECK OUT MY HORO-SCOPE.

Still, before I met Cosmo's astrologer, Aurora Tower, I wasn't convinced that astrology had much to do with Cosmo's mission: to give young, modern women all the inspiration, tools, and ideas to take the world by storm. But Aurora explained to me how, as an astrologer, she actually puts together her monthly forecasts. It was fascinating. She's not the kind of person you'd ever find hunched over a crystal ball, tossing back her long scarf. She's a modern woman who graduated from Brown University, and she treats astrology like a huge mathematical puzzle. She brings a serious and exciting approach that has resulted in her doing astrological readings for many famous people—something she keeps irritatingly private. Believe me, I've tried to get it out of her! But more important than gossip, she taught me things beyond horoscopes, such as what a rising sign and a moon sign can tell you, and her descriptions of my character based on my birth date and time seemed almost eerily accurate.

We are thrilled to have her insight in the pages of Cosmo every month and in this groundbreaking book. Working in tandem with editor Laura Brounstein, Aurora created a gorgeous, useful, and comprehensive modern guide to astrology. The book reveals how you can use your sign's strengths to your advantage and not be held back by potential weaknesses. Ultimately, your future is in your own hands, but astrology can help you anticipate when to be open to opportunities, when to keep logic at the forefront of your decision making, and when to follow your heart. And I think you'll agree with me that the Sexscopes guide will be deeply important for all of us as well!

Cosmopolitan Bedside Astrologer: The Ultimate Guide to Your Star Power is an invaluable tool in your journey to connecting with the universe, trusting yourself, and living your biggest life. So settle in, read on, takes notes, and get ready for a powerful year ahead!

—JOANNA COLES

HOW TO TAP INTO YOUR
STAR POWER

WHY AM I THE WAY I AM?

What career will I thrive in? How will I find true love? When is the right time to make a significant change in my life? These are some of the questions we can answer with astrology. We've all known our zodiac signs forever and eagerly flip to the Cosmo Horoscope each month for inspiration and entertainment. Which day will I feel sexiest? Is there any insight I can gain from knowing my crush's sign? Horoscopes help us get a sense of our environment at a particular time and to better understand ourselves and the people we care about. And they are really fun to read! But astrology is even more fun and insightful when we scratch beneath the surface, go a little deeper and learn to use it as a tool that can help us in all aspects of our lives.

For example, have you ever wondered why you react differently in certain situations than friends who have the same sign as you do? It's because there are signs other than our sun sign—specifically our moon sign and rising sign—that are just as important and influential in our personalities. Learning about these other two signs, and their role in our lives, helps us unlock and decode other parts of ourselves.

Everyone has a unique combination of sun, moon, and rising signs, based on how the stars and planets were aligned at the exact time of birth. Your moon sign and rising sign shape the way you express your sun sign. You already know your sun sign; it's the sign you've always associated yourself with, such as Taurus or Virgo. But once you determine what your moon and rising sign are as well, you will gain a deeper understanding of the different layers of your personality. For example, when you know that you are a Pisces with a Cancer moon sign and Capricorn rising sign, you can use that information to help you realize your dreams and get the most out of every day!

Here's the super simple formula:
YOUR SUN SIGN = What you want.
YOUR MOON SIGN = What you need.
YOUR RISING SIGN = How you get what you want and need.

Your Sun Sign

Our sun sign is the zodiac sign that we look for in horoscopes. It's your answer to the classic "What's your sign?" question. Since the sun stays in each sign for about 30 days, people born in early July have a Cancer sun sign and people born in early August have a Leo sun sign, etc. With the sun being the center of our solar system, the sun sign provides essential insight into who we are at our core. The sun sign indicates our natural gifts and abilities and what we most want to do, express, and achieve in life.

Your Moon Sign

The moon changes signs about every three days based on the moon's position relative to the earth. So even though everyone born in early October has a Libra sun sign, depending on the day and year of their birth, they will have different moon signs. The moon sign indicates our emotional nature and deepest needs, especially as related to relationships. In order to better understand what makes us feel safe, loved, and nurtured, we look to the moon sign. For example, if Libra is your sun sign but Pisces is your moon sign, you may want to analyze every issue, but you may also need to sometimes let whimsy rule your actions.

Your Rising Sign

The rising sign (also called the ascendant) is the sign that was visible on the eastern horizon at the time you were born. Every zodiac sign rises on the eastern horizon at some point every day so depending on what time of day you were born, any sign could be your rising sign. For example, a Scorpio can have a rising Aquarius sign. The rising sign indicates our outer personality and the skills and techniques we use to get what we want and need. It is like our outermost shell and we often embody the characteristics of our rising sign as we go about our daily lives.

When you combine your sun sign, your moon sign, and your rising sign, you will gain a much deeper understanding of what you truly want and need, and—best of all—how to get it! *To find out your moon sign and rising sign, flip to the Ephemeris, starting on page 180.* Follow the instructions to find your signs. Then come back to Chapter 1, The Zodiac Signs, on page 12 and read the sections related to those signs as well as the section for your sun sign.

And just for fun, on page 178, we have added two work-book style pages where you can record the birth info and the signs of your family, friends, and other important people in your life. Just as you'll learn so much more about yourself from exploring the different facets of your personality, likewise, your understanding of others will be strengthened by recognizing their core wants and needs as well.

In each of the zodiac sign sections in Chapter 1, we explore love, style, travel, and education as well as many other areas of life to describe preferences that feel right and natural for you. We differentiate how each of the signs expresses itself depending on whether it is your sun sign, your moon sign, or your rising sign. You will now have three times as much information about what makes you tick!

Everything Else You Need to Know

In Chapter 2 on page 134, we dive into the world of guys, romance, and sex. Have you seen references to elements and modalities and wondered what they were all about? And what astrology can tell us about our perfect match? We will explain all that and more here. And if it is extra insight about guys you're after, then flip straight to our Definitive Guy Guide on page 146 to find out everything you need to know about turn-ons and dream dates for each of the zodiac guys!

In Chapter 3 on page 160, we will explain more about how astrology works and help you decode your daily and monthly horoscopes. If you have ever wondered what the heck a trine is and why it matters anyway, then this is the section for you. We explain the lunar cycle and eclipses and give you some survival tips and tricks for that least favorite of celestial events, Mercury retrograde.

But before we get started, let's get back to the basics and take a quick look at astrology and its meaning and purpose in our lives.

What Is Astrology, Really?

Astrology is all about patterns and cycles.

We are all familiar with some basic astrology—we all know that the sun rises every morning and sets every evening. This is the most basic of all patterns and cycles that rule our daily lives. Beyond this, we also know that the seasons change throughout the course of the year. Without these changes (day to night, summer to winter), life on earth would cease to exist. That is because each of these different periods has their purpose. At night, we must sleep; during the day, we must rise and interact with others (to shine!). During the summer, we harvest the bounty of the earth and during the winter, we allow ourselves— and our environment—to rest and replenish.

These are some of the visible surface-level patterns and cycles that we can observe on earth. Yet there are many more cycles and patterns happening around us that aren't quite as obvious. But that does not make them any less real or important! It is these cycles that astrologers keep track of and describe. When a planet is in a certain sign or position, it is fulfilling a certain purpose and will act a certain way. That position will impact our lives

just as much as the fact that it is nighttime will impact the energy and environment around us, albeit in a more opaque way.

Humans have been recording the movements of the planets since they first gazed into the night sky. Ancient Babylonian, Egyptian, and Greek civilizations all employed some form of astrology in their quest to understand the world. Our interconnection with nature and the universe was taken for granted for millennia, but in our modern society, people are just now rediscovering the human connection to the greater universe.

Just as we are likely to wear different clothes in July than we do in January, horoscopes give us a sense of the greater celestial weather that is happening at any given time so we can "clothe" ourselves appropriately. Astrology also believes that someone who was born in July will have a different experi-

ence of the energy in July than someone who was born in January. Think of this as the difference between being a "local" versus a "visitor" in a certain city or country. Neither experience is inherently good or bad, just different in terms of comfort and familiarity. Thus, daily, weekly, and monthly horoscopes reflect how the energy of a given period will affect each of the signs in a different way.

Your Journey Through the Stars

This book is designed to be a visual journey through the zodiac and a personal road map for achieving your most intimate needs and wants. So now that you have a grasp of the background of astrology, and how there is much more to explore than just your sun sign, you are ready to put the heavens to work for you!

Congratulations! You are one step closer to understanding and achieving your desires.

1

THE ZODIAC SIGNS

ARIES

MARCH 21

— *through* —

APRIL 19

03.21–04.19

ARIES

ELEMENT	MODALITY	RULING PLANET	SYMBOL	COLOR
Fire	*Cardinal*	*Mars*	*The Ram*	*Red*

You are the universe's original gold medal winner! You have a thirst for life that is contagious, and you are always ready to take on new challenges and adventures. Boredom and routine are your least favorite things and you ward them off by sprinkling your daily life with small doses of fun and spontaneity. Never one to sit around if you can help it, you enthusiastically go from one activity to the next, getting a rush from every new experience or relationship. Not having companions for these escapades doesn't hold you back at all; you're perfectly happy to pursue your interests on your own when none of your friends are game. In fact, you'd rather go off on your own than be forced to do anything you're not personally excited about or interested in. You can be quite rebellious if others are cramping your style or trying to overmanage your time.

Not to overstate the obvious, but you like to win! You can be so competitive, sometimes, you're not even sure what game you're playing; you just know you're going to rule it. The better you are at setting goals for yourself and focusing on your own best outcome, the less time you'll waste tangling with others and being annoyed. When something doesn't go your way, you can be short-tempered. Fortunately, this usually blows over just as quickly, because you're already on to the next thing. Your independent spirit and disdain for the limitations of others make you an innovative thinker and even a visionary. When you care about something, you're a true believer and won't let anything— or anyone—get in your way.

Once something captures your imagination or heart, you jump in enthusiastically. And while your burst of passion helps you get projects off the ground, you can easily become bored with the more mundane details and follow-up. Learning how to delegate effectively and to extricate yourself from situations gracefully, so that there are no hard feelings, will keep your relationships in smooth running order. You are usually quick to forgive and forget when someone steps on your toes—unless he or she has truly been disloyal to you. When that happens, you can hold a grudge. Cutting certain people out of your life may be for the best, and once you do, you can quickly move on. Staying busy and active is very important for you, as is finding groups and organizations with like-minded people. Once you have found your passions and positive channels for your endless energy, you are unstoppable!

STELLAR GIFTS
You know what you want and you know how to go for it.

BLIND SPOTS
Your take-charge attitude can leave others in the dust.

FASHION FAVES
Always on the go, you favor comfortable sporty styles in warm, rich colors.

INDULGENCE
There is a slight chance that you have enjoyed the occasional post-victory gloat. Slight.

SEDUCTION STYLE
Getting what you want is your spe-cialty. And once you've landed your prize, you don't like to come up for air either!

Image

Bright, alert, and quick on your feet, you're always ready to spring into action, and your clothes have to be comfortable and easy. You like to look good and put effort into your style, but that comes second to functionality, so you may prefer an active, tomboy look. Your tendency toward constant motion means you stay in shape easily and are usually found out on the go. You are likely to have balanced facial features and a slim, athletic build.

Money

You have a knack for managing money and know the difference between investment pieces and inexpensive whims. You like to put your money into art and stable investments, rather than pie-in-the-sky fantasies. But your eye for quality means you can have quite luxurious tastes! Imitations or fakes are so not for you. Gorgeous flowers, fine foods, and objects made from exquisite materials draw your attention. But you know how to budget your resources and rarely overspend on impulse buys.

Education

You are curious about lots of different things and enjoy dabbling in all the areas that interest you. But you don't necessarily love to commit yourself for the long haul, so one week, African dance could be your passion, and the next week, you are on to Russian lit! Reading and writing are both great outlets for you, so spend time cultivating these hobbies. Getting involved in many different things will always appeal to you, but be realistic with yourself and others about how much time you're willing to commit.

Home Life

Even though you're always raring to go, having a cozy nest to come home to is important to you. Welcoming, traditional styles appeal to you more than anything too modern or edgy, and the kitchen is often at the heart of your home. You care about creating an environment where people feel happy and taken care of, and you are known as being fiercely loyal and protective of those in your inner circle.

Fun

"Go big or stay home" tends to be your motto, so when you decide it's time for fun, not much can get in your way. Embarking on extravagant adventures, and mixing in a hefty dose of glamour, thrills you. You treasure making memories you will have forever. You love family, so gatherings with loved ones of all ages, especially where your own inner child can connect with little ones, can be particularly meaningful. Your competitive nature gives you an edge when it comes to winning at games, but don't spend too much time at the casino!

Health

You are a naturally active person who likes to spend time in the great outdoors. As far as working up a sweat goes, you prefer to do it the old-fashioned way—with a jog or a hike or a game of soccer with friends. Gimmicky exercise fads rarely interest you. Likewise, as far as your diet is concerned, you stay healthy with fresh ingredients and lots of fruits and vegetables, rather than fussy or complicated diets.

Relationships

You're quite a romantic at heart. Chivalry and old-fashioned manners attract you, as does honesty and a palpable sexual connection. Despite having many suitors, you are happy to dismiss the ones who don't ignite a certain spark. But once your attention has been won, you jump in headfirst and can rush into love. Your best relationships, personally and professionally, are ones where you have open and diplomatic lines of communication and you are both getting your needs met.

Intimacy

As a hot-blooded person, you feel things intensely. Once someone you care about scratches beneath the surface, you can be self-protective and deliberate about what you reveal and to whom. Opening up the deepest parts of yourself to others can be a struggle for you, but a journey that you are willing to embark on with people you truly trust. Strong female friends and confidantes are an important part of your life.

"IF YOU DON'T LIKE SOMETHING, CHANGE IT. IF YOU CAN'T CHANGE IT, CHANGE YOUR ATTITUDE."

—MAYA ANGELOU

Travel

You love to travel and explore different cultures. You are curious about how people live in other parts of the world and prefer to get your hands dirty and live like the locals rather than cloister yourself away at isolated resorts. Your love of adventure also comes out when you are traveling, and the rush of a once-in-a-lifetime experience is hard for you to resist. A safari or ski vacation captures your imagination and boundless energy. So get exploring and challenge yourself to get as many stamps in your passport as possible!

Career

Whatever profession you choose, you don't shy away from challenges and are practical and strategic when it comes to working toward advancement. You know who are the important people to impress, and you spend your time slowly sowing the seeds for your success. You keep your eyes on the prize and maintain a long-term perspective about your goals. You are a natural at networking and know how to maintain and leverage a solid network of business contacts.

Friends

Having a strong, wide, and varied group of friends is important to you. You are very loyal, but you also believe in giving people space to do their own thing. Following your own path is important to you, so you're naturally non-judgmental about your friends' quirks and varying outlooks. Staying in touch online helps you keep up with one another on the go. You can make great and lasting connections with the people you meet through teams, clubs, or other activities that matter to you.

Privacy

Everyone sees you out and about, but what they may not realize is how much you love your private time! A long soak in the bathtub, listening to your favorite tunes, and just getting lost daydreaming are some of your favorite relaxation activities. You are also very creative and if you don't use your artistic side at work, carving out time to paint or indulge in your imagination is important. The world you create for yourself at home is so restful and reassuring, you might want to luxuriate in your bubble bath for days at a time. Savor your solitude, but know when it's time to get back to the real world!

SUN SIGN

WHAT YOU WANT: Quite simply, you want to be free to do whatever you want! You are one of the most independent people in the zodiac and generally don't like being told what to do or how to live your life. You are very driven and motivated to succeed, but your goals need to come from within, rather than being imposed on you. You are a curious person and when something sparks your interest, you like to follow the lead until it bores you and then you are off on a new lead!

When it comes to your family and projects that you have wholeheartedly committed to, you are as loyal and protective as they come. You assume responsibility naturally and will work hard to ensure that everyone is okay and being taken care of. If you encounter injustice, you'll fight to right wrongs and make sure the underdog is given a fair shot. You are a fiery person and can sometimes view life as a battle. There is nothing wrong with that, except you need to define your own code of conduct, so you don't run anyone over (and cause them and yourself pain) as you reach for your goals.

Just as you want to be free to do what you want, you also accord others the same freedom. You rarely impose constrictive rules on the people in your life, but you don't hold back either when you are disappointed or frustrated. Managing your expectations and your temper is a good lesson for you. Staying busy is important, and you should always have a few goals or projects you are working on or you'll become restless and cranky. Your confidence makes you a beacon of light for many people and you are a natural and inspiring leader.

> "I THINK THAT IT IS VERY IMPORTANT IF YOU KNOW WHAT YOU WANT, UNDERSTAND WHERE YOU ARE HEADING TOWARD, AND TRY YOUR BEST TO GET IT. IT IS ONLY WHEN WE USE OUR HEARTS TO DO IT AND FALL IN LOVE WITH WHAT WE ARE DOING, THEN CAN WE REALLY GET REAL DETERMINATION."

—EMMA WATSON

MOON SIGN

WHAT YOU NEED: You need to have freedom and spontaneity in your life. You can become frustrated and impatient if you feel you are being restricted in any way, and this can cause you to act out or even run away! Excitement and novel experiences are very important for you. Falling in love is something that stirs your heart, but you prefer the hot and heavy early days and can feel the itch to move on after boredom and routine set in. For this reason, you are well suited to other fiery-type personalities, where there is lots of passion between you when you are together, but you also give each other room to grow and spend time apart.

Often a visionary, you are a natural pioneer and are fearless when it comes to getting involved in projects that you believe in. It is here where your aptitude for commitment shines, because you will be tenacious about seeing things through till the end. You dislike inequality and injustice, so charities or humanitarian organizations provide a perfect outlet for your energy and determination.

Your need for new and different experiences can lead you down some dead ends until you realize that you should do more due diligence before charging forward. Figuring out which projects and people are worth your enthusiasm will be an ongoing lesson for you. Learning how to pace yourself will help you feel less restless and will also lead you toward the right type of exciting adventures!

IF ARIES IS YOUR

RISING SIGN

HOW YOU GET WHAT YOU WANT AND NEED: Your open-minded and curious attitude makes you likable and easygoing. You have a "try anything once" perspective on life, which means that people warm up to you quickly and are eager to share their ideas and dreams with you. Being present in the moment and having fun with life will continuously open new doors and possibilities for you.

Your spontaneous and positive approach to life means you sometimes find yourself having a blast in the most unexpected places with the most unexpected people! Your easy charm and lack of agenda turn strangers you encounter along the way into supporters and allies, eager to help you with your goals and desires. When you get excited about something, your enthusiasm is contagious! But your natural exuberance can feel to some like you're coming on too strong, so take the time to read others' signals and be diplomatic. The better you get at pacing yourself and being strategic about moving forward with people and projects, the more successful and satisfied you'll be.

You draw strength from staying active and spending time outside. You can be competitive, and it's important for you to have a positive outlet for your energy. Playing team sports and aligning yourself with groups and associations with similar interests is both fun and buoying for you. If you feel your competitive side taking over, remember that you have unique goals and perspectives and your only real competition is yourself!

> "SOMETIMES IN LIFE YOU DON'T ALWAYS FEEL LIKE A WINNER, BUT THAT DOESN'T MEAN YOU'RE NOT A WINNER—YOU WANT TO BE LIKE YOURSELF."
>
> —LADY GAGA

TAURUS

APRIL 20

— *through* —

MAY 21

04.20–05.21

TAURUS

ELEMENT	MODALITY	RULING PLANET	SYMBOL	COLORS
Earth	*Fixed*	*Venus*	*The Bull*	*Pink, Cream, Sea foam*

Y ou are strong and steady without ever losing your dignified, feminine air. Deeply in touch with your body and the world of the five senses that surrounds you, you navigate your way through life based on a desire to create and cultivate your own personal magical world. Keenly aware of your own preferences, you steer clear of things that displease you and focus on attracting things you enjoy and maximizing time with people who bring you pleasure. This practical approach to life helps you to use your natural instincts and sensory perceptions for maximum benefit. Indeed, you can be quite determined and strategic once you set you mind to something, leading to your notoriously stubborn streak.

Yet you can also be as tender and hopeful as a fresh flower in the spring. You possess an extraordinary amount of patience with people and situations that might make others run for the hills, and your loyalty and dedication are legendary. You want to believe the best about people and the world, and you look for ways to improve and beautify your surroundings. Your eye for beauty and artistry are innate, and you are likely to possess some amount of creative talent, either in music, performing, visual arts, or cooking. You can truly get lost inside of your craft and leave all other cares and concerns behind.

As a very physical person, it is important for you to maintain your health through diet, exercise, and calming practices such as yoga and meditation. Daily physical activity nourishes you. You are also deeply connected to nature and spending time outdoors; either taking walks or lying in the grass will rejuvenate you in many ways. Escaping the pace of hectic city life for serenity and beautiful scenery is your idea of bliss. With such strong preferences, you can sometimes get stuck inside your own routine or way of viewing things and have trouble empathizing with others whose path may be more meandering. Make it a priority to always leave yourself open to different perspectives and positive change.

STELLAR GIFTS
A true friend, you are loyal and patient to the core.

BLIND SPOTS
You can be single-minded and resistant to change.

FASHION FAVES
Cashmere, silk: You go wild for soft, luxe materials.

INDULGENCE
You would rather pay top dollar for the best than cut corners.

SEDUCTION STYLE
Wine, flowers, candles, music…you love a romantic atmosphere! And you like to take your time. Warming up with a massage and a hot bath will get you in the mood for a decadent marathon between the sheets.

Image

You know what you like and stick with it, cultivating a kind of uniform in your wardrobe and rarely deviating. Fine fabrics, feminine lines, and pretty colors often appeal to you. Maintaining your style becomes part of the consistency that others grow to expect from you. You tend to be strong and well-proportioned, with pronounced and alluring features. You dislike rushing and hurrying and instead you maintain a stately and calm presence that pacifies more frazzled types around you. Yet your tenacity shines through when you have a set purpose or goal.

Money

You are very financially savvy. And you enjoy having a clear and long-term savings strategy. That said, you can also be charmingly whimsical and enjoy spontaneous fun with your friends and small guilty pleasures. But you know what you can afford and keep yourself in check. Holidays are at the top of your list of splurges, as are educational opportunities that interest you, especially in the arts. You have a knack for making good investments, whether it is playing the stock market or discovering an up-and-coming-artist.

Education

How you feel about school depends on the day or the week! Sometimes, you are in a positive groove and other times, you are loath to get up and go to school, wanting to do almost anything else. Over time, as you have more control of the subjects that you take, you will feel more content. Sign up for as many PE and arts classes as you can to balance out all the classroom learning. You will make lifelong friends in school and your relationships with them are as important as the educational aspects of school life.

Home Life

You often come from a close-knit clan. Time together may be a big priority and you are encouraged to shine. The more time your family spends cultivating your unique interests the better. If you aren't close, it could be because your parents prioritize a glamorous or fun-centric lifestyle over personal intimacy. Or they may set firm expectations, assuming that you will follow in their footsteps. As you get older, your desire to have a family of your own becomes very strong, but you may be picky when it comes to making a commitment. Once you do settle down, you enjoy creating a cohesive magical world for your children.

Fun

Even if you go through a wild phase at some point, you tend to become moderate when it comes to partying. You enjoy taking care of yourself, and as health becomes more of a focus, time spent taking hikes or hanging out at the beach with your friends takes precedence over epic nights out. One of your great delights in life is finding ways to truly make a difference. Charity work, helping others, and giving back all bring you joy, and you like doing small, considerate things for people you love. And then, of course, having them return the favor!

Health

It's all about moderation when it comes to your health. Being so set in your ways, you can sometimes overdo it with a certain diet or exercise routine. Ultimately, you need to come back into balance and simply practice common sense. Great food is one of your biggest joys in life and you may find yourself wanting to overindulge. Not limiting your options will help you feel good about occasional indulgences, as will sticking to a consistent fitness schedule. Then you can have fun and enjoy yourself when you are satisfying your sweet tooth!

Relationships

Passion and intensity are of paramount importance to you in your relationships. Unless a fire inside you is lit, you can hardly be bothered to make an effort. You have many suitors who are attracted to your calm and careful ways, and the ones who spark you will bring out your passionate side. You can become attached to the object of your affection and seek a constant togetherness, which one or both of you may eventually find tiring. Giving each other space will keep the flames hot. In your work relationships, you also seek kindred spirits with whom you can share a strong and long-lasting bond.

Intimacy

Being so in touch with your body, you love exploring sensual pleasure in its many forms and are up for a healthy dose of sexual experimentation. Your YOLO attitude will bring you varied experiences in this part of your life that will only help you in further refining your preferences. You also care about having a spiritual bond with the people you are most intimate with and enjoy discussing your beliefs about the world. When you see eye to eye about these subjects, you become even more closely bonded.

SEX ISN'T JUST FIRE AND HEAT; IT'S NATURAL BEAUTY."

—JANET JACKSON

Travel

You bring your refined senses with you when you travel. You tend to prefer tried-and-true destinations that have services (and food!) you can depend on, rather than winging it at new or unknown locations. Your love of nature is also a priority for you when you travel, so places in gorgeous settings where you can bask in the great outdoors are also high on your list. Sometimes you will choose a remote location where you can go off the grid for a while, but otherwise, you tend to prefer places where you love the food and you can have fun with your friends.

Career

Over the course of your career, you refine your specialty until you have quite a niche expertise. Whether this is in the realm of the arts, technology, the media, or any other field, you know how to bring out your own best qualities and find a job that complements your skills and interests. Through this process of refinement and specialization, you may end up being quite an innovator in your chosen profession. Your career is an area where you are not bound by tradition and instead enjoy doing things in new and original ways. Following your instincts and passion will set you on your own unique path.

Friends

Your closest friendships are the ones where you feel like you don't have to make a big effort. You are simply connected to one another in the most magical and comforting ways. You cherish these types of soul-level relationships and together you can get lost for hours simply listening to music, relaxing, and daydreaming. You are loyal to the people you care about and may idealize your close friends. You get hurt when you are disappointed or let down by those you trust. It will take a while for your confidence to be regained, if you don't just let their friendship slip away.

Privacy

You cherish your private time and don't like others to impose expectations or requests of you when you are in your zone. Rather, you use this time to relax and ponder your next steps. You are quite a bit more ambitious than your calm and consistent demeanor reveals. Since you have such great success reaching your goals once you focus, you have an innate understanding that you can do just about anything you set your mind to. You are also competitive and hate to lose, so you choose what you focus on carefully, aiming for targets you know you can reach. Your confidence grows with every victory.

IF TAURUS IS YOUR

SUN SIGN

WHAT YOU WANT: You want to create your own mini-world and infuse it with the things and experiences you enjoy. As such, you tend to exercise a lot of control over your environment, which can lead others to find you stubborn. Your stubbornness does not necessarily stem from a desire to control others, but instead it is rooted in your heightened senses and desire to avoid things you dislike. In extreme cases, you will sort experiences and people into yes vs. no categories and once you assign these labels, you are very hesitant to change the designation. This can lead to complications when people you like show less- than-desirable qualities, yet you are unwilling to reassess the relationship. You can then cling to things or people when they should instead become part of your past.

Your hesitancy about change comes from a fear that shifting things will destabilize you and the environment you have so carefully and purposefully cultivated for yourself. Growth will come when you realize that pruning dead flowers aids the health of the whole garden, rather than imagining change as pulling a thread that will unravel the whole sweater. It will also help you to realize that your beautiful, artistic dedication to creating a life of your own imagining can only benefit from being reassessed and reimagined from time to time. If you stay open to your needs and desires adapting and growing, then transitions can become experiences that you relish and enjoy, rather than fear.

Once you strike the right balance between consistency and change, your life becomes truly spectacular. The magical paradise you imagine, where all your five senses are engaged in the most wonderful ways, is well within your reach. When you stop resisting change, you can use all of your creative energy in gaining what you truly want, which is to enjoy as many beautiful, pleasurable things in life as possible. Then indulging your senses, spending time in nature, and taking care of your loved ones take on a whole new level of fun.

> **THE BEST THING TO HOLD ONTO IN LIFE IS EACH OTHER."**
>
> —AUDREY HEPBURN

MOON SIGN

WHAT YOU NEED: You need consistency and stability in your life. You also have high standards and strong aesthetic tastes and seek to have as many pleasurable and enjoyable experiences as possible. Your desire for sensual and tactile delights can lead you down the road of love and lust quite easily. You may also overindulge when it comes to food and treats since you gain a huge amount of satisfaction from delicious things. Yet, because you are quite stubborn and determined, you may just as easily swing in the other direction and become quite fixated on a certain health or diet regimen. Finding a balance in this area will be good for you, rather than jostling between extremes.

Your innate need for stability makes you a very dedicated and unwavering partner. You are reliable and relish the happiness that comes from stable, long-term relationships. You are very patient with your loved ones and derive a lot of joy from building a life together. When things aren't working out the way that you want, you have difficulty knowing whether or not you should pull the plug. But once something is past the point of no return, you are able to move on.

With very strong creative senses, you may have talent in the arts. Spending time cultivating your creative side will bring you rich rewards. You are financially savvy, and with your eye for detail and fine taste, you are also very attracted to beautiful things. This can lead you down a path toward materialism and a desire to build a collection of objects or prized possessions. As long as you are working within your budget, there is no problem with this. But if you are spending above your means, you will regret it at a later date. Likewise, if you are collecting items because you feel lonely or to show off to others, they may quickly lose their luster. You are at your best when your desire for beauty and consistency is augmented by quiet time enjoying nature and life's small pleasures.

IF TAURUS IS YOUR

RISING SIGN

HOW YOU GET WHAT YOU WANT AND NEED: You are steady and reliable, which helps you to achieve all of your needs and wants. Once you set your mind to something, there is little that can get in your way. You are capable of maintaining focus and direction for long periods of time and are unwavering in your commitment to your priorities. Failing to reach your goals or being thwarted can be a tough blow for you. You are also a bit competitive and dislike losing. Sometimes it takes you a while to recover from a situation that has disappointed you, and in these cases, you can become stuck. But once you have set your sights on a new goal, you will move on and pour your energy exclusively into that.

Since you are so consistent and determined, others have faith in your ability to get things done. So whatever your priorities may be, you can easily win other people over to helping you achieve your aims. Yet your determination can border on fanaticism and you can be very stubborn and unwilling to listen to differing perspectives. Practicing patience and cultivating good listening skills will help you even more. You like to move at your own pace, whatever that may be, and can become frustrated when others are rushing you or slowing you down. You know where you are going, and you know how and when you want to get there!

You have an eye for art and may possess creative talents. Finding a career or lifestyle that allows you to work creatively will be a major boon to you. You also have a knack for money and finances so you may enjoy a job in that field. With your artistic talents and financial acumen, you gravitate toward beautiful things and may become quite a collector. Just make sure your desire to have beautiful possessions comes from your appreciation of them, rather than a desire to show off to others or make you feel more important or happy. Instead of collecting things to soothe your emotions, you will be better off spending time in nature and appreciating the beauty that surrounds you.

> **SEXINESS IS ABOUT BEING AN INDIVIDUAL AND HAVING CONVICTION ABOUT WHAT THAT IS."**
> —CHRISTINA HENDRICKS

GEMINI

MAY 22

— *through* —

JUNE 20

GEMINI

ELEMENT	MODALITY	RULING PLANET	SYMBOL	COLOR
Air	*Mutable*	*Mercury*	*The Twins*	*Yellow*

Y ou see the world as a kaleidoscope of possibilities, and your quest to experience and understand all its endless combinations guides you through life. You are open, curious, and versatile and love to learn and have new experiences. Your agile mind is always working overtime to devise new, innovative ideas and solutions, which come naturally to you because you see the connections between things that others often overlook. You dive headfirst into whatever new topic fascinates you, and once you feel you have learned and absorbed enough to satisfy your thirst, you often move on. Others can misunderstand this as being inconsistent or two-faced, but in reality, you are just exploring different options and moving forward with the ones that suit you best. You enjoy an interdisciplinary style of learning that leaves you free to explore different ideas and subjects at your own pace.

Naturally witty and articulate, you are everyone's favorite dinner party guest. Your interests and experiences are so varied, you light up the room when you describe your passions. You have innate gifts in storytelling, writing, and speaking. Developing these skills will greatly benefit you, no matter which career path you end up choosing. Not surprisingly, you tend to be social and like to stay busy in your community. Whether it's a book club or yoga class, you enjoy finding activities that make use of your active mind—or help to calm it down!

When you are able to prioritize and channel your immense mental activity into a single, purposeful direction, you are unstoppable. But zeroing in on a single direction can be a challenge, especially since there are always so many different things that capture your fascination. Articulating your values will help you narrow your options. Having freedom in your daily life and schedule is important to you, especially since traveling and seeing more of the world fires your creative spark. Avoid getting stuck in routines that stifle your spirit. Finding a job that encourages you to be creative and use the many different aspects of your personality and skill set will ensure that you stay engaged and keep your cheerful smile in place.

STELLAR GIFTS
You are a five-star flirt who makes sparkling connections wherever you go.

BLIND SPOTS
Because breezy is what always comes easy to you, others may feel like you gloss over their feelings.

FASHION FAVES
Accessories are your secret weapon; you kick ass with your killer shoe collection.

INDULGENCE
Hours pouring over blogs and online shopping—all those pretty things! You want 'em all!

SEDUCTION STYLE
You are all about the mental spark, and once you have seduced his mind, the body isn't far behind.

Image

No matter your age, you are girlish and youthful in your appearance and have a spring in your step. You have a mega-watt smile and bright inquisitive eyes. Typically quite lean, you have an active metabolism, but your nervous energy may make you fidgety. You gravitate toward accessories to complement whatever mood you are in at any given time. You tend to use your hands a lot to punctuate your latest brilliant and insightful observation!

Money

You view money as a safety net and use it to comfort and nurture yourself. This could include splurging on group dinners for your friends and family or saving up to buy a dream home. Although you love to travel, you also enjoy having a sanctuary and are likely to pour your time and money into making it as cozy as possible. You are generous when it comes to supporting friends and family; if someone you love is in need, you are there.

Education

With your bright mind, you tend to do well at school without too much effort. The flip side of that is you can also become bored quite easily and find ingenious ways to avoid doing things that don't interest you! Thus, you can cultivate a twin persona of being a superstar at subjects you love and a bit of a flake with subjects you don't. Learning is a lifelong passion for you, and you often continue to take classes and add degrees to your résumé throughout your career.

Home Life

Often you grow up in a home that's extreme in terms of structure, either providing a lot or hardly any. So finding a comfortable routine and daily lifestyle is something of a challenge that you continue to work at throughout your life. The more you focus on health and fitness, the more grounded you'll be so you can spread your wings elsewhere in life. You prioritize small, considerate gestures as ways to show the people you are closest to that you care. You also tend to be something of a collector and like to keep mementos and souvenirs in your home.

Fun

You are a social creature and your biggest smile emerges when you're at a stylish party surrounded by the people you love. Staying up-to-date with all the latest social goings-on is important to you, and even though you need private time, you suffer with too much isolation. You are also very inspired by beauty and a trip to an art museum or a park or anywhere that gives you a sense of joy and appreciation is a happy day for you.

Health

This is a part of your life you tend to be private about. You prefer to come up with a specific diet or fitness routine that works for you, rather than jumping on the bandwagon from one trend to another. Because your mind works so fast, exercises that ground you and calm you are very therapeutic, so yoga and meditation could be very powerful for you if you give them a try. Over time, you will find that your sense of personal power and concentration improves the more committed you are to your health.

Relationships

You are an optimist when it comes to relationships and often fall hard and fast! A sense of possibility and adventure is important to you when it comes to both your love and business engagements, and while you tend to rush in, you need to remind yourself to give one another space to grow and evolve as well. You are often attracted to people from different backgrounds and cultures and can start meaningful relationships while you are traveling.

Intimacy

Despite sometimes jumping into relationships quickly, for you, trust and intimacy grow slowly and over time. Special bonds with childhood friends stand the test of time, and you strive for relationships that start later in life to have the same solid bones and longevity. You also often end up having business relationships with close friends and, conversely, forge intimate relationships with people you meet through work.

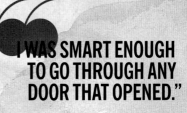

I WAS SMART ENOUGH TO GO THROUGH ANY DOOR THAT OPENED."

—JOAN RIVERS

Travel

You love to explore the world—the more exotic and off the beaten path the better! If you can also satisfy your love of learning while traveling, all the better. Your travels usually spark a new interest or hobby that you will then integrate into your life once you return home. You often meet unique people who become lifelong friends on your journeys. Your spiritual life is inspired by your roaming. Professional epiphanies frequently come to you when you are exploring and outside your comfort zone. You also love quick weekend getaways.

Career

If you aren't meaningfully and emotionally connected to your work, you're likely to become discontented. You may feel from an early age that you have a purpose or calling, and if so, you should do your best to follow this passion. If not, your passion often comes to you in subtle ways and usually involves creativity and often also helping others. The healing professions, the arts, teaching, writing, and charitable activities are all natural outlets for you.

Friends

People fascinate you and you make new friends easily. However, not all of these friendships are made to stick! Your social media might be clogged with people you haven't spoken to in ages, yet a wide circle of acquaintances works for you. Because no matter how many people are part of your wider group, you know who's in your loyal tribe. Together, you love to be spontaneous and spend time outside or trying new things.

Privacy

In your alone time, you prefer to take it easy and pamper yourself. You love going for a spa day or creating one for yourself at home. Music is also a big stress relief for you and going to concerts or dancing is one of your favorite things. But you are also just as likely to be caught binge-watching a TV show that lets you zone out completely. The only problem is, regaining your momentum and motivation afterward can be a challenge.

IF GEMINI IS YOUR

SUN SIGN

WHAT YOU WANT: You want to be free to learn and communicate about the things you are passionate about. With your natural affinity for writing and speaking, you are a born communicator and feel frustrated when you can't join the conversation or share your perspective. You have an inquisitive mind and often come up with new and clever ideas about how to do things. Not all your ideas will pass muster, but it's still important for you to be able to share them and then decide if you want to proceed or not.

You have such a wide bandwidth, you often see the hidden interrelated links between things that others fail to see or notice. As such, you can draw unique conclusions and come up with innovative ideas. But since you can jump from one thing to another so quickly, others are apt to misunderstand your intentions, which earns Gemini the negative label of two-faced. More accurately, you are open-minded and will adjust your perspective if a better solution or idea comes to light, but others can view this as flakiness. Never fear, you will ultimately prove them wrong when you show just how tenacious and loyal you can be when you truly believe in something.

Continuing to learn and grow, long past school age, is important for you, and surrounding yourself with books, blogs, and people keeps your brain active and happy. With so much going on in your mind, you can sometimes struggle to decide where to focus your attention. It is a lifelong process for you to separate what is truly meaningful for you from among all the mental stimulation in your life. Take a step back every now and then to distill a cohesive vision. This will help you set a plan of action and break down your big goals into smaller manageable steps.

> "ANYTIME I FEEL LOST, I PULL OUT A MAP AND STARE. I STARE UNTIL I HAVE REMINDED MYSELF THAT LIFE IS A GIANT ADVENTURE, SO MUCH TO DO, TO SEE."
>
> —ANGELINA JOLIE

MOON SIGN

WHAT YOU NEED: You need open lines of communication in your relationships. Your emotional connection with others comes through chatting, gabbing, texting, and really any kind of sharing. You love to be in touch with the people you are close to, and sharing your ideas as well as just silly stories makes you feel connected. You are naturally bright and talkative and make others feel at ease with your effortless conversation.

You make friends quickly and are usually good about keeping in touch, even if it's primarily via social media. But with so many different things and people occupying space in your mind, you may also get easily distracted. So keeping organized and on top of things is important for you. Likewise, given your proclivity for easy banter, there are times that you find yourself slipping into gossip or glossing over sensitive topics, so cultivate your listening skills and remember that your bright mind is better used for constructive activities. Travel is a passion for you and you often have ability with foreign languages. You are also gifted as a writer and speaker.

You have a strong love of learning and need to satisfy your curiosity with new ideas, books, and social activities. When you can't immerse yourself into something that will keep your mind busy, you can feel restless and unproductive. So be sure your slew of electronic devices are charged up and close at hand! Your mind is a major erogenous zone, and nothing turns you on more than feeling like you and your people are on the same page when it comes to major issues. Learn to speak up about what you care about, even when it seems intimidating, because expressing yourself is essential for you to feel loved and cared for.

IF GEMINI IS YOUR

RISING SIGN

HOW YOU GET WHAT YOU WANT AND NEED: You are a great communicator and have an innate ability to talk to and connect with just about anyone, anywhere. Due to your bright mind and curious nature, you're a keen observer of human behavior and you use that gift to tailor your message to whomever you are addressing. By speaking to people in their own "language," you are able to make your words and ideas resonate with others. It is your highly verbal and expressive abilities that will help you to achieve your objectives.

You love to travel and experience new places and things, even if it's only a quick weekend getaway. Sharing a wide range of experiences and interests is one of the ways that you bond with others. You know at least a little bit about lots of different things so you usually can find a way to relate and connect to whomever you meet. This chameleon-like quality comes naturally to you, since different people bring out different sides of your own eclectic personality.

You may have a natural aptitude for foreign languages and may find yourself in personal or professional relationships with people from other countries. You are naturally curious and your horizons will be expanded greatly from travel. This will also help you build a strong network of acquaintances and contacts you can call on for personal and professional assistance. Indeed, this constellation of friends and supporters is one of your greatest assets in getting your needs and wants met, and keeping those relationships strong is important to you.

"WE ARE ALL OF US STARS, AND WE DESERVE TO TWINKLE."

—MARILYN MONROE

CANCER

JUNE 21

— *through* —

JULY 22

CANCER

ELEMENT	MODALITY	RULING PLANET	SYMBOL	COLORS
Water	*Cardinal*	*Moon*	*The Crab*	*Blue, White, Silver*

You are at once a tough and tender soul.

More disciplined and tenacious than your gentle exterior would indicate, you set goals for yourself privately and slowly but surely set out to achieve your aims. And your aims can be quite lofty indeed! You are ambitious and will not settle for less than what you feel you need and deserve. Your strategic approach is not always evident to those around you, thanks to your other, more visible, caring nature. You are a consummate nurturer who feels drawn to taking care of others and derives great satisfaction from your role as the reliable friend and family member who is always there to help out or offer words of wisdom. You care deeply about being there for the people you love and assuring them of the constancy of your affections.

You connect to others from the heart, and when you feel you are in a situation where you need to censor yourself or don't quite feel comfortable, you can become withdrawn and cranky. You generally don't like to blurt out your thoughts and opinions, preferring instead to gauge your audience and respond in kind. Yet you also don't like to feel that your point of view is being overlooked, so you may end up asserting your perspective and your independence in some unexpected ways. Take care that your tactics don't slip into the realm of passive-aggressive behavior where you may say one thing and then do another. It is better for you to learn to be clear in expressing what you need and want.

Your close friends, family, and home life are areas of great joy for you. And if you find a job that you love, you may also see your colleagues as an extended family, and embrace a role as the nurturer and caregiver to the team. The satisfaction you gain from these relationships is nourishing to you—just be careful that you do not become overly dependent on your relationships with others as a barometer of your own success and well-being. You tend to navigate life cautiously and deliberately. But when you are truly comfortable in a situation or relationship, you can open up like a flower and expose your soft, romantic, and hopeful underbelly.

STELLAR GIFTS
Everyone knows you are a true friend to lean on in tough times.

BLIND SPOTS
You can get over-involved in other people's personal business.

FASHION FAVES
A true summer baby, you love classic white and nautical stripes.

INDULGENCE
A great meal with close friends is your favorite way to spend an evening.

SEDUCTION STYLE
The art of romance is not dead for you! You love to set the scene with music, candles, lots of cuddling, and a delicious meal, of course!

Image

Your image can be quite changeable, depending on your mood. Your features are very expressive, so it is easy for others to tell how you are feeling. If you're aware of this, you may attempt to mask your changing feelings with a certain image or persona. But this will be exhausting to you over time. You are better off rolling with the currents of your emotions and allowing your naturally quite glamorous presentation to entice new people and relationships into your world.

Money

You have high standards and enjoy spending on the most expensive things that you can afford. Besides, fine food, beautiful clothes, and the occasional extravagant vacation never hurt anyone! But you also take special pride in your home and like to spend time and money entertaining. And you derive great joy from sharing with the people you love. You are also keen to make the best investment of all: in yourself. If you have a passion or vision, you are willing to put whatever resources you have toward realizing your dreams.

Education

Once you find a subject that interests you, you are happy to work hard. If, however, you do not enjoy school or don't feel emotionally connected to your environment, you may reject academia wholeheartedly. Thus, it is extremely important for you to find subjects you enjoy so you can propel yourself toward success in those areas. Fields that involve studying people or helping others appeal to you. And once you find a path that works for you, you will excel through careful dedication and carve out your own niche.

Home Life

As a child, your home life was likely quite social and festive. Various friends and family members may have come together to contribute to a lively and group-oriented environment. This is part of what leads you to prioritize the people and relationships in your life. However, with so much going on, it is possible that many of these relationships remained at the surface level and more intimate connections were missing. You strive to recreate this festive dynamic with your own family and will never lose your joy at being surrounded by a large group of people you love.

Fun

Observing others and analyzing situations is your idea of fun. Using your keen eye and sharp perceptions, you like to dig beneath the surface. This helps you decide whom to trust and how to proceed with your goals. But you thoroughly enjoy this kind of analysis since it comes so naturally to you. And spending time bonding with your most trusted allies is your idea of a dream day. Being around the people you feel safe enough with that you can truly be yourself nourishes you.

Health

When you are young, you may take your health for granted and not put very much thought or effort toward this area of your life. But when you do truly get in touch with your body and its needs, proper health, diet, and fitness become a lifelong passion. You have a strong and resilient body that thrives on activity. But you may have an emotional relationship with food and need to pay close attention to its role in your life and whether it's a healthy one. Spending time in nature or doing competitive sports are some of the best outlets for you to stay in shape, because they offer you the chance to exercise while also being social and enjoying the world.

Relationships

When you decide to settle down, you want it to be for the long haul. You bring both romanticism and pragmatism to this area of your life. You love the fantasy of love, but safety and security are some of your top priorities when you are considering a partner. You may find yourself attracted to much older (or younger!) partners. Since you are also often in your own little world pursuing your ambitions, having an organized and efficient partner is very appealing to you. You hate saying good-bye to loved ones, but once a relationship is no longer functional, you can be realistic about your need to move on.

Intimacy

As in many other areas of your life, you are inclined to be quite specific about what you enjoy behind closed doors. You are experimental and are generally game to give anything a try at least once. But after you have found your favorite treats, you are likely to want to return to them again and again. Because your trust is hard won, once you have found people you can bond with on an intimate level, you are very loyal. You may have quite different types of relationships with each person you are intimate with, since each one brings out a different aspect of your personality.

MY FAMILY IS MY LIFE, AND I'LL NEVER LOSE THAT."

—JESSICA SIMPSON

Travel

Travel is a romantic and whimsical experience for you. It is here that you can relinquish some of the control and focus that you exert in other areas of your life, and simply let yourself be swept away. You particularly love being near the ocean or the water because that really recharges your batteries. You allow your softer, more wild and romantic side to emerge when you are traveling and you cherish these times of carefree abandon. Bonding with people you love and learning about the local arts also especially attract you when you're on the road.

Career

Often, you're something of a pioneer and a visionary in your field. While you tend to be cautious in many of your daily life choices, your big-picture goals can be bold and forward-thinking. When it comes to your chosen career path, you don't like to follow tradition, preferring instead to trust your own instincts about how things should be done. You tend to shy away from areas where you don't feel you can succeed, and even if you don't always show it, you can become frustrated when things aren't going your way.

Friends

You are loyal for life! It takes you a while to warm up to new people, but once you have bonded at a soul level, you are in it for the long haul. Together, you enjoy the simple pleasures, like eating well and spending time outside. You like to believe the best about everyone you love, but if you feel that someone has wronged you or betrayed your trust, it is hard for you to forgive. You may at times have to make the difficult decision to end certain relationships permanently.

Privacy

Behind the scenes, you are quite a bit more hyperactive and busy than people realize. Staying up to date on the news, reading about topics that interest you, and cruising social media are some of your favorite ways to distract yourself when you're alone. You also have some interesting and unique hobbies that others don't realize you have. For the most part, you are fine keeping these interests casual and light, but occasionally they will lead you to a wonderful work-related brainstorm!

IF CANCER IS YOUR

SUN SIGN

WHAT YOU WANT: You want a steady and secure home life that you can use as a stabilizing base for your explorations in the world. You have a need for security and consistency that guides many of your decisions. Even when you are making bold choices in your career, you feel most settled and grounded when you know exactly what you will be returning home to. Hence, you put a lot of time and effort into cultivating the relationships that make you feel most secure, whether they are with your family, colleagues, close friends, or lovers. When all is well in those areas of your life, you are content indeed.

Because so much of your emotional well-being is based on your desire for security, you can become somewhat single-minded in your pursuit of it. Beware of your tendency to evaluate people, situations, or ideas based solely on their perceived impact on you and your life. Instead, recognize that there is value and legitimacy in many different ideas and perspectives and try not to take everything so personally. Once you are able to put some healthy space between yourself and all the daily stimulations that surround you, you will find you are less defensive and emotionally charged when things don't go your way.

You are an extremely caring and compassionate person who wants to nurture and support others. You are always available to listen and lend your advice and support to people you care about. And you have the patience and tenacity to nurture large projects from inception through completion. These skills make you a natural in the world of business and in demand in whatever profession you choose. You have a gentle touch and don't like to be in situations that are too aggressive or hostile. Instead, you want your life to be filled with comfort and constancy, from which you derive your admirable strength and stamina.

CARRY OUT A RANDOM ACT OF KINDNESS WITH NO EXPECTATION OF REWARD, SAFE IN THE KNOWLEDGE THAT ONE DAY, SOMEONE MIGHT DO THE SAME FOR YOU."

—PRINCESS DIANA

MOON SIGN

WHAT YOU NEED: You need comfortable and stable intimate relationships. You are a sensitive and giving person who can be hurt easily by people who are not as gentle and considerate as you are. So you have, over time, learned to go slowly and steadily into new relationships and feel out situations before you commit yourself wholeheartedly. This helps you to balance the romantic and practical sides of your personality. You have a gift for naturally knowing when, how, and with whom to open yourself up. When you trust your own instincts, you become organically attuned to the people and situations that will most nourish you.

You relish your role as caretaker and need to be appreciated for the efforts you make in this area. You often have a talent for hosting, decorating, or cooking and enjoy pampering your friends and family. You are usually the first one someone comes to when they need advice or a shoulder to cry on. You take your duties as a trusted confidante seriously and will always give your best, most thoughtful advice and assistance. If you feel as though you are being taken for granted or your efforts in this area are not being appreciated or reciprocated, you can feel wounded and withdraw your affections. Because your feelings are strong, you may not be able to articulate exactly what is bothering you. Taking the time to understand your own emotions and communicate them clearly will help you avoid confusion and misunderstandings.

Your need to be needed by others can also spill over into your career. You are thoughtful when it comes to choosing your profession, and whatever your field, you will try to assist others and make a positive difference. Your talent for nurturing people also makes you a natural in jobs that require coaching, teaching, or seeing projects through from start to finish. If you love your job, you become passionate and attached to the projects that you work on. You can use your ability to build relationships to boost your career; just make sure you remain in sync with your own instincts, and don't get swayed by a need to please others.

IF CANCER IS YOUR

RISING SIGN

HOW YOU GET WHAT YOU WANT AND NEED: You have very strong intuition and instincts, which helps you to navigate your choices wisely. You are a master at "feeling things out" and then proceeding accordingly. Even if your goals and objectives are crystal clear, you nonetheless enter situations slowly and cautiously, waiting to see what kind of signals you pick up on from other people and the environment. If you receive favorable signals, you proceed to put your plans into action in the most subtle and effective ways. If it feels to you as though it would be better to wait until a later date, you patiently retreat and form another strategy or circle back around.

When things don't turn out the way that you want, you can get thrown off your game and become overemotional. In these instances, you may have an emotional outburst or retreat privately to lick your wounds. Learning to become more clear and expressive about your own needs and expectations will help you to find the kind of support that you need from the people in your environment. But you are often hesitant about putting all your cards on the table and letting people into your private world. You have a chameleon-like quality and are quite skilled at adapting to new situations. Since others are never quite sure exactly what to expect from you, you may end up being seen as unpredictable. But you are simply following your heart and your intuition.

You present a glamorous and alluring image, attracting many admirers, and you have a natural talent for nurturing people. You may play a mother hen role among your group of friends and family, always taking care to support and nurture those in need. You derive great satisfaction from this and can build very strong, loving relationships. These relationships then become a central focus in your life. But since you are slow to reveal your most private self, you may remain a beautiful mystery or enigma to others. You can use these alluring qualities to your advantage. Yet you are at your most powerful when the relationships you are building truly meet the needs of everyone involved.

"I CAN TURN AROUND AND SCREAM AND GET ANGRY, BUT THEN I TURN AROUND AND FORGET ABOUT IT."

—SOFIA VERGARA

LEO

JULY 23

— *through* —

AUGUST 22

THIS IS
HOW WE
DO IT!

LEO

ELEMENT
Fire

MODALITY
Fixed

RULING PLANET
The Sun

SYMBOL
The Lion

COLORS
Orange, Red, Gold

All hail Queen Leo, one of the most energetic and creative ladies of the zodiac. When you are engaged and passionate about something, you are unrivaled in your zeal, determination, and enthusiasm. You put your whole heart on the line when you pursue your dreams and inspire those less daring and assertive souls around you. Your sometimes larger-than-life persona belies a raw vulnerability that sits just below the surface where you may secretly harbor pangs of self-doubt and insecurity. When those voices grow loud, your behavior too can grow rather boisterous as you display a need for attention and reassurance. But when you feel calm and emotionally connected with your loved ones, you don't resort to over-the-top displays and instead emit a dignified and regal air of positivity.

You are engaged and enthusiastic about both your personal and professional lives, and care about succeeding in both of those areas, however you define that. You are loath to fail at things you try and will retreat quietly to lick your wounds when you feel you have been bested. But if you feel you have been wronged, you will roar with disapproval and hurt. You expect the game of life to be played fairly and will not tolerate cheaters or people who disrespect or ignore your contributions. You need your outsized efforts to be acknowledged and appreciated and when they are, you purr with happiness.

When things are running smoothly in your life, you go out of your way to make things fun and enjoyable for others as well. You are incredibly generous and take your time picking just the right cards and gifts for those you love. You know how to lavish people with praise and attention and exactly how to make them feel special. When you turn your sparkling eye on a new friend or suitor, they become the center of your warm and bubbly universe. You have strong leadership skills and enjoy the challenge of creative projects. You are not afraid of hard work and love the thrill of seeing your grand and beautiful visions come to life.

STELLAR GIFTS
Your sparkle and zest for life light up any room you walk into!

BLIND SPOTS
You can easily intimidate others with your dramatic style.

FASHION FAVES
You know just how to pick the perfect styles that flatter you. You love to accessorize and light up dramatic black looks with gold sparkle.

INDULGENCE
A hostess with the mostest, you love to entertain and thrive when you are surrounded with happy admirers.

SEDUCTION STYLE
You go for what you want! And you keep the courtship phase of the relationship alive for the long haul, continuously lavishing one another with flowers, presents, and extravagant date nights.

Image

You have a magnetic presence and tend to take over the energy when you enter a room. You are strong and well-proportioned and usually have a nice warm glow to your skin. You radiate light and are known for your luscious mane of beautiful hair. True to your symbol of the lion, you often have feline features, including large alluring eyes. You take great care with your self-presentation and even if your style is more laid-back than high gloss, you still pick items of the best quality that you can afford.

Money

When it comes to your personal business matters, you tend to be very detail oriented. You may even have a color-coded organization system that rivals the efficiency of major banks! You like to know exactly where everything goes and derive a sense of peace from having everything in its rightful place. You don't like to overspend so you will do your due diligence before making a purchase, but you'll save up for big-ticket items. You have an eye for detail and are willing to spend for unique items and quality craftsmanship.

Education

School is enjoyable for you as much for the social aspect as for the lessons. You are quick to make friends and have fun palling around in a big group. You make a sincere effort with most subjects but will try extra hard in classes where the teacher encourages you or where you show a natural affinity. You dislike authoritative learning environments and do best when the instruction is flavored with warm doses of humor and fun. You love putting your own creative and artistic stamp on whatever you do.

Home Life

You often come from a close-knit, strongly bonded tribe, which encourages your love of home and family. There may also be a significant amount of pressure on you to succeed or to share the family's values and priorities. When you feel aligned with your clan and their values, this can bring peace and contentment. When you don't, you may feel the need to strike out on your own and create your own tight family unit. You are a natural with children and have a very strong maternal instinct.

Fun

Travel and exploring the world are some of your greatest sources of happiness and enjoyment. You are spontaneous and open-hearted and go full force into new pursuits. You make friends with people from a wide variety of different backgrounds and are always seeking ways to keep learning and growing together and from one another. You are also a bit of a daredevil and will try things that others may shrink away from. Your courage will lead you into many exciting new adventures. You also love playing games and can be more than a little competitive.

Health

Consistency is key when it comes to maintaining your health. You tend to feel physical imbalances quickly and tangibly, which helps you correct your course accordingly. Taking care of your back and shoulders and not carrying too much stress in those areas of your body is important for you, as is maintaining your bones with proper calcium intake. Long hikes and time in the great outdoors are some of your favorite ways to exercise, rather than simply toiling away inside a gym.

Relationships

Long-lasting committed partnerships are very important to you. That means you may jump into marriage and decide to settle down and have children early in life. It is important that you find someone who can match your own level of emotional enthusiasm, because partners who are emotionally reserved may not be able to give you the warmth and nurturing you desire. But when you do find a like-minded mate, you two are able to co-create a unique lifestyle that makes both of you happy.

Intimacy

You are very romantic and love to get swept away in love once you find someone you can truly open your heart to. Candles, music, bubble baths, you want the whole nine yards, and since you work so hard when you are in career mode, you relish lazy days when romance is the only thing on the agenda. You tend to idealize your partner and can feel disappointed if they don't live up to your expectations. Likewise, you can brush aside less than stellar qualities in others in an effort to preserve your image of them. Be aware of these tendencies so you don't confuse your dreams with reality.

> "THE MOST COURA-GEOUS ACT IS TO STILL THINK FOR YOURSELF. ALOUD."
>
> —COCO CHANEL

Travel

You are an intrepid traveler who is unafraid of charging into new territory. Whether it is up the highest ski slope, to the farthest reaches of a remote country, or to the newest restaurant at a five-star resort, you embrace each of these challenges and new experiences with gusto. You can even become a bit competitive as you add ever more daring and exotic locations to your list of destinations. Just make sure you balance your enthusiasm with careful planning since you can have a short fuse if hiccups or complications impede your progress.

Career

Building your career is important to you, so you are diligent and responsible about work. You take a long-term perspective when it comes to success and are willing to work your way up slowly and gradually. Even at entry-level jobs, you take your tasks seriously and will always seek to do the best job you can do. You have a knack for finances and know how to position yourself to make a good living. You excel at jobs that reward your long-term commitment and ones that engage your refined aesthetic and creative know-how.

Friends

You have lots of friends and relish spending time with them. You make connections very easily and you have a smile for everyone in your neighborhood, from the mail-delivery guy to the local grocer. You and your gang have your favorite hot spots and have been going there for years. When you get together, you let out your playful fun-loving side and don't take things too seriously. You are good at keeping in touch with your vast network of friends, even if it's just by checking in with a quick text message. If you have siblings, you tend to be very close with them as well.

Privacy

When you get some downtime, you love nothing more than just curling up at home and taking it easy. Sweats, some yummy food, and a TV binge night is your idea of a dream evening when you have a moment to relax. Your loyalty to your family and best friends is also very strong, so you always want people to come to you when they need help and support. Therefore, your home is often a haven for the people you love. When you have your own family, piling into bed together and chilling are some of the happiest times for you.

IF LEO IS YOUR

SUN SIGN

WHAT YOU WANT: You bring light and enthusiasm to everything you do. Your sense of personal creativity and passion is strong and it is important for you to find channels to pour that energy into. You don't believe in limits and will work hard to create a life that allows to you succeed in all the different areas that you deem important. You are very determined and won't let minor setbacks derail your progress, even if they cause you temporary anguish. You feel everything very strongly and put your full heart into each of your endeavors.

You are a natural optimist and believe that hard work, passion, and determination will win the day. You want to surround yourself with others who have the same level of boundless enthusiasm and can become disappointed easily when people bring down your high energy, poo-poo your big ideas, or don't appreciate the depth of your passion. Finding an environment where you can shine and where your passion and big-picture creativity is encouraged is very important to you. Otherwise, you may feel lost and misunderstood.

Beware of becoming too dependent on the approval and encouragement of others, lest you begin to let this dictate your choices, rather than allowing your natural talents and creativity to light your path. When your moods are dictated by the response you get from others, you will know you have gone too far in this direction. If that happens, realign yourself with what you love to do and the admiration and appreciation of others will naturally follow. You have a flair for drama and want to be free to inject each of your projects with your own unique stamp. It is not enough simply to imagine all the amazing things that life has to offer; you want to feel them and experience them to truly get 100% out of your life.

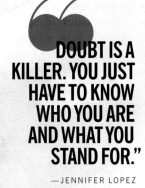

DOUBT IS A KILLER. YOU JUST HAVE TO KNOW WHO YOU ARE AND WHAT YOU STAND FOR."

—JENNIFER LOPEZ

MOON SIGN

WHAT YOU NEED: Deep feelings, passion, and excitement stir your heart. When a person catches your attention, it is usually because they have as much enthusiasm and zeal for life as you do. You don't give your heart away very often, but when you feel that certain spark, you become full of optimism. You have a big heart, and you don't play halfway. Instead, when you believe in something or someone, you give 100%, trusting that there will be a good outcome. Hence, you can sometimes feel wounded when your passions or overtures aren't reciprocated. It is important for you to pay attention to the messages you receive from your partner, rather than merely idealizing them or putting them on a pedestal.

When you are single, you are a master of cat-and-mouse games. While you do go after what you want, you also love to be chased and pursued. You draw others in with your gregarious and flirtatious charm. You are very creative and take special pride in your home and tend to enjoy hosting get-togethers and bonding with new and old friends. You have a natural affinity for children and retain the enviable ability to see the world as a wondrous, fascinating place throughout your adult life.

When you settle down, you need to feel you are with a partner who is worthy of your love and who also appreciates your generosity and passion. A person who fails to notice your considerate nature or thoughtful actions will hurt your feelings. Yet someone who is too emotional and needy may likewise wear you down and dampen your energetic spirit. It is important for you to not become too trapped in the image of the type of person you would like to be with, lest you find yourself with someone who appears to have it all but can't truly connect to you at the deepest level. You will be happiest when you let your heart guide you to a deep bond based on mutual admiration and care.

RISING SIGN

HOW YOU GET WHAT YOU WANT AND NEED: Your boundless enthusiasm is one of your greatest tools for getting what you want and need out of life. You have a warm, sunny, and dynamic disposition that piques many people's interest and curiosity. And you are a pro at playing your glamorous persona to your advantage. When you turn your attention on a friend or potential suitor, they feel like the most special person in the world, as you radiate light and positive energy their way. However, you may at times become overly concerned with the response you get from others and become touchy or wounded if you are not receiving the attention or respect you believe you deserve. In these instances, you can become haughty or self-righteous, which will derail your attempts to connect with others.

You are a very passionate person and feel life very strongly. You see the world as your oyster and are keenly aware of the fact that you have unlimited creative potential. You have an added dose of charisma and creative capabilities at your disposal to help you achieve your most personal wants and needs. But sometimes all this energy can feel overwhelming, even to you. It is very important that you find outlets such as physical exercise and calming daily routines that help you channel all that dynamic energy—otherwise, you're in danger of feeling restless and frustrated.

You're a natural performer, knowing just how to cater to your audience and get the response that you want. However, unless performing is your actual career, you must be careful not to let your ability to put on a show take over your personality. If this happens, you can feel trapped within a self-created role and as though you must appease people or behave a certain way in order to gain the love you want. This will cause you some loneliness and isolation as you feel you cannot show people your true self. You can prevent this from happening by courageously sharing all parts of yourself with others and trusting that the originality of your perspective and your heartfelt motivations will earn you everything you want and more.

> "I'M OVER TRYING TO FIND THE 'ADORABLE' WAY TO STATE MY OPINION AND STILL BE LIKABLE!"
> —JENNIFER LAWRENCE

🍃

VIRGO

AUGUST 23

— *through* —

SEPTEMBER 22

VIRGO

ELEMENT
Earth

MODALITY
Mutable

RULING PLANET
Mercury

SYMBOL
The Virgin

COLORS
*Green, White,
Earth colors*

Y ou are a rare combination of earthy and playful. You know your values and priorities and rarely deviate from them, yet manage to be as open and supportive to others and their way of life as possible. This balance takes time and effort to achieve, but you are aided by a huge level of patience and self-discipline that guides you in many areas of your life. Your pronounced work ethic comes from your sense of duty to being the best possible version of yourself that you can be, and your commitment to bringing your unique talents and perspective into the world. You have a tremendous eye for detail and elevate any job or profession that you choose by tweaking and refining until a new level is reached.

You are very caring toward

the people in your life, and small considerate gestures mean the world to you. It is much more meaningful for you to have the people you care about listen to your perspective and assist you with the things that are important to you than to be part of elaborate spectacles that will mean little in the long run. Your caring nature could even spill over to a career in the healing professions or at a charitable organization. But you also like to have fun! You have a cheeky sense of humor and are always up for an adventure with your friends. Travel is often a wonderful escape for you; it opens you up to new perspectives and provides a fresh dose of creative inspiration.

You are a thoughtful person who enjoys learning and is always seeking avenues for self-growth.

You are especially in touch with your body, and diet and exercise may play a major role in your life. You simply feel better when you are in sync with your body and take care of yourself. But it's possible that your self-discipline may be taken to extremes. Be gentle with yourself and strive for balance, rather than perfection, in your life and with your body. Since you are so caring and thoughtful, you have high hopes and can become easily disappointed by others' actions. Setting clear expectations in your personal and professional relationships will help you bring your sizable talents to the world in as productive a way as possible. You are at your best when you are aiming to do good and help others while simultaneously nourishing your own need for growth and productivity.

STELLAR GIFTS
You are very observant and sensitive to your environment, which gives you the ability to fit in anywhere, anytime!

BLIND SPOTS
In your desire for perfection, you can sometimes make others feel like they can't live up to your high expectations.

FASHION FAVES
You love to walk the line between classics and more edgy pieces with a flair for unique geometric details and accessories.

INDULGENCE
You are a hard worker, so when you do take time off, you really love to kick back and unplug!

SEDUCTION STYLE
A master of subtle flirtation, you never come on too strong. You like to bond with your crush over shared interests and then slowly become the person they depend on the most. That's because you pride yourself on always delivering what you promise, in and out of the bedroom.

Image

Classic looks and staying under the radar appeal most to you. Blending in gives you a perfect vantage point to view others! And you are very alert and observant. You are generally petite with small features and bright eyes. You can be a bit of a chameleon when it comes to your look, but you're consistent when it comes to your underlying style. As comfortable in sweats and a T-shirt as you are in the most elegant of eveningwear, you nonetheless prefer clean lines and unfussy styles. But your creativity and eye for detail are evident in the small touches, such as accessories, that you carefully select.

Money

You tend to be cautious financially, but your favorite way to spend money is on fun social events with your friends. Group dinners, trips, and nights out are well worth the expense, especially if there's a special setting and good times involved. You also have an eye for fashion and may love staying up to date on all the latest designer trends. In this case, you can become quite a collector and have an epic closet filled with unique and beautiful finds. Purchasing art may also become a passion of yours. Your collection of lovely things brings you joy.

Education

How you feel about school is based in large part on how well you enjoy the atmosphere there. If you enjoy the people and the vibe, you can dedicate yourself quite single-mindedly to the subjects that you enjoy. You have a long-term approach to education and the ability to focus on distant goals rather than being distracted by short-term circumstances. If you dislike the environment at your school, you could become withdrawn and unhappy. Balancing academic work with creative pursuits and outdoor activities will help you unwind.

Home Life

You may be exposed to lots of different ideas or cultures as a child. This gives you a sense of the broader world and helps fuel your desire for learning and personal growth. If travel was a part of your life when you were young, the seeds for a lifelong love of exploring were planted. It's possible, however, that there was little structure or consistency in your household. This may have made you quite self-sufficient. As long as you feel you have strong and loving roots to come home to, you, too, will want to introduce your own children to different cultures and ideas, and may even create a flexible or mobile lifestyle for your family.

Fun

You are very loyal to your group of friends and love to spend time together. Often your closest friends are people you met in childhood or at school, and together you form a tight crew. You are able to balance chic parties and fine dining experiences with much more low-key hangouts. Being together in nature, someplace beautiful and remote, is especially appealing to you and you may enjoy glamping in the great outdoors. Collaborating on business projects with your friends also often brings you success.

Health

You are specific about your fitness and diet. Since you are very much in tune with your body, you know exactly what works for you. You may even veer away from standard diets and workout trends and come up with your own unique routines. As long as you do not become too fanatical or set in your ways, you may find great success with these custom solutions. This area may capture your attention to such a degree that it becomes your career focus, in which case you could become a celebrated pioneer.

Relationships

Nothing feels better to you than being swept away by love. You can be very romantic when it comes to your relationships and cherish time together simply relaxing, listening to music, and basking in one another's glow. Together, you can just check out of the world for a few days and luxuriate in each other's company. So finding a partner who wants a similar level of intimacy and bonding is important for you. Emotional connections are also important to you in your work relationships. You will benefit from setting clear priorities and having open lines of communication in your relationships so that there is no confusion when it comes to the less romantic aspects of life together.

Intimacy

Behind closed doors, you can be quite a bit feistier than you appear! You aren't afraid to go for what you want, and you can be somewhat insatiable when you are in the mood. You like to mix things up and are always game for experimenting. When you feel a connection with someone, you want to jump right in and open up to that person quickly. But you can just as quickly realize that they are not for you and move on. You tend to be a trusting and open person who is inclusive and seeks connections with others.

> **THE BEST THING IS TO REALIZE THAT YOU ARE WHO YOU ARE AND YOU GOTTA WORK WITH WHAT YOU GOT."**
>
> —ZENDAYA

Travel

You adore traveling in style. Places with gorgeous scenery, good food, and some level of artistic atmosphere are especially appealing to you. You love lounging and being pampered. Spa retreats and foodie holidays are dream vacations. You also crave time in nature and are inspired by natural beauty so you can rough it when you are somewhere gorgeous. Destinations that have a thriving arts scene where you can dance the night away or check out museums and galleries also appeal to you.

Career

When it comes to your career, you are multifaceted. With your bright mind, you see lots of different possibilities and don't like to limit yourself to any one specific path. While you tend to have a niche expertise, you nonetheless will find new and innovative ways to work in several different areas. You may eventually end up with two different careers. You enjoy balancing more than one interest and finding creative ways to fulfill all your different endeavors. Writing, media, and the arts are areas where you have natural talents.

Friends

Friends are like family for you. Your emotional connections with them run deep and they may be the first people you turn to when you need a shoulder to cry on. You take pride in taking good care of those closest to you and being an emotional support system for them as well. You are likely to make your home as welcoming a sanctuary as possible for your crew and enjoy quiet chill time at home with them. When a friendship ends, you feel a great loss, but you also understand that it's important for some relationships to grow apart.

Privacy

Your innate sense of confidence shines behind the scenes. You know that you are a star and can do anything that you set your mind to—you are just picky about what you choose to go after! And living a low-key lifestyle is usually a deliberate choice, because you could easily climb your way to the top of the social ladder if you so desired. The home you create for yourself might be quite luxurious since you revel in spending time there and surrounding yourself with the things that bring you pleasure. You take pride in your taste and quietly enjoy the appreciation and admiration that comes with being celebrated for your great style. You are human after all!

SUN SIGN

WHAT YOU WANT: You want to be able to take care of yourself, as well as others, to the best of your ability and to improve the world around you. Whether that means pursuing a service-oriented profession or just taking great care with the small details of your day-to-day life, you want to be a force of positivity and beauty. And you don't need massive rounds of applause everywhere you go for your efforts. You are happy to work diligently behind the scenes as long as you feel like your contributions are respected by the people you care about the most. You are sincere in your efforts, as well as consistent and hardworking, which wins you many admirers. You can become a trailblazer in your field simply by virtue of the fact that you take such great care with everything you do, and stay true to your values and beliefs.

Your dedication and humility fuel you and contribute to your success in your profession of choice. They also grant you a measure of privacy, which you relish. Working away behind the scenes with consistency and integrity means that people respect you and for the most part give you freedom and autonomy to do your own thing, however you see fit. You will seize the opportunity to carefully craft a career, and life, of your own making. With your alert mind and eye for details, having creative and executive control over your life is exciting but can also lead to confusion when you feel overwhelmed by many different possibilities. It is in these instances that your famous pickiness and fussiness can take over and you can feel that nothing is quite right and become critical of yourself and everything around you. You can soothe these tendencies by being less demanding of yourself and others and remembering that every failure is a learning opportunity.

As a grounded earth sign, you are very connected to your body. The more in touch with your body you are, the calmer and more centered you become, as you learn to trust your own path and instincts even more deeply. Having a daily diet, fitness, and work schedule that is customized for your lifestyle and health needs will make a world of difference in your overall happiness. Take care to keep refining and tweaking your routine as you get older, rather than becoming too stuck in a rigid way of doing things. When you are feeling healthy in both mind and body, a luminous and fun-loving side of your personality comes out. You know how to kick back and enjoy yourself along with the best of them! It is a well-deserved reward for your careful and considerate approach to life.

"POWER MEANS HAPPINESS; POWER MEANS HARD WORK AND SACRIFICE."

—BEYONCÉ

MOON SIGN

WHAT YOU NEED: You need to feel healthy, centered, and in sync with the people around you when it comes to the small, considerate nuances of everyday life. You have a special relationship with your body, and learning the proper ways to take care of yourself and cater to your own unique needs may become a central theme of your life. You may even make a career in the world of food, health, or fitness. You are attuned to these fields because you don't look for shortcuts or easy answers but rather are willing to take your time and patiently understand the best ways to achieve the results that you want. And your eye for detail helps you to accomplish everything you set out to do in the best possible way.

You are blessed with both a bird's-eye view of the big picture of what is important to you as well as an understanding of the daily steps that are necessary to get where you want to go. However, when the smooth running of your daily life is thwarted or an obstacle to your goals arises, you can become cranky and anxious. Learning to soothe yourself and navigate life's normal ups and downs with tolerance and compassion, toward yourself and others, will help you to stay centered. The better you get at easing up on your natural perfectionism, the farther you'll go.

It is important for you to feel as though the great care you take with the small things in your life is seen and appreciated by the people you love. You don't need massive amounts of approval or reassurance, but you do want your efforts to be acknowledged and reciprocated. You care deeply about your close friends and family and will always try to do nice things to make life easier and better for them. You may tend to become a victim of your own considerateness and make yourself a martyr, always helping others and feeling like they do not put in the same amount of effort toward you. Remember that only giving from a place of abundance and genuine care, rather than a need to please, will satisfy you in the long run. And once you have corrected any tendency toward this, the level of care and attentiveness you give and receive will come beautifully into balance.

IF VIRGO IS YOUR

RISING SIGN

HOW YOU GET WHAT YOU WANT AND NEED: You can achieve just about anything that you set your mind to, because you are a good listener and able meet others' needs, while simultaneously working to achieve your own aims. Even if you are as tenacious and driven as they come, you are skillfully able to employ a mask of caring and consideration to others who then believe that you indeed have their own best interests at heart as well. If you are in the habit of using the trust that others give you exclusively for personal benefit, then you may keep bumping up against small delays or annoyances that derail your progress. You are at your most powerful when you truly care about meeting both your own needs and those of others. Then you are a strong force of positivity who can fuel great success for yourself and all the people whose lives you touch.

Staying flexible and open-minded is one of your best paths to achieving what you want and need. New information and ideas are always presenting themselves to you, so you can use your keen mind and eye for details to keep integrating and reimagining your strategy. You have a tendency to be a perfectionist and you can become quite fussy and dissatisfied if your environment falls into discord or disarray. Ease up on yourself, and others! Creating a daily routine that works for you is also essential. Taking good care of your health will make a big difference in your life. Your body is very sensitive to your emotional environment, as well as what you eat and drink. Small imbalances will show up quickly so it's best to be preventative and curate a customized health and exercise regimen that keeps you feeling strong and empowered.

You have an amazing eye for details and are also very thoughtful and considerate. You take pride in the small and caring gestures that you make for the people you care about, and you would like to receive the same level of attentive care from others in your life. Dealing with people and relationships that are more fluid and unpredictable may be simultaneously a source of attraction as well as repulsion for you. On the one hand, you can be emotionally drawn into the glamour of the mysterious. But on the other, you may end up trying to save, fix, or correct a situation to your own, as well as everyone else's, chagrin. You are better served channeling your caring attitude toward people who reciprocate your kindness or into the world of service and philanthropy.

IMAGINATION IS THE HIGHEST KITE ONE CAN FLY."

—LAUREN BACALL

LIBRA

SEPTEMBER 23

— *through* —

OCTOBER 22

09.23–10.22

LIBRA

ELEMENT
Air

MODALITY
Cardinal

RULING PLANET
Venus

SYMBOL
The Scales

COLORS
Pastels

You are the zodiac's consummate charmer. Beauty enchants you, wherever you find it, be it in art, fashion, or people. You're never happier than when creating lovely and harmonious environments for your friends. Bringing together the interesting and varied mix of people you love gives you a sense of peace and purpose. Nobody ever feels left out or out of place at a Libra-planned party. One of your hard-won gifts is the ability to keep relationships, both personal and professional, even-keeled. When you were younger, you may have had some friendships and romances that felt unbalanced; you knew just what to give but not always how to show or ask for what you really wanted. You're so naturally empathetic, it can be easier for you to respond to a partner's desires. The more confident you are about making sure your own needs are met, the more smoothly your relationships will flow.

Despite a light and breezy demeanor, you are very hard working and are seldom without a project (or five!) going on. That said, when you are in relaxation mode, there is almost nothing anyone could do to get you off the couch. You cherish your down time and rightly feel you deserve to be pampered and to bliss out every once in a while. No matter how much you pack your schedule, finding time for the people in your life who matter most is always a priority. This can be a real challenge during your single years: You have so many love interests, sometimes you have a hard time remembering who's who! But once you settle down, you devote lots of time to creating a happy and balanced partnership.

No matter the setting, you are a natural diplomat and always seek to maintain peace and equilibrium. You are proud of the fair and open mind you bring to every conversation, and you dislike aggressive and dogmatic people who don't strive to be considerate enough to listen to others' points of view. Because creativity comes so naturally to you, careers that involve art and aesthetics appeal to you, especially those where you can see projects through from idea to execution. Then you can use your practical, detail-oriented mind, as well as your refined tastes, to complete the task at hand.

Image

You are very aware of the image you project. As such, it is important to you to always come off as a lady and you avoid being rude and hostile to others. You have good manners and other people feel that they can count on you or rely on you to ease conflict-laden situations and smooth over ruffled feathers. In keeping with your harmonious vibe, you tend to have balanced facial features and a well-proportioned physique.

Money

When it comes to money, you can be quite secretive and private. Shrewd and careful observation of others' habits and practices is endemic for you, so you may have picked up a few financial tips and tricks from those you admire and respect. You gravitate to more long-term calculated investments, and trust in advisors whose power and authority have been tested and validated. You err on the side of conservatism, but when you truly believe in something, you will take a big risk.

Education

As an astute observer of people and culture, much of your learning takes place outside the classroom. One of your greatest joys is having new experiences and you're open to illumination wherever you find it. Exploring the world, locally and in far-flung locales, is one of your favorite ways to learn, and you relish immersing yourself in diverse cultures. You will buckle down when you need to but facts, figures, and tests can feel limiting to you. You are open-minded and curious and prefer to let your mind and spirit roam all available avenues of enlightenment.

Home Life

You don't feel the need to buy into society's expectations, but a traditional family and home life appeals to you. You celebrate family rituals, finding that stability and routine comforting. Respecting your parents and your background provides a safe and reassuring base for you. Your family is often a source of support in your career by providing you with connections and advice. You're grateful for your network and enjoy doing the same for your children and inner circle.

Fun

Nothing brings you more joy than spending time with your various circles of close friends. Your bonds run deep, and you make sure everyone knows you have their back, no matter what. Someone's birthday? You are the one who throws them the party they dream of. Celebrating holidays and special occasions with unique traditions is what your favorite memories are made of. You are inclusive and always feel like the more the merrier.

Health

You feel your way through this part of your life on a day-by-day basis, rather than committing to a strict or regimented health or fitness routine. But you do like to stay active. Dancing and yoga are great options for you because they allow you to get in touch with your body in a more fluid way. Getting plenty of rest and taking care of yourself is especially important for you since you can sometimes focus on taking care of others before yourself.

Relationships

This is one area where you like to throw caution to the wind and jump in headfirst! You love the thrill of the chase in relationships and being pursued by ardent admirers. Together, you like to explore uncharted territory and go on spontaneous adventures. Passion and excitement are important for you in romance, and you keep the sparks flying long after the courtship period has ended.

Intimacy

Slow and steady is your MO when it comes to intimacy. When you find someone with whom you can combine the excitement you love and who also has the patience and sensitivity to get you to truly open up, you fall hard. You value trust and dependability above all. When someone betrays you, you are not likely to forget. However, once someone has earned your trust, you are loyal for life.

"I'M REALLY EXCITING. I SMILE A LOT, I WIN A LOT, AND I'M REALLY SEXY."

—SERENA WILLIAMS

Travel

You love to pop around to various fun locations and destinations, often places you have traveled to with your family or where you have friends. You always seek "the neighborhood feel" wherever you are and revel in living like the locals. Seaside towns and family-friendly communities especially appeal to you, as do places where you can socialize with old and new friends.

Career

Any career that lets you use some of your nurturing energy to help others or provide a comforting and safe environment will feel right for you. As such, jobs in the hospitality or counseling worlds let you shine. You also excel in creative endeavors, so writing, fashion, or jewelry design are pursuits that not only tap into your love of beauty but also give you the opportunity to nurture your ideas from creation through finished product.

Friends

You are drawn to bright, warm, and extroverted people. Your friends are a funny, generous, and dynamic crowd and you are proud of them. Together, you boost each other up and give each other confidence to tackle your challenges and dreams in life. And best of all, when there is something to celebrate, you pull out all the stops to make your squad feel special. You definitely know how to party in high style.

Privacy

Behind closed doors, you're more of a worrier than most people realize. Because you have your mind tuned to so many different things, sometimes you can get overwhelmed. So you like to keep yourself organized to a degree that can sometimes border on OCD! But when you're taking care of yourself and your health, you feel calm and confident that you can come up with solutions to any problem.

IF LIBRA IS YOUR

IF LIBRA IS YOUR

SUN SIGN

WHAT YOU WANT: A harmonious life filled with fun, friends, and social revelry is what brings you joy. You are hardworking and determined, but you care about balancing that with a rich and rewarding social life. Many of your great victories in life come through alliances and teamwork. As such, the relationships in your life, both professional and personal, are very important to you. But if anyone becomes a source of ongoing strife or negativity, you find ways to distance yourself diplomatically.

You are thoughtful and fair-minded, naturally evaluating all sides of any situation. Since balance is so important to you, you are a skilled negotiator, peacemaker, and matchmaker. Yet, because you're so diplomatic and aware of everyone's point of view, you may find choosing sides to be stressful. You will strongly resist being pressured, and you need time to weigh the pros and cons and analyze all perspectives in any conflict. However, once you determine a course of action, you act decisively and rarely second-guess yourself. You dislike aggressive, bullying behavior and will fight for justice. In these instances, you can become an enthusiastic and articulate crusader for your chosen cause.

You care about beauty and pleasure and want your surroundings to be as harmonious as possible. You are enormously creative and enjoy finding many different ways to express yourself. Making art or music or even DIY projects can be a great source of fun. Whipping up gorgeous dishes to delight guests or creating artfully designed adornments for your walls or outfits is both relaxing and joyful. Since relationships are so important to you, you may find yourself searching for "the one." When you embody the qualities you seek in a partner, you will find the dream mate you are looking for.

> "GLAMOUR TO ME IS ABOUT REMAINING GRACEFUL AND UNDERSTATED."
>
> —KATE WINSLET

MOON SIGN

WHAT YOU NEED: You need your professional and personal relationships to flow smoothly and harmoniously. If you feel your life or your liaisons are off-kilter, you can become cranky and critical. You garner much of your energy and sense of well-being from productive and enjoyable engagements with others, so when that's not working, it can be exhausting and cause you a lot of stress. The good news is that since you are quite thoughtful and analytical, you can usually pinpoint exactly what's throwing things off and take steps to bring things back on track.

You love being around people and are a great communicator. You see all sides of a situation and enjoy lengthy debates and discussions. Even though you instinctually weigh all perspectives in any given argument, you can become quite set on your way of viewing things. Take care to not waste your precious energy fighting one-sided crusades, or endlessly debating trivialities. You enjoy people, but it's also important for you to spend quiet time alone. When your life is in social overdrive, you can start to feel burned out and drained. You thrive when you strike the right balance between mellow you-time and time engaging your vast social and professional networks.

You dislike it when people are rude or aggressive, and if anyone comes on too strong, you distance yourself. You can sometimes be emotionally reserved, because you tend to see things from a rational and pragmatic perspective. It can be a challenge for you to empathize with the intense feelings of others since you are so thoughtful and balanced when it comes to your own emotional needs. Letting yourself feel deeply, and not just rationalizing your needs, will help you connect to others at an even more profound level.

RISING SIGN

HOW YOU GET WHAT YOU WANT AND NEED: You get what you want and need by charming people and winning over anyone who might help you or—heaven forbid—get in your way. When you meet someone new, you have an uncanny ability to connect quickly, which makes you new friends and fans wherever you go. You can easily ingratiate yourself to others with your easy conversation and good manners. You are attracted to beauty and harmony and frequently find yourself playing peacemaker and smoothing ruffled feathers among your friends and colleagues.

You are rarely very flamboyant in your personal presentation, preferring instead to fit into most social contexts unobtrusively. You use these chameleon-like qualities to help you better understand other people and your environment so you can relate to them. Being social is important to you, and you become distressed when things are out of harmony in your relationships and will work hard to find ways to remedy the situation.

Since you are polite and engaging, you can work pretty much every situation to your advantage. With so many skills at your disposal, you may be tempted to use your interpersonal skills to climb the social ladder or manipulate others. Your casual and sociable facade can mask your ambition, so you have to remain aware of the effect you have on others and use it to assist them as well as yourself. You are a natural connector, so matchmaking, both romantically and professionally, is one way that you can give back to others and benefit everyone with your keen social abilities.

> "A THING THAT YOU SEE IN MY PICTURES IS THAT I WAS NOT AFRAID TO FALL IN LOVE WITH THESE PEOPLE."
>
> —ANNIE LEIBOVITZ

SCORPIO

OCTOBER 23

— *through* —

NOVEMBER 21

84

10.23–11.21

SCORPIO

ELEMENT
Water

MODALITY
Fixed

RULING PLANET
Pluto

SYMBOL
The Scorpion

COLORS
Dark red, Black

You are one of the most powerful and complex creatures in the zodiac. Your quest for success and stature comes from your internal drive to be the best that you can be. You have an innate understanding of your personal power and a deep desire to channel that as positively and potently as possible. For you, life is about identifying and tapping into your inner vision so you can harness your potential and make your mark on the world. This requires being carefully attuned to your intuition as well as committed to your ever-unfolding process of growth, change, and transformation.

You tend to have a love/hate

relationship with change. You embrace new goals and recognize the need to leave behind relationships you've outgrown, so in that respect, you charge fearlessly into the future. But you are also a creature of habit and when you don't feel ready to make changes or move on from something or someone, doing so can be an agonizing process. Learning to trust in the flow of life, and in other people, is one of your big challenges. You also have an inclination to micromanage people and situations, often out of fear that they will make an error or disappoint you if you don't control the process. Easing up on yourself, and others, will unlock a whole new world of possibilities for you.

You are fascinated by how the world works and are an especially astute observer of people. Your insights and words carry power, so resist the urge to shoot poison arrows when you feel betrayed or hurt. You vigilantly guard your privacy and let only a select few into your innermost world, but you are very loyal to those who win a place in your life. Setting your own standards for success is important to you—and those standards tend to be high and defined by your personal values and principles. Once you truly know what matters to you, you are capable of achieving just about anything you set your mind to.

STELLAR GIFTS
You have an eagle eye for details and know how to make others feel like they are the most special person alive.

BLIND SPOTS
When you are feeling introspective, you can come off as cold and give off mixed messages.

FASHION FAVES
You love to keep people guessing with gorgeous outerwear and sexy underwear.

INDULGENCE
Known for your prowess in the bedroom, all-day love-fests are one of your favorite things.

SEDUCTION STYLE
You know just when to turn on the charm and when to back off and give your suitors the chance to pursue you. Maybe that's because you know prospective partners usually fall under your thrall completely and quickly. When you finally let go and really connect emotionally, you do so with just as much intensity and fervor.

Image

As a keen observer of human nature, you are very aware of your image and the impression you make on others. As such, you cultivate your presentation carefully. Sometimes you prefer an Earth Mama vibe, while at other times, you choose to tap into your ripe sensuality. Your purposeful personality radiates from the intense gaze you fix upon whatever or whomever you desire, be it objects, objectives, or other people.

Money

Travel and spontaneous adventures are high on your list of indulgences. You are curious about the inner lives of people in other parts of the world, so when you roam, you tend to return home with treasures. Despite your naturally cautious nature, you are generally optimistic when it comes to money, always believing you'll find a way to get your hands on it when you need it, which for the most part tends to be true.

Education

You work hard at school and generally see good results. You understood from a young age that achieving good grades and excelling in your studies will help you realize your passions later in life. Hence, you've always been willing to put in the time. You particularly enjoy subjects that offer you a vantage point to study people and things related to business and politics. You have a knack for finding the perfect internships to suit your interests.

Home Life

You may have grown up in an unusual household. There may have been an untraditional family dynamic or perhaps your parents lead an eccentric lifestyle. Depending on how much you enjoyed this environment, it pushes you either to embrace the same path or to find your own equally unique and rewarding home life. You don't believe in doing things a certain way just because everyone else does, and social conventions don't restrain you from creating a personal world that's as one-of-a-kind as you are.

"I FALL IN LOVE EVERY TIME. AND I DON'T REALLY FALL IN LOVE A LOT, BUT WHEN I DO, I FALL HARD."

—KATY PERRY

Fun

There is a romantic undercurrent pulsing below the surface of your personality and this manifests in everything you do. You especially love lounging with your closest friends. You revel in carefree days lazing at the beach, listening to music, and daydreaming. Time near the water particularly soothes you and makes you happy. But be aware of your tendency to drift off into la-la land during your escapes so you don't go on a permanent vacation!

Health

You tend to be quite vigilant about keeping up your health and enjoy being active. You are a natural at sports, and outdoor activities like running, hiking, and swimming get your blood pumping. Your not-so-secret competitive streak means that gym classes or activities where you can race to the top appeal to you. You might even enjoy trying your hand at boxing or martial arts.

Relationships

When it comes to relationships, yours are built to last. Shared values and priorities are crucial components of your personal and professional partnerships. Once you decide you're all in with something—which doesn't happen every day—you commit yourself for the long haul. You relish the process of slowly and deliberately building a life or a durable business with someone. Together, you enjoy indulging your senses and appreciating the best that life has to offer, including quiet private time in nature.

Intimacy

If you feel really comfortable with someone, the hidden goofy, silly side of your personality comes out. You love communicating with the people you are closest to and exploring all different kinds of ideas. You will know you have reached a whole new level of intimacy in relationships when you are comfortable enough to say anything that comes to mind. If you have siblings, it's likely that you have an especially close bond with them.

Travel

Exploring the world with your family and inner circle of friends is one of your great delights. For you, part of the joy of travel is that special time together with people you love. Destinations near the water appeal to you as well as those that have a rich cultural history or a personal significance to you and your family. The spice and surprise of local foods thrill you when you travel and you often pick up some recipes to bring home.

Career

You're determined and unstoppable, so once you have decided on what type of career you want, you go for it full throttle. Even though you like to guard your privacy, you are a natural at performing and being in the limelight, so whatever your chosen profession, being a company spokesperson or the face of a brand appeals to you. You are also attracted to glamour and your ideal job could have you mixing with powerful people.

Friends

You are a very thoughtful and considerate friend. Small gestures mean the world to you, and you are always looking for ways to show the people you love how much you care about them. When others don't show you the same level of consideration in return, you quickly become disenchanted. You crave one-on-one time with your closest pals, whether that means cooking and savoring a healthy meal together or just lying in the grass and talking about life.

Privacy

Even though your privacy and alone time are carefully guarded, you become bored when you are left to your own devices for too long! Instead, you will find ways to reach out to your loved ones and find someone to connect with. Being surrounded by peaceful, beautiful things is important to you, and you work to create an environment that inspires you, where you can rest and recharge your batteries. You may collect art or gorgeous objects that hardly anyone sees but you! That's okay. They bring you joy.

IF SCORPIO IS YOUR

SUN SIGN

WHAT YOU WANT: You want to feel empowered in your life and in your career. For you, strength comes from deep within and fuels your energy, creativity, and passion. Finding your own personal gifts and how to channel them is of utmost importance for you. Early in life, you may take cues about what to do or say from people around you, but you realize quickly that when you aren't in tune with your own perspective, you feel off-balance. Much of your energy is then dedicated to a process of uncovering your passion and purpose.

This quest for self-knowledge will likely lead you down all kinds of interesting paths. Your natural confidence and self-assurance guides you through lots of different types of situations. You notice and analyze everything and everyone around you, and use your observations to better understand yourself and others. You trust your intuition, and if something doesn't feel right, you move on. In this way, you are a master of transformation, constantly absorbing new insights and information and discarding what is irrelevant or no longer necessary. You can run into obstacles when you don't know quite what you want to keep and what you want to discard. In those moments, returning to your personal values and core beliefs will guide you through.

Once you have found your path, you are tenacious and driven. You want to feel your core energy and power flowing through you and as such can become extremely focused on success. As you rise to the top, be sure to curb any tendency to manipulate or control others with your dominant personality. Just be careful that you don't put blinders on and limit your field of vision too much. When this happens, you can feel stuck and your life can seem limiting. When you stay open to new possibilities for learning, growing, and giving back, you are truly limitless!

> "PEOPLE CAN JUDGE ME FOR WHAT I'VE DONE. AND I THINK WHEN SOMEBODY'S OUT IN THE PUBLIC EYE, THAT'S WHAT THEY DO. SO I'M FULLY COMFORTABLE WITH WHO I AM, WHAT I STAND FOR, AND WHAT I'VE ALWAYS STOOD FOR."

—HILLARY RODHAM CLINTON

MOON SIGN

WHAT YOU NEED: You need intimacy and passion in your relationships. You are also very determined and tenacious, so maintaining a clear vision of your goals is important. Your questioning and curious nature makes you a keen observer of the world and the people around you. Your emotions are strong and it may take you a while to come to grips with them. Separating yourself from your feelings, so you can manage a clear view of things, can be a challenge. Taking time to honestly and carefully appraise your feelings and motives can be a lifelong project. But it is precisely your strong intuition and desire for strengthening and self-improvement that will, over time, help you transform less useful emotional habits into newer and healthier ones.

Often drawn to psychology, astrology, or the occult, you are very insightful and have an insatiable curiosity about how people tick. You are unafraid to poke below the surface of life's great mysteries. You tend to have an "all or nothing" approach when it comes to relationships, a trait that, eventually, you may attempt to grow out of. Likewise, you will benefit from recognizing, and releasing, a tendency to try to control or micro-manage others. You emit a strong personal energy that attracts interesting and powerful people to your orbit, who sometimes give you the intense connection and passion you desire. Resisting the urge to rush into relationships when you feel a spark will be one of your learning lessons. As with many things, you will learn this through trial and error.

Scorpio is associated with regeneration, so you have a unique capacity to grow and develop at all stages of your life. You may have many incarnations both personally and professionally, rising each time to an ever more elevated and powerful position. However, your need for intense experiences and transformation often leads you to relationships that require personal evolution, which can be a painful process. The limits of your trust and faith may be tested time and again. Yet your desire for closeness and intimacy with others can ultimately provide the impetus for you to better understand yourself. Once you have found peace with yourself, which you gain from genuine self-acceptance, you can truly achieve all your desires and connect with others in the most intimate and rewarding way.

RISING SIGN

HOW YOU GET WHAT YOU WANT AND NEED: You can be somewhat of an enigma to others. You are passionate, intense, and very private. You are keenly aware of the image that you project and decide quite consciously what you want to reveal and to whom. Although you can be very charming and engaging, you are certainly not an open book. In fact, you are a mystery to many, which enchants potential admirers and suitors. Your wants and needs thus have a powerful mask behind which they can operate, since others are likely to project their own fantasies onto your mysterious persona. You can use this to your advantage, allowing others to believe what they want about you, all the while maneuvering in the direction you want from behind the scenes.

Your magnetic appeal may boost you to the status of a sex symbol. Certainly, you're drawn to intimacy and are driven to get to know people in highly personal ways, in and out of the bedroom. You don't much care for trivialities and prefer to focus on what you think is most important. Powerful and glamorous people are often attracted to you, so you could easily find yourself rubbing shoulders with the elite. Just make sure that you don't get lost inside the romance of your own enigmatic persona since you could end up as its slave rather than its master. Although you are very private, resist the urge to keep too many secrets from those you care about as you may find it draining and destabilizing in the long run.

You tend to have rather fixed preferences and can become cranky if things don't go your way. Learning to be gracious and to control your temper will help you immeasurably. You may find spending time with others to be quite emotionally and physically taxing and thus need to offset that with privacy and alone time. Nature is especially restorative for you. Over time, you could become more and more drawn into your private world. Just make sure that you keep the lines of communication open with the people who care about you. It becomes easier for you to be around other people when you don't take everything and everyone (including yourself!) so seriously. When you feel content and have learned to use your sharp intuition and personal magnetism for positive benefits, you will find that you can have a profound healing and empowering effect on others.

IT TAKES A MINUTE FOR ME TO LET MY GUARD DOWN, BUT ONCE I DO AND I GET TO KNOW SOMEONE, I'M VERY OPEN, VERY TRUSTING."

—ANNE HATHAWAY

★

SAGITTARIUS

NOVEMBER 22

— *through* —

DECEMBER 21

11.22–12.21

SAGITTARI

ELEMENT	**MODALITY**	**RULING PLANET**	**SYMBOL**	**COLOR**
Fire	*Mutable*	*Jupiter*	*The Archer*	*Purple*

You are a dynamo who is determined to make the most out of life. You don't worry very much about what everyone else is doing. Instead, you set your own course and blaze ahead to create the life that you desire. You are naturally open, curious, and spontaneous so you can find yourself doing all types of unusual things. "Sure, why not?" is usually your attitude. But you have a strong sense of who you are and don't let yourself get overtaken by insecurity or peer pressure. Instead, you dabble in new activities to see if they suit you and then move on if you aren't having fun. Having a good time and enjoying yourself is important to you and you can hardly see the point in doing anything that isn't engaging.

US

You are naturally confident and self-assured and your trust in yourself guides you on your personal journey.

Your curious spirit extends from your home and family and into the wide world around you. You should seize any opportunities you have to travel since you will gain a huge amount of inspiration and perspective from exploring different lifestyles and cultures. Likewise, you will benefit from studying as many subjects as possible in school and going as far as you can in your education. You are likely to enjoy learning and studying more as you grow older and your interests in the world become more nuanced and specific. Your interest in other people and different cultures often leads you to ponder the "big" questions in life. You may feel naturally drawn to religion and spirituality as you have a sense that there is something bigger out there.

You are an optimist who looks for the best in people and situations. You tend to be quite open-minded, but if your interest in religion or world affairs has been activated, you may become passionate and single-minded in your support of a certain belief system or political perspective. Remember to always leave room for growth and differing opinions. Your faith in people and positive outcomes can lead you to make bold choices that others would deem risky. As long as you are making these choices from the heart, you tend to find great successes following your instincts and your passion.

STELLAR GIFTS
You are nonjudgmental and easygoing, which makes you first on everyone's list for a wingwoman.

BLIND SPOTS
You don't realize more sensitive types can misunderstand your sense of humor or feel overshadowed by your big personality.

FASHION FAVES
You love colors and patterns! Your whimsical style matches your outgoing and ever-seeking personality.

INDULGENCE
A great escape! You have serious wanderlust and are always ready to pack your bags for an adventure. The more exotic the better....

SEDUCTION STYLE
Just go for it! You aren't shy when it comes to catching your guy.

Image

Self-confidence and trust in yourself ensures you are noticed wherever you go. You have a fun-loving and no-fuss attitude, which puts others at ease. You are also known for your great sense of humor and warm people up by making them smile. Your personal style suits your active lifestyle and may include clothes and accessories you find while traveling. You are not precious or dainty, and usually have an athletic body that can take you wherever you want to go.

Money

You are quite business savvy and have a big-picture approach to finances. Even though you like to spend money on exciting escapades, you also care about saving for a rainy day. You may decide to start your own business, in which case you will be responsible and diligent. You also thrive working at larger corporations, provided they give you some freedom and flexibility. Even if it appears you are just out there enjoying yourself, at the end of the day, you have usually quietly built yourself a nice nest egg.

Education

School can be something of a mixed bag for you. If you find something you are passionate about and excel at, you can be a veritable prodigy. A single-minded focus on something you love appeals to you more than splitting your time between lots of subjects that don't really interest you. But if you don't find something that really interests you until later in your education, you may become restless and move on to more amusing pursuits. Try your hand at as many things as you can from a young age, so you can find something that truly excites you. Because when you are focused, you soar.

Home Life

You gain a great deal of peace and calm from your home life and can happily retreat into your own private world. In your childhood, your family may have a close-knit and cozy vibe or could be quite loose without much structure. In either case, you enjoy creating a little paradise for yourself at home where you can surround yourself with music and create an environment that soothes you, free of the demands of others. Just make sure you come up for air once in a while and don't flake too often on obligations to friends and family.

Fun

You are always first in line for a new adventure and up for whatever merriment presents itself to you during the course of the day. You pride yourself on making the best of whatever situation you find yourself in and can enjoy yourself virtually anywhere, with anyone! However, you can also become bored easily so you often make a quick exit once the good times are over. Outdoor activities and good old-fashioned competition also get your heart beating and you have a blast taking a hike with friends or triumphing during a heated game night.

Health

You tend to be very in tune with your body and can easily feel imbalances or health issues when they arise. You love to enjoy the finer culinary things in life and may be quite a foodie. Building in a good exercise regimen will help you indulge in your savory delights more often. Staying grounded and connected to your body through yoga, meditation, and spending time in nature will be very calming and stabilizing for you.

Relationships

You want your relationships to be full of fun! You tend to gravitate to those who are as lively and energetic as you are. You love to be able to talk for hours about your shared interests, and enjoy when your partner introduces new ideas and activities. Without that stimulation, you can feel bored and restless. Together, you like to socialize and have a trusty group of friends to hang out with. You dislike feeling trapped, so learning, growing, and traveling together will keep things fresh.

Intimacy

Behind the scenes, you can be much more traditional than others realize and you want your partner to court and pamper you. You enjoy the more gentle, sweet aspects of taking care of one another in and out of the bedroom. You can lose yourself to passion and delight in burrowing indoors, spending whole weekends bonding. Feeling nurtured and cared for on a deep level is important to you and you coax your partner into meeting these needs by taking care of them the way you would like to be cared for.

I'M ALL ABOUT ZAGGING WHEN EVERYONE ELSE IS ZIGGING."

—TYRA BANKS

Travel

Since you love to travel and explore new places, you tend to blaze forward optimistically into the unknown. You especially gravitate to destinations where there is strong cultural creativity, such as artistic centers or places filled with spiritual energy or dramatic nature. You are also drawn to glamour and like to be surrounded by other creative souls. The right balance of being pampered and feeling excited and invigorated makes a perfect holiday for you.

Career

You are a bit of a perfectionist when it comes to matters of your career. As you define your interests and narrow your focus, you tend to develop a niche skill or speciality. You then focus diligently on improving your skills and refining your talents in a certain area throughout the course of your career. You may have artistic talent and this should be used in your work. You have an eye for detail and can discern patterns that others fail to recognize. Cultivating your own niche focus will be a source of satisfaction and continuous personal growth for you.

Friends

A sumptuous and raucous dinner party in a beautiful setting, where you can just sit back and enjoy good friends, food, and vibes is your idea of paradise. You dislike drama and want things to be easy and fuss free. You adore meeting new people but many of them remain cheerful acquaintances as you often keep these relationships at a pleasant surface level. Engaging in cultural pursuits with your friends, like going to museums or concerts, feeds your imagination and spirit.

Privacy

Despite your fun-loving personality, you are actually quite a private person, and few people truly get very far beneath the surface to know your innermost workings. This is not necessarily out of any calculating forethought, but rather because you require a certain amount of personal space and freedom and prefer to keep your own counsel when it comes to most matters. It is here too that your spiritual and religious nature provides you solace and where you trust in your own inner guidance.

IF SAGITTARIUS IS YOUR

SUN SIGN

WHAT YOU WANT: You want to have fun in life! You tend to see the world as a playground (or an amusement park!) where anything and everything is a possibility and you don't like to limit your options. You want to have the freedom to explore whatever comes around the next corner and will resist relationships or situations that try to prevent you from following your naturally inquisitive nature. The more you learn and see, the more inspiration you have for your own life, which you enjoy building and creating with an artistic eye and an enduring self-confidence. Even if others don't have the same vision of life that you do, you diligently stick to your own path and trust in your vision for what you want.

You can have a fiery temperament, especially if you feel that something is unfair or if it doesn't go your way. Small outbursts usually smooth over quickly and it is simply important to you that you can voice your opinion and be heard in these instances. Sometimes you take your natural confidence and curiosity to rebellious extremes. In these instances, you can be goaded on by the awe and enthusiasm you inspire in others when you engage in ever more daring behavior. As long as you are expressing your creative spirit and not merely behaving recklessly because you are intoxicated by the attention it brings you, you will meet with positive results. And certainly your bravery, when rightly harnessed, will help you become a trailblazer in your profession.

Especially as you get older, your natural curiosity about the world extends into an underlying quest to understand "the truth." Your need to understand the inner workings of the universe leads you to explore religion, spirituality, travel, and education as realms where deeper understanding about the world can be found. You have a philosophical outlook and may become quite engaged with certain teachers, spiritual leaders, or politicians you believe have direct access to a powerful message. Your need to feel this bigger connection can turn into extremism in some cases. Strive to assimilate everything you learn into your own unique truth and remain open to continuously growing from, as well as teaching, everyone you encounter.

IF YOU'LL JUST STAND UP AND GO, LIFE WILL OPEN UP FOR YOU."

—TINA TURNER

MOON SIGN

WHAT YOU NEED: You need to have freedom and flexibility in your life and in your relationships. You are a naturally curious and spontaneous person who likes to explore whatever new paths become available. You need to feel that life is a positive adventure and that a fun person or situation is just around the next corner. This helps you feel confident and gives you a natural positivity and playfulness. You place a lot of importance on humor and try to infuse laughter and joy into all your activities. Rather than being rigid and structured in your methods of dealing with others, you prefer to be spontaneous and trust in a positive outcome.

Your casual and optimistic attitude easily wins you many admirers, but is not geared toward bonding with others at an intimate or emotional level. You have difficulty understanding the emotional nuances of others, and since you rarely pause to reflect on your own deeper needs, you can be dismissive of the quirks and irrationalities of others' emotional needs. Taking the time to try to understand what is motivating others at a deep level will require patience and listening skills that don't necessarily come easily to you but that will help you to connect with others in a more meaningful way. Your love of freedom may lead you to traveling and exploring the world. In this case, you may find you connect strongly with people from other countries and different cultures.

You tend to have a naturally spiritual or religious attunement to life and believe in a bigger picture. These beliefs help fuel your optimistic and upbeat attitude. However, they can also lead you to believe that you have the "right answers" about life, which can further distance you emotionally from others who see things differently. Learning not to impose your view of the world or how things should be on others will help you build long-lasting relationships. You are at your best when your own need for freedom and flexibility is matched with a sincere desire to understand and embrace others' values and priorities as well.

IF SAGITTARIUS IS YOUR

RISING SIGN

HOW YOU GET WHAT YOU WANT AND NEED: Your gregarious and positive attitude is infectious. You have an adventurous spirit and a playful sense of humor that wins you many admirers. You tend to charge fearlessly into situations, even if they are sometimes a bit dangerous or risky, and trust that the outcome will be good. Your optimism is admirable, and usually you emerge unscathed, but you would be wise to slow down from time to time and assess situations more thoroughly before jumping in. Yet, your fearlessness and positivity are your greatest assets at getting you what you want and need.

No matter what you set out to do, you bring a great deal of energy and enthusiasm with you. Because of this, others tend to trust you and look to you for guidance and encouragement. But since you prefer to be spontaneous rather than rigorously organized, make sure you have a strong plan of action. Otherwise, you could end up the leader of an army with nowhere to go and no war to win. Since you naturally inspire others, you make a fantastic teacher and keep your students engaged through a mix of humor and education. Many things in life come easily and naturally to you, so you may have a casual attitude that rubs more steady and diligent types the wrong way. This does not concern you much. However, you may begin to feel that you have uncovered the "right way" to do things and become dismissive of others who see things differently. Take care not to steamroll others and to continue to learn and grow from differences of opinion.

Your sense of humor is a great asset to you. But you may accidentally step on the toes of people who don't understand or appreciate your humor. Maintaining sensitivity to your audience without losing your natural charm will help you translate even more successes. You like a good time and want to make the best of any situation. And you thrive in any number of situations, from your favorite Saturday night bar to a remote destination in a faraway land. Travel inspires your curiosity and you should seek to adventure to as many places as possible, where you are sure to enjoy your travels and gain a new and inspiring perspective.

I THINK IT'S ONLY HARD IF YOU'RE TRYING TO BE SOMETHING YOU'RE NOT."

—MILEY CYRUS

CAPRICORN

DECEMBER 22

— *through* —

JANUARY 19

CAPRICOR

ELEMENT
Earth

MODALITY
Cardinal

RULING PLANET
Saturn

SYMBOL
Mountain goat

COLORS
Browns and earth tones

A brilliant driven achiever, you are an endlessly engaging enigma to most of the people in your life. You are modest and patient, while being very hardworking and ambitious. You have a fun-loving and playful side, yet you always manage to hit the nail on the head when it comes to work. Your innate prowess for prioritizing helps you determine the best ways to channel your time and resources. When you are in work mode, you give 100% and when you are in play mode, you give 100% too. And best of all, you know when to start and when to stop. You can seem nearly superhuman to others! If your achievements seem supersized, it is all the more so because you are rarely boastful. In fact, you are naturally humble and gracious. But you're also a born charmer and your personal and professional relationships are of paramount importance to you.

Indeed, one of the greatest boons to your success is your network of connections. You are a people person, and being diplomatic and strategic in your alliances helps you build the firm foundation you require to reach your goals. You are very loyal and will nurture people and projects until the end if you believe in them. You feel a strong sense of responsibility and will always make good on your commitments.

You are a planner and take a long-term approach to success and happiness. You have self-discipline and a guiding sense of personal values and goals, so you are willing to sacrifice fleeting pleasures when you know it will lead to a greater victory down the road. This determination keeps you centered and even-keeled. You are very practical and find it challenging to do things in which you don't see a purpose. If you sometimes seem unyielding and stern to others, it's because they have not seen your more gentle and nurturing side. Cultivating the softer side of yourself and allowing it to come out in your work and daily life will empower you even more.

Image

You are an earthy beauty who eschews an ultra-flashy presentation in favor of a highly curated mix of classics, with some boho flair thrown in for good measure. You prefer to look natural, and your active, disciplined lifestyle means you often grow into your good looks, aging very gracefully (to the envy of all the other zodiac ladies!).

Money

When it comes to how to spend and invest your money, you have very specific tastes and habits. If a nifty financial trick or tip that you picked up early in life proves fruitful, you are fiercely loyal to that particular perspective. One area where you love to spend is on your friends and bonding activities with the people you love. You can also be a strong patron of charities and groups that you believe in. Your analytical mind leads you to do well with investments in technology.

Education

This can be hit-or-miss for you. If you don't feel personally called to a particular subject, then it can be an uphill battle for you to focus on schoolwork. You excel at creative pursuits, and music, art, and performing may appeal to you more than lots of hours in the library. But you are consistent and dedicated when you want to be, so when you do set a goal for yourself, you always work hard enough to ensure you realize it.

Home Life

The haven you create for yourself is a sacred space, where you feel your most free and at peace. You tend to stay organized, because you always want the stage to be set for a spontaneous gathering. Your home is often a place for impromptu parties that mix all kinds of interesting people. You love collecting beautiful things and despite the fact that your practical side keeps you from amassing too much clutter, you are loath to part with items that you treasure.

> **I WANT YOU TO UNDERSTAND THAT EVERY SCAR YOU HAVE IS A REMINDER NOT JUST THAT YOU GOT HURT, BUT THAT YOU SURVIVED."**
> —MICHELLE OBAMA

Fun

Spa days, sumptuous dinners at the highest quality restaurants, and being in artistically appointed surroundings are paradise for you. Indulging in exceptional things and experiences is your greatest treat. You can rack up quite a bill living the high life, but you know good value when you spot it. You can also be very connected to nature and being in the mountains or the fresh air is a thrill for you. Pampering the people you love gives you great joy.

Health

You vacillate between being high-strung and lethargic so it's important for you to find ways to calm your nerves. Finding fun athletic pursuits or gym classes motivates you and you like to buddy up and work up a sweat with your friends. You enjoy trying new and innovative physical challenges that keep you motivated. Dancing is another activity that you love and it does double duty as being both healthy and sexy.

Relationships

Trust and longevity are characteristic of your deepest relationships. A sense of feeling supported and cared for is important to you. It is often within your most intimate relationships that you let out your softer side and you tend to be very nurturing toward your partner. When you believe deeply in someone else and the connection you share, be it personal or professional, you're patient and loyal to a fault. You are willing to see things through to the end and hate to give up on people you care about.

Intimacy

When you feel safe with someone, you let the full force of your warm personality and big heart shine. Elaborate displays of affection for the people you love are often characterized by gifts and unfettered adoration. You can idolize your partner and dream of receiving the same level of adulation from them. Your feelings may get hurt if you don't feel your warmth and caring are being reciprocated in the same way. Teaching people how to please you will help you get the love you want in return.

Travel

When you want a getaway, you often look for pristine places where natural beauty shines. Mountaintop or seaside escapes, where you can really let your hair down and retreat from your intense daily life appeal to you. Health- or fitness-related travel is also a good option, so investigate yoga retreats or beach boot camps that are a good opportunity for a break but also help you stay healthy and active.

Career

You are an ambitious and hardworking person with lofty career goals. Your strong network of personal and professional acquaintances is advantageous to you in your climb to the top. You are an ace at mixing business with pleasure and people you work with often become confidantes. And your friends often do double duty as professional allies. You thrive in careers where you work closely with others or play matchmaker, such as fund-raising, head-hunting, sales, and business administration.

Friends

If you strike a true bond with someone, you are loyal for life. You often forge deep connections that others can barely understand, let alone break. When you feel like someone is disloyal or betrays you, this can be very difficult and disorienting for you. But fortunately, it's a problem that you don't have very often, thanks to your naturally keen perceptions about people. But when it does, you may cut them out of your life for good. You cherish your private time with your trusted inner circle.

Privacy

Since you are so accomplished, others don't often see the goofier, sillier side of your personality! In your own private world, you don't take yourself too seriously and you delight in going on spontaneous adventures and engaging with ideas or people that may be far removed from your "normal" life. You may also have a more hidden spiritual side, and spending time reflecting and getting in touch with your intuition could be calming and affirming for you.

IF CAPRICORN IS YOUR

SUN SIGN

WHAT YOU WANT: You strive to be successful and accomplished in your chosen field. You relish hard work and immersing yourself in pursuit of a chosen goal, so finding people and causes that matter to you will help you to channel your vast energy and ambition. Even if your goals are modest, you value accomplishment and a job well done. Once you have decided what you want to achieve, you are patient, prudent, and deliberate on your path. You understand how to work well with others, and healthy, mutually beneficial relationships are a backbone to your success.

You take pride in nurturing the people and projects you believe in. You intuitively understand that anything worth doing takes time to achieve and that every step is a worthwhile one. You can become impatient with others who have a less developed sense of practicality than you do. Since you are so reliable, you often end up taking on a lot of responsibility. So choosing exactly what pursuits and alliances you want to dedicate yourself to becomes an important step in your growth.

As you achieve more responsibility, and the power that comes with it, your goals can change and grow as well. Staying mindful of others' needs and sticking with your core values will help you to navigate an increasingly complex web of relationships, achievements, and goals. Just like your symbol—the mountain goat—you will carefully climb your chosen mountain and find your way to the summit. But your real achievement is knowing how important it is to have fun along the way and celebrating your major milestones as they come!

DON'T COMPLAIN, DON'T EXPLAIN."

—KATE MOSS

MOON SIGN

WHAT YOU NEED: You need to feel like you are making a meaningful contribution in the world. At heart, you are a very practical and hardworking person whose happiness requires being taken seriously and respected by others. You feel hurt when anyone underestimates your skills or abilities, so you will work overtime to ensure that you meet expectations. When it comes to relationships, you offer a unique combination of practicality and sensitivity. There is one part of you that feels like a relationship where both partners' needs are equally addressed and realized is sufficient. Another part yearns for a warm and enveloping partnership where you can get lost in affection and feel provided for and taken care of.

Balancing these two aspects of your own personality, and how they reflect in your relationships, is one of your ongoing challenges. Early in life, you may vacillate between being with partners who satisfy either your need for parity or your need for passion but not both and then you feel disappointed. You can be hard on others, but this is because you are hard on yourself. Remember that not everyone needs or wants the same things you do.

You will feel lighter and achieve your needs more easily after you stop trying to be all things to all people and narrow your field of vision. Setting your own bar for success will be a big relief to you, since you will no longer find yourself at the mercy of having to live up to others' expectations. You are an ace at networking, and nurturing important business relationships will be always be instrumental to your success. Determining which responsibilities are worth shouldering, and which will prove to be more of an unnecessary burden, will be liberating for you. Then when you accomplish the goals you put your heart and soul into, it will be on your own terms, and you will be able to celebrate your achievements wholeheartedly!

IF CAPRICORN IS YOUR

RISING SIGN

HOW YOU GET WHAT YOU WANT AND NEED: You are a pragmatic and shrewd observer, which helps you achieve anything you set your mind to. You have a natural ability to understand the give and take involved in business relationships, and hence, you are perfectly situated to create positive and mutually beneficial alliances. You take your time getting to know people, cautiously watching their behavior before you form an impression of them. You then decide if it is a relationship worth pursuing. Once you commit to a personal or professional relationship, you tend to be loyal, but if a relationship has outworn its benefit, you acknowledge that and are confident in your decision to move on.

You don't shirk away from responsibility and are unafraid of taking on big commitments. You may be entrepreneurial from an early age, because you have a knack for seeing how processes can be streamlined and improved. If early efforts to accomplish something fail to ignite, you simply regroup and try a different strategy or approach. Once you decide that you believe deeply in something, you see it through till the end, no matter the complications or obstacles. Your tenacity, modesty, and reliability are admirable and attract a wide pool of potential personal and professional suitors.

In your quest to reach your heart's and mind's desire, you can be hard on yourself and others. You don't suffer fools gladly and prefer to surround yourself with those who are as competent and consistent as you are. Yet, you often find yourself drawn to more carefree and whimsical types, who don't necessarily relish the same level of responsibility that you do. Giving yourself permission to indulge in the more sensitive and mysterious sides of your nature will be liberating and help you ease up on yourself. And it may even provide you with more inspiration for your next great achievements!

> **WE ALL HAVE A WONDER WOMAN INSIDE US."**
> —DIANE VON FURSTENBURG

AQUARIUS

JANUARY 20

— through —

FEBRUARY 18

115

AQUARIUS

ELEMENT	MODALITY	RULING PLANET	SYMBOL	COLORS
Air	*Fixed*	*Uranus*	*The Water-Bearer*	*Bright blues and metallics*

Effervescent and fun, with an air of mystery, you are a bit of an enigma even to those who know you best. You draw others in effortlessly with your kind, open, and easygoing demeanor. Yet, beneath your breezy exterior, you know just who you are and what you want and are not likely to budge an inch from your chosen path. You are endlessly curious about other people and make friends easily, but you are staunchly resistant to others imposing their views, beliefs, and priorities on you. You have a charmingly "live and let live attitude" that grants others the freedom to be themselves, while also fiercely guarding this right for yourself.

You are very independent and resist being stereotyped. Your

friends often say quite rightly, "You are one of a kind!" Indeed, you march to the beat of your own drum, which makes you an inspiration for others. Your visionary POV captures the attention of other unique souls, and your tribe of friends, colleagues, teammates, and acquaintances is always growing. You also have a giving and humanitarian spirit and are often drawn toward people and organizations that are trying to make a positive difference in the world. You are loyal to those who matter to you, and you're sympathetic when you encounter someone who needs a hug or a pick-me-up. But you're not one to go too far down the rabbit hole of mushy feelings, preferring instead to assess situations, including your own emotional inner workings, analytically and practically.

Once you have picked your path and set sail, you can be a creature of habit who is resistant to big changes, especially those that others try to impose on you. But when the need to alter your course comes from your heart, you don't hesitate to pull the plug and move in a totally new and different direction, without so much as a glance behind you. This means that others may have a hard time anticipating your next move. But you hardly notice others' reactions to your decisions, much less let them bother you. Instead, you are totally focused on creating the life you have envisioned for yourself. And if you can help others and inspire people along the way, well, then all the better.

STELLAR GIFTS
You always speak your mind and are 100% loyal to your friends!

BLIND SPOTS
You can be super-stubborn and resistant to changes that you don't initiate.

FASHION FAVES
Sticking to what you know and love makes you shine. You have a flair for experimenting with modern metallic, saturated colors and bright accents.

INDULGENCE
Nothing makes you happier than QT with your pals, so a group dinner—or trip!—to a unique locale is your fave way to spend time.

SEDUCTION STYLE
With your friendly charm, you win over many admirers. But you know how to transform a friendship into a romance once someone captures your interest.

Image

You tend to stick to your own personal uniform, whether it's tutus and tiaras or Birkenstocks and backpacks. You know exactly what suits you and you are loyal to it. You have a certain look and it's as much a part of your persona and life as your witty sense of humor and friendly smile. Your strong personal confidence and easy charm command the spotlight and people notice when you walk into the room. This is especially true when you roll with your squad of friends.

Money

When it comes to finances, you can be quite mysterious and somewhat whimsical. Just as your preferences tend to be unique and fixed in other parts of your life, so too you may have some financial quirks that others can't quite understand. Large personal collections of mementos or nostalgic items may vie for space in your life with the top-of-the-line techie gadgets you are known to love. You also can't resist a beach holiday and are willing to splurge on a few days in paradise where you can just unwind and listen to the sound of the waves.

Education

You are a quick learner with a sharp and unique intellect. In subjects that interest you, especially in the realm of math and science, you may be a veritable genius—you're able to crack puzzles in an instant that others ponder for hours. But you are hard-pressed to make a big effort in subjects that don't grab you. You are a bit competitive and will move on from something if you realize you don't have a natural knack for it. You are creative and should make an effort to diversify and experience as many subjects and extracurriculars as possible in school to see which ones you find a passion for.

Home Life

While your home life might not always be traditional, it tends to be stable. There you find a sense of consistency that you can rely on, even if your parents' choices or lifestyle are different from what you have in mind for yourself. There could be a large focus on money or achievement in your house, or you could come from a family of artists. You likely have a strong reaction in one direction or the other, either following in your family's footsteps or choosing a path that is quite different.

Fun

You are always up for a quick get-away with your friends. Especially if participating doesn't require too much effort or commitment from you. You enjoy exploring new places and tend to have a passion for intellectual pursuits like reading, making book clubs a favorite social outlet. You are also a superior connoisseur of staycations, so you go out of your way to get to know interesting people, places, and events in your community.

Health

Connecting with your body can be a challenge for you, since you are so mentally focused. Meditation and yoga are both effective tools you can leverage to slow down and be present in your physical self. You have an emotional relationship with food and can be prone to skipping meals or overeating when you're feeling sad or stressed. Applying the same level of consistency to your diet as you do to other areas of your life can be a good thing, but make sure you are truly meeting all your body's needs.

Relationships

Close relationships, especially those in which you feel comfortable enough to show your passionate and playful side, bring out the best in you. Proud, courageous, and fiery types who display magnetic charm and open-hearted warmth win you over. You know what you like and won't settle for anything less, so you're a careful and selective dater. You'd rather wait for the real thing than settle for pretty good. You love true individuals, who proudly show their quirks. When you do fall, you are totally loyal and committed.

Intimacy

Different partners bring out different sides of your sexuality. With one person, you may be blasé and with another, you could be a hot-as-fire dynamo. Everyone sparks something different within you. But you tend to have quite an earthy sensuality, despite your otherwise airy nature, and revel in long and sweaty sessions between the sheets. You can uncover mysterious erogenous zones that others overlook, which aids you in being quite an attentive and detail-oriented lover.

"BEWARE OF MONOTONY; IT'S THE MOTHER OF ALL THE DEADLY SINS."

—EDITH WHARTON

119

Travel

All aboard! The more the merrier is your motto when it comes to travel! You like having your friends and family by your side when you explore new places. And you tend to stick to destinations that are easy and where you can simply relax, rather than overly complicated trips that involve lots of precise agendas or arduous adventuring. Dragging yourself away from the pool for a lovely candlelight dinner or a trip to an art museum or two is usually all the stimulation you need. But when you occasionally decide to take a real adventure somewhere exotic, you go all in and immerse yourself totally.

Career

You are quite strategic and determined when it comes to your career. You take a long-term view of what you want to achieve and have the patience and diligence necessary to take you all the way to the top. It is also very important to you that your career feel authentic and rewarding. You will follow the guidance of your own inner wisdom in making choices, rather than society's conventional expectations. You are capable of reaching positions of great power and seek to use that power to support others.

Friends

There are few things you enjoy more in life than time with your friends. Around them, you can be wild and silly and show off all the different sides of your personality. You are likely to attract lots of different types of friends, potentially those from diverse parts of the world. Together, you can talk about politics and big-picture philosophical ideas but also just relax and chill. You enjoy traveling with your friends and make a lot of new ones while you are exploring. Even if you don't see each other for ages, once you are reunited it's like you never parted.

Privacy

You are more serious and hard-working than people realize. Your outwardly easygoing nature belies the more cautious and pragmatic approach to life that you foster behind the scenes. You think very carefully about major decisions and weigh all your options diligently. Likewise, you can be quite political and strategic about your alliances and connections. It comes naturally to you to look for win-win situations and you will work hard to get yourself to where you want to be and help others out along the way as well.

IF AQUARIUS IS YOUR

SUN SIGN

WHAT YOU WANT: You want the freedom and flexibility to explore life in your own way. You are a hard worker but are resistant to conventional expectations and instead seek to forge your own path. The more people try to get you to do something you don't want to do, the more you will resist. You may even shut the door on relationships and people who refuse to accept you for who you are. You have a strong connection to your inner voice, and when you follow it, you can become something of a visionary and trailblazer. Whatever your area of interest, you are capable of making new discoveries and being a pioneer.

Finding a tribe of like-minded people is important for you. Since you are guided strongly by your own personal vision and inner wisdom, you feel most connected and supported when you connect with others who share similar interests. Otherwise, you may end up feeling isolated and misunderstood. Once you have found colleagues or friends with similar interests, you thrive and become a source of leadership, unity, and support for the whole group. You connect to others mentally and through your shared interests, objectives, and hopes for the future.

You are quite a brave person who is unafraid to challenge expectations and conventional wisdom and instead trust your own inner guidance. This can lead you through peaks and valleys in life as you can alternately be celebrated for your visionary successes or isolated for your independent lifestyle. You are happiest when you strike a balance between these two extremes and can live life by your own terms while also feeling supported and encouraged by others who understand and appreciate you. When you find that balance, you are truly able to share your unique and insightful gifts with the world.

"USE YOUR LIFE TO SERVE THE WORLD, AND YOU WILL FIND THAT IT ALSO SERVES YOU."

—OPRAH WINFREY

MOON SIGN

WHAT YOU NEED: You need to have the freedom to follow your own interests and manage your own time. You gravitate toward unconventional intimate relationships and the constant give-and-take of close partnerships may be a challenge for you. Because you're so set in your ways and resistant to others demanding too much of your time and energy, you thrive in relationships with those who appreciate you intellectually and who don't crave constant reassurance or emotional connection. You will quickly feel drained and depleted by a partner who wants to analyze every nuance of their latest dream or fantasy.

You are curious, open, and socially minded and thus can attract a lot of friends and admirers. You are friendly and can engage with people from across a wide range of backgrounds and socioeconomic strata. Yet, despite your curiosity and ability to easily connect with others, you rarely take these connections beyond a superficial level and will find ways to gracefully extricate yourself should someone try to overconfide in you or dominate your time. When you find a partner or friends with whom you share interests and can relax and have fun, you are loyal for life.

Your strong need to safeguard your freedom and personal space may cause you to avoid emotional issues and topics. You feel more comfortable disconnecting from complicated intimate feelings than confronting and exploring them. You will benefit from recognizing your tendency to shut down emotionally when feelings are running high. Instead of allowing yourself to shrug it off, try to re-engage with your feelings and articulate them. This will help you reach a whole new level of intimacy in your partnerships, without opening you up to the type of draining emotional dependency that you seek to avoid.

IF AQUARIUS IS YOUR

RISING SIGN

HOW YOU GET WHAT YOU WANT AND NEED: You allow others the freedom to be independent because you know how important that liberty is to you. Rather than making stringent demands on others, you instead give people personal space. Thus, others rarely make heavy demands on you, which is exactly the way that you want it. This leaves you the freedom and independence to follow your own interests and manage your own time unimpeded. You have specific habits, patterns, and little rituals that are important to you and you dislike being thrown outside of your own routine for too long.

With this level of freedom and independence, you have every opportunity to work behind the scenes to accomplish your wants and desires. You may have quite a nontraditional lifestyle that sets you apart from others. It does not bother you that others may find you unique, but it is important to you to find close friends and allies, otherwise you can become lonely and isolated. A tribe of confidantes who understand and support you and let you do your own thing makes you feel safe and loved.

You may find yourself feeling very drawn to a particular social cause or political issue. In fact, you may get so heavily involved that it comes to define you or take up almost all your time. In this case, you will find yourself at the forefront of whatever movement you've committed yourself to and embrace a communally oriented lifestyle. If, however, you maintain a more balanced lifestyle, you will attract many different types of friends and acquaintances from a variety of backgrounds. Your open-minded and independent personality helps you achieve all of your wants and needs.

"ONCE YOU FIGURE OUT WHO YOU ARE AND WHAT YOU LOVE ABOUT YOURSELF, I THINK IT ALL KINDA FALLS INTO PLACE."

—JENNIFER ANISTON

PISCES

FEBRUARY 19
— through —
MARCH 20

02.19–03.20

PISCES

ELEMENT	**MODALITY**	**RULING PLANET**	**SYMBOL**	**COLORS**
Water	*Mutable*	*Neptune*	*The Fish*	*The shades of the sea*

You are driven by deep desires, and plunge headfirst into love and life. But like waves that soar, crash, and retreat, you seldom take a straight or steady path to achieve your desires. Instead, you follow the dramatic rise and fall of your emotions. Creativity and passion swirl inside you, seeking outlets in both your professional and romantic exploits. You enjoy showering the people you care about with affection, but things get complicated when the balance of giving and receiving is out of whack. Because you have such a giving nature, you often don't know how to ask for your own needs to be met, which can lead you to feeling frustrated and disappointed. Once you become confident in receiving as well as giving, your life will bloom in a whole new way.

More than just working a steady nine-to-five job, you want to connect emotionally and intuitively with your purpose. Otherwise, you are prone to feeling drained and unhappy. Finding situations where you feel truly appreciated is a key to satisfaction and joy. Being creative and contributing to the greater good also nourishes your soul. Even if the way you earn a living doesn't give you much opportunity to satisfy those desires, finding a way to incorporate philanthropy and artistic pursuits into your life will bring you rich rewards. Volunteering for a cause that matters to you will make you feel vital and alive. And expressing your unique vision will give you peace of mind. Whether that means experimenting in the kitchen, making inspiration boards to guide your dreams, or just taking the time to journal and reflect, tapping into your rich imagination is an endless source of fun and inspiration.

You are so tuned in to the emotions of others and the vibes in your environment that finding techniques to ground yourself and stay centered is especially important. Meditation, writing, and exercise are all effective strategies. Rest is especially important to you as well, so don't feel guilty about taking time for yourself. You need privacy to restore your natural equilibrium so that you can return to the world to bless it with your abundance of love and creativity.

STELLAR GIFTS
You are creative, elusive, and wildly romantic, attracting admirers at every turn.

BLIND SPOTS
Always open to new ideas and interests, you change your mind quite a bit and your seemingly contradictory desires can be confusing to those around you.

FASHION FAVES
You are an ace at combining whimsical touches—think sparkles, feathers, lace—with edgier looks like studs or leather.

INDULGENCE
Art feeds your soul. When you find someone whose work you connect with, you love to bask in the glow.

SEDUCTION STYLE
The romance and fantasy of new amour thrills you. You get swept up in the thrall of desire, by the possibilities of new connections, and the fun of unlocking each other's secrets. You have to be careful not to idealize your partner too much.

Image

Your style changes depending on how you feel on any given day, as you are always guided by your instincts in the present moment. But your vibe is always confident, comfortable, and beautiful. You love gauzy layers and surprising combinations, like lace and leather or sequins and sneakers. You also enjoy nostalgic looks and may take style cues from a bygone era.

Money

When it comes to spending, your spontaneity and free spirit make you a little impulsive. You revel in having the freedom to change course and set out on a new adventure at the drop of a hat, and that can be expensive! You're also generous, showering the special people in your life with surprise gifts. Spending money to feed your creative and artistic pursuits is one of your best investments.

Education

This is one area where you tend to prefer a fixed routine, which means adhering to your own rituals. Beware anyone who holds you back from your pre-class or pre-work cappuccino! This bit of structure helps you to get grounded in what you are learning, and you can have a lot of patience when it comes to studying. You are disciplined and committed to subjects that you love, but are loath to study things that don't interest you.

Home Life

Often your family background is lively or even a bit chaotic. With so many different things going on, you can feel alternately inspired and unsettled. Your searching spirit may lead you to move around and travel quite a bit and you are always on the hunt for a romantic paradise in which to set down roots. You may even fall for a few different locations that each inspire different sides of your soul. If finances allow, you very well might find yourself splitting time between two homes or destinations you love.

I AM IN LOVE WITH BEAUTY AND THINGS AND PEOPLE AND LOVE AND BEING IN LOVE. AND THOSE THINGS I THINK ON THE INSIDE SHOW ON THE OUTSIDE."

—GLORIA VANDERBILT

Fun

Nothing brings you more joy than quality time with your friends and family. When you all get together, you know how to let loose! And even better, you are great at supporting one another and making each other feel special, celebrating each other's wins, and bolstering one another during tough times. Some of the friends you make in childhood are your soul mates for life and you guys support each other like a family, sometimes even spending holidays together. Closeness can come with occasional conflict, but familial loyalty always wins the day.

Health

It is very important for you to do plenty of cardio and to keep your energy levels high. You're so empathic that you become easily drained by others, so keeping your own vitality strong is essential. You can feel wounded or hurt by others' insensitivity, so keeping your expectations of others reasonable will protect you from feeling emotionally and physically exhausted. You also care about how you look so that is another perk to staying healthy. Just don't let vanity override your good senses!

Relationships

It's the little things that matter to you in relationships. A kind gesture or thoughtful card go a long way for you. Things don't need to be expensive or elaborate, but you really appreciate consideration and a personal touch. Connecting over shared values and goals is also meaningful to you. Together, you both seek to be of service in the world but must also find a way to balance this with a healthy personal life.

Intimacy

You like things to be as fair and balanced as possible when it comes to your intimate connection with others. When a relationship feels out of balance, you find it difficult to relax and trust. Making sure your needs are clearly expressed is very important since sometimes you can be indirect and simply assume that others know how to please you. Your desire to please others can also get in the way, so make sure you don't discount your own needs.

Travel

Some of your most intense and profound experiences can come through travel, especially to different cultures. You are fascinated by the intimate details of how others live. But you innately need plenty of privacy so you do best in places where you can escape from the crowds into your own secluded space, preferably overlooking the ocean! Luxurious places surrounded by nature or in an authentic community stir your soul.

Career

It is important for you to feel like you are doing something meaningful in your career, and thus, you often branch out on your own with a unique vision for your own path. It can be a challenge when others don't understand your big-picture goals, but as long as you keep the faith in your own vision and stay true to it, you're assured of success eventually. You thrive in careers related to the arts, travel, education, and publishing.

Friends

You are loyal for life when it comes to your friends. Confidantes you meet through your parents, school, and work are especially significant. You often end up doing work and creative projects with them and you know you can trust and lean on one another! When you get together, you love to indulge, especially in fine meals in luxe restaurants.

Privacy

Your personal space is very important to you, and when you are in your own world, you don't like to be disturbed. You create a unique environment and rituals for yourself that help you relax and connect to your spiritual center. Meditation and the study of esoteric subjects can help you to access guidance as well as creativity. Carve out some time daily to rest and replenish your energy.

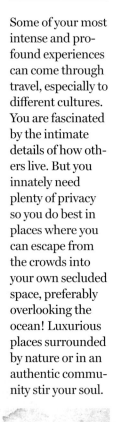

IF PISCES IS YOUR

SUN SIGN

WHAT YOU WANT: You want the freedom to express yourself creatively and emotionally, without being overly constricted by others. You are a naturally very giving and caring person, which can lead others to depend on you and drain your energy. You are very sensitive and intuitive, which is a great blessing. But since you can also pick up on others' feelings so easily, it can be hard for you to tell where your feelings end and another's feelings begin. It is important for you to find the right balance between giving and receiving in your personal as well as professional relationships.

You have a vast imagination and usually exhibit a fair amount of creative or artistic talent. Even if your career pulls you in a more routine direction, finding outlets that nourish your creative side will be good for you. Spending time at concerts or appreciating art will boost your spirits and keep your connection to the world of mystery and artistry alive. Your sensitivity can lead you to have spiritual or even psychic experiences. Be open to this, but take extra care with your health and body to keep you grounded as well.

You thrive on close human contact, but establishing more clear boundaries and protection for yourself will shield you from feeling like all of your love and creative energy is going down a bottomless well. You can establish those boundaries by tapping into your natural urge to retreat and reflect as a way to replenish and restore yourself. Through focusing on creative activities, health, and calming meditation, you can center and focus yourself so that you are not as susceptible to being thrown off balance. Once this is achieved, you can watch your creative visions come to life and contribute an abundance of love and inspiration to others.

> "I'VE ALWAYS SAID THAT ONE NIGHT, I'M GOING TO FIND MYSELF IN SOME FIELD SOMEWHERE, STANDING ON GRASS, AND IT'S RAINING, AND I'M WITH THE PERSON I LOVE. AND I KNOW I'M [NOW] AT THE VERY POINT I'VE BEEN DREAMING OF GETTING TO."
>
> —DREW BARRYMORE

MOON SIGN

WHAT YOU NEED: You are a very romantic and sensitive person and need to feel a sense of limitless possibility in your relationships. You can easily get swept off your feet in love and adore the sensation of getting lost in another person or a new affair. This is all fine and dandy—until you realize that you may not have been seeing the other person or situation clearly. That is when a feeling of being lost and confused can set in.

You have a keen sense of magic, mystery, and imagination. You are very creative and often have skills in the arts. While you may be resistant to having a fixed routine, dedicating yourself to nurturing your talents will pay off in the long run. You may be very spiritual and feel that there is something greater "out there." Follow your intuition and explore these feelings, but remember to remain pragmatic, lest you find yourself swept away by a spiritual fad.

You will benefit from balancing your dreams of fairy-tale romance with a more practical and discerning perspective. All that glitters is not gold and only when you can accurately assess whether a person's actions and daily behaviors are in line with the image they project will you know that you are truly connecting with who that person is, not just your idealized version of them. After you have learned to see people for who they really are and not who you want them to be, then you can properly channel your tremendous abundance of love and giving energy into the right people and situations. In those relationships, you will achieve the sense of end-less creative and emotional gratification that you crave.

IF PISCES IS YOUR

RISING SIGN

HOW YOU GET WHAT YOU WANT AND NEED: Your tremendous intuition and powers of perception help you achieve your personal desires and goals. You are quite flexible and easily adapt from one situation to the next. You have a knack for fitting in and making friends wherever you go. This is due to your keen ability to pick up on the energy of people and situations and go with the flow. Others tend to open up to you, which helps you meet their needs and concerns as well.

However, you can be quite idealistic and naturally tend to see the good over the bad. That is a lovely quality, but you have to keep your eyes open behind those rose-colored glasses so you can effectively watch out for "red flag" situations. Until you master that, you may find yourself in situations you don't like, saying "I knew this was going to happen!" You have a very giving and caring nature and want to be as supportive and helpful to others as possible. Again, this is an excellent quality, once you have learned not to sacrifice your own goals, desires, and needs in the process.

You are very creative and find inspiration wherever you go. If only everyone could see the magic that you see in the world! Channeling your insights into creative projects helps you make your unique vision more tangible. You may also be quite spiritual, which enforces your positive belief system and encourages your empathy toward others. Once you have learned to avoid the situations that keep you trapped and to stand up for your own needs and desires, you are capable of achieving most anything you set your mind to. The trick is to have faith in your own unique vision and to ground yourself in a daily routine that supports your health and efficiency.

> "I LOVE READING PEOPLE. I REALLY ENJOY WATCHING, OBSERVING, AND BEING ABLE TO FIGURE OUT A PERSON—THE REASON THEY WORE THAT DRESS, THE REASON THEY SMELL THE WAY THEY DO."
>
> —RIHANNA

2

ROMANCE & SEX

SEDUCTION AND THE STARS

How do you interact with others? What types of people are you most attracted to, as friends and as lovers? If indeed you have a type, you may be drawn to one of the zodiac "groups."

There are several ways that astrological signs are grouped and organized, including by element, modality, and opposites. We will explore exactly what that means for you and for the people in your life.

And in this section we give you not one, but two quizzes to help you identify your astrological type when it comes to love! We also share a ton of intel on the dating and mating rituals of every sign in the zodiac.

Unlock the Elements

The universe is composed of the elements earth, air, fire, and water—and so are all of our personalities. But based on our zodiac sign, we tend to identify with, and embody, certain elements more than others.

Some signs are associated with water, some with earth, others with fire or air. What our element tells us is how we experience life and our natural orientation to the world around us.

Compatibility in relationships and friendships often has to do with having a shared vision and experience of life, so our element tells us a lot about the types of people we get along well with.

We will give you an overview of the elements beginning on page 138 and also a fun dating quiz on page 139 to help you identify the element you are most attracted to based on what appeals to you in relationships.

The Modalities: Make the Most of Your Mojo

While we may be familiar with the four elements, the three modalities are a lesser-known astrological category. Each zodiac sign is associated with a modality and your modality describes how you express the energy of your sun sign. Your modality is one of the following three types: cardinal (someone who initiates action), fixed (a stabilizing influence), or mutable (a change agent).

Knowing your modality helps you uncover the strengths you can bring to the workplace and to your relationships. On page 140, we will show you which modality your sign is and provide a quiz so you can determine which modality you're most attracted to. Then check out our modality grid to see exactly how your modality and your crush's modality stack up in the sack!

Opposite Signs: Partnerships with Power

We tend to think of opposites as having nothing in common. But in astrology, opposites are more like a pair. They often have the same concerns and interests but are likely to approach them from a different perspective.

When we feel overwhelmed or bogged down, it's a good idea to look to our opposite sign for inspiration! Taking the perspective of our opposite sign can help us find different answers to the same question. Friendships or romances with people whose sun sign is opposite our own can be some of the most memorable and significant relationships of our lives. Beginning on page 144, we run through each of the six pairs of opposite signs so you can identify your own power combo. As the saying goes, "Opposites attract!"

The Definitive Guy Guide
Have you ever wondered what a roll in the hay with a Virgo would be like? Or what it takes to get a Pisces man to settle down? You will find your answers in our Definitive Guy Guide, beginning on page 146. This essential rundown of the idiosyncratic love lives of the men you know and date will surely prove invaluable as you puzzle over their latest bizarre text messages. Does Aries only want the chase? What on earth is Scorpio really like beneath that broody exterior? And who is the biggest flirt? (Spoiler: It's Libra.) All that and more as we take a very up close and personal look at the men of the zodiac.

Sexscopes
Finally, we invite you to get to know all the signs intimately, by exploring their bedroom style in the privacy of your own home each year when the sun is in their sign. For example, neither you nor your partner may be a Taurus, but when the sun is in Taurus between late April and mid-May, why not experiment with Taurean pleasures? Refer to Sexscopes on page 158 to see exactly when and how to add some of the signs' sexy sparkle into your love life.

UNLOCK THE ELEMENTS

HOW DO YOU EXPERIENCE THE WORLD?

The answer to this question can be found by identifying your element. Do you experience life like a fire sign, as a fun game ready to be explored (and won!)? Or more like an interesting puzzle that you are curious about, the way that air signs do? Each element has its own approach to life. And while all four elements are part of our personalities, we tend to identify most with the one that's related to our sun sign. So find your sun sign and element group below. Then take our quiz to see which element is your ideal date.

Earth Signs
TAURUS, VIRGO, CAPRICORN

You are practical, loyal, and patient. It takes a moment for things to catch your interest, but once you are excited about something (or someone!), you are steadfast. You delight in simple pleasures, like nature and delicious food and wine. In love, you want a considerate partner who can indulge in these luxuries with you. You take pride in taking care of yourself, and you have high standards and excellent taste. Neutral colors and luxurious textures, like soft cashmere and slinky silks, make you feel your sexiest.

BEST MATCHES
Earth and Water signs

Water Signs
CANCER, SCORPIO, PISCES

You are intuitive, nurturing, and a romantic at heart. Music and art arouse your passions. You are generous with your time and will always help those who need assistance. Passionate and romantic mates often spark your curiosity. Once you make a strong emotional connection with someone, you don't let go. You have a style that's whimsical and changeable. While always feminine, some days you're into cozy, casual styles, and other times you can be a full-on diva!

BEST MATCHES
Water and Earth signs

Air Signs
GEMINI, LIBRA, AQUARIUS

You are curious, sociable, and articulate. Because of your passion for learning, you have a wide variety of interests. Having a strong mental connection with your guy is very important to you because great conversation turns you on. Sharing your thoughts and feelings is how you build intimacy in all your relationships. You have a flair for finding flattering clothes and meaningful keepsakes, and your closet and home are always full of beautiful things.

BEST MATCHES
Air and Fire signs

Fire Signs
ARIES, LEO, SAGITTARIUS

You love to have a good time! You are open-minded and adventurous and enjoy getting swept away by the excitement of new people and experiences. You tend to jump headfirst into unfamiliar situations and have a naturally optimistic nature. Friends and lovers who are similarly extroverted and enthusiastic bring out the best in you. You are always one step ahead of the latest fashion trends. Bold colors and sporty styles that let you stay comfortable during your active lifestyle are your go-tos.

BEST MATCHES
Fire and Air signs

WHICH ELEMENT IS YOUR BEST MATCH?

1. THERE IS NOTHING SEXIER IN A MAN THAN:
A. Athleticism in and out of the bedroom.
B. A healthy bank account and a fondness for well-cut blazers.
C. A passion for talking global politics and big ideas.
D. A serenade with a song he's written just for you.

2. PERFECT FOREPLAY IS:
A. A glass of your favorite wine, candles, and a bubble bath prepared just for you. Oh, and a foot massage too!
B. Listening to your favorite playlist while cuddling and kissing for hours.
C. A session of stimulating verbal sparring that sparks your intellectual and passionate appetites.
D. Let's get physical! A little wrestling in the sheets gets you frisky!

3. YOUR IDEAL FIRST DATE IS:
A. Rock climbing or surfing. You want to see what he's made of!
B. A romantic stroll through the park or a long hike where you can walk and talk to get to know each other.
C. A theater show or art-gallery opening, then a post-event cocktail.
D. Dinner at an underground, hidden gem of a restaurant that serves only local farmers' market produce.

4. A FIGHT BETWEEN TWO GUYS BREAKS OUT AT A PARTY. YOU EXPECT YOUR GUY TO:
A. Jump into the fight to break it up.
B. Be there with a first-aid kit to patch everyone up when it's over.
C. Make a beeline straight to you to make sure you're okay.
D. Use his way with words to get the guys to talk—instead of punching—through their problems.

5. VALENTINE'S DAY OF YOUR DREAMS INCLUDES:
A. Champagne and diamonds! Duh!
B. The puppy you've been wanting for ages.
C. A hot, passionate night in bed exploring some of your fantasies.
D. Breakfast in bed, a gift book of all your Instagrams together, and a personalized playlist.

SCORING: 1. A–4 , B–1, C–3, D–2; 2. A–1, B–2, C–3, D–4; 3. A–4, B–2, C–3, D–1; 4. A–4, B–1, C–2, D–3; 5. A–1, B–2, C–4, D–3

EARTH SIGN GUYS: 5 TO 7 POINTS
Taurus, Virgo, Capricorn
PRO: Steadfast and passionate
CON: Picky and demanding

The Earth sign guy's mix of rugged and sophisticated tastes and raw passionate nature turns you on! These dudes rise in their careers and love the good life but still keep their feet planted on the ground. Speak up with him; you don't want his needs to overwhelm yours. Note: This earthy lothario is a master of sexual positions, so don't be shy in the bedroom!

WATER SIGN GUYS: 8 TO 11 POINTS
Cancer, Scorpio, Pisces
PRO: Seductive and thoughtful
CON: Hard to read and shy
A sensitive romantic turns you on big-time! Water sign guys have a sixth sense for knowing—and giving—women what they want. He's always compassionate but not always good at expressing his true feelings, so you may have to help him along at first. He likes familiar surroundings, so plan on dates at favorite neighborhood restaurants and bars and, of course, sexy stay-home nights.

AIR SIGN GUYS: 12 TO 15 POINTS
Gemini, Libra, Aquarius
PRO: Witty and wise
CON: Distractible and high-strung
You love smooth talkers! Air sign men are great conversationalists who'll keep you up all night chatting. They enjoy cultural events, post-work drinks, and barbecues where they exchange points of view. They're super turned on by women who can hold their own in social situations. Communication is key with these guys, so up the data plan on your phone and keep the love alive with flirty texts and witty e-mails.

FIRE SIGN GUYS: 16 TO 20 POINTS
Aries, Leo, Sagittarius
PRO: Magnetic and fun
CON: Unpredictable and restless
You're thrilled by the adventurousness of the Fire sign stud! They like to rush into romance, so buckle your seat belt and get ready for a wild ride. Make active dates; they'll burn up his endless energy. He loves the thrill of the chase, so keep your schedule full and drop hints about how in demand you are.

THE MODALITIES

MAKE THE MOST OF YOUR MOJO

Just as each sign is associated with a certain element, each sign is also associated with a modality. While our element is related to how we experience the world, our modality demonstrates how we engage in the world. How we act and the type of influence we are likely to have on people and situations can be seen by looking at our modality. So find your sun sign below and learn about how your modality affects the way you go through life. And similar to our element dating quiz, you can also investigate which modality you are most attracted to. Then flip to our Modality Matchmaker on page 142 to see how you two are likely to spark in the sack!

⚡ Cardinal

ARIES, CANCER, LIBRA, CAPRICORN

You are the doers and problem solvers of the zodiac! You get restless sitting still. You are innovative and purposeful and will take calculated risks to achieve your aims. The rush you get from accomplishment pushes you forward to your next challenge.

◬ Fixed

TAURUS, LEO, SCORPIO, AQUARIUS

You are strong-willed and value consistency. You take a slow and steady approach when getting to know people, but once you find something or someone you love, you're loyal for life. You dislike change being imposed on you, but when you decide you are ready to make a shift, it is swift and total!

◎ Mutable

GEMINI, VIRGO, SAGITTARIUS, PISCES

You can get along with anyone, anywhere. You have a knack for fitting in that's aided by how observant and curious you can be as well as your love of exploring. While you have your preferences, you're more likely—and happy—to go with the flow than dig in your heels.

WHICH MODALITY IS YOUR BEST MATCH?

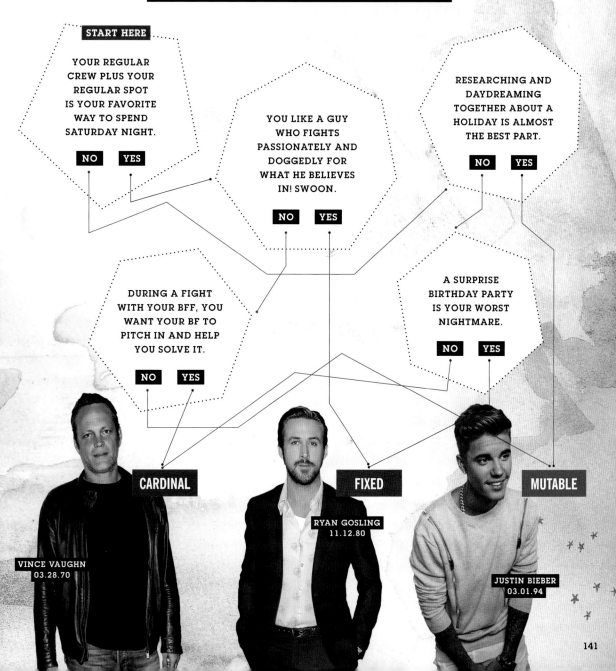

START HERE

YOUR REGULAR CREW PLUS YOUR REGULAR SPOT IS YOUR FAVORITE WAY TO SPEND SATURDAY NIGHT.

NO   YES

YOU LIKE A GUY WHO FIGHTS PASSIONATELY AND DOGGEDLY FOR WHAT HE BELIEVES IN! SWOON.

NO   YES

RESEARCHING AND DAYDREAMING TOGETHER ABOUT A HOLIDAY IS ALMOST THE BEST PART.

NO   YES

DURING A FIGHT WITH YOUR BFF, YOU WANT YOUR BF TO PITCH IN AND HELP YOU SOLVE IT.

NO   YES

A SURPRISE BIRTHDAY PARTY IS YOUR WORST NIGHTMARE.

NO   YES

CARDINAL

FIXED

MUTABLE

VINCE VAUGHN
03.28.70

RYAN GOSLING
11.12.80

JUSTIN BIEBER
03.01.94

MODALITY MATCH-MAKER

Our modalities are indicative of how we engage with the world and with each other! As such, they are a good barometer of our sexual chemistry. Here, we break down how you and your Romeo connect in and out of the bedroom.

YOU ARE CARDINAL
Aries, Cancer, Libra, Capricorn

HE IS CARDINAL

CARDINAL SIGN: You have a lot of respect for each other's ambition. Your calendars are both jam-packed with work, errands, and time with friends. Doing outdoor activities like sports together keeps you bonded. Just make sure you two power players slow down and check in with each other!

G FORCE: As the zodiac's alpha couple, you'll reach your highest peak (read: orgasm) in this high-impact position that lets you both control the action.

HE IS FIXED

FIXED SIGN: This is a great match! You have endless enthusiasm and drive, and he has strong and clear preferences, which you respect and admire. He helps give you focus, while you lighten him up and explore new things. Slow down and let him catch up to you. It'll be worth it.

GET DOWN ON IT: This intimate but steamy position lets you take control...as usual. Your libido's more raging, but your steadfast lover is happily along for the ride.

HE IS MUTABLE

MUTABLE SIGN: Your passion and zest ignite him. He loves discovering new possibilities so he's up for the exciting ride you take him on! You will both need to exercise patience, since you're both apt to change your mind and direction unexpectedly. Experimentation is the name of your game.

BOOTYFUL VIEW: He's game for anything and you're impatient for your O. So slip 'n' slide to your heart's (and clit's) content while he thrusts and enjoys the view.

CARDINAL SIGN: While you tend to dig in your heels, he helps you explore new ways of approaching problems. He can go hard and fast in the bedroom, while you appreciate a slower pace, but if you teach him your preferences, he'll be eager to please!

REACH FOR THE HEAVENS: You're set in your ways, but he's an explorer, so let him push you out of your comfort zone (and...against the headboard) while you squeeze your legs teasingly.

CARDINAL SIGN: His can-do attitude and zeal for life inspires you. You love exploring new horizons and he has lots of escapades on tap, so together you are in constant motion. He's adventurous sexually, and you are more than happy to be led by an enthusiastic guide.

THE STANDING SPREAD-EAGLE: He's dominant but addresses your needs too with this passionate upright sex position.

FIXED SIGN: You both have your quirks and preferences, but if they click, you totally just get each other. You respect one another's determination and values, and your relationship will be a true expression of the things you both love. All that intensity makes your sex life combustible!

THE SENSUAL SPOON: You are both stubborn and sometimes disagree—but not on this acrobatic spoon that gets you both off.

FIXED SIGN: He is a man with a clear idea of who he is and what he wants, and that appeals to you. . .when you agree with him! You urge him to reach for the stars, while he can be a fabulous teacher and support system.

THE DIRTY DANGLE: He tends to stick with one position, but he's as intent on pleasing you as he was on acing his SATs, so it won't be hard to get him to agree to this head-rushing take on missionary.

MUTABLE SIGN: You prioritize life differently. You know what matters most to you and are willing to fight for it, while he seems to be constantly changing and adopting new interests. You could be frustrated by this or embrace it.

THE SPIDER WEB: Rein in his short attention span with this intimate orgasmic tangle, then keep things focused with some super-hot slow grinding.

MUTABLE SIGN: The world is your oyster! You both enjoy getting swept away by your curiosity and intuition. One weekend, you're uncovering a nearby town together or bingeing on a new show. The next, you're enjoying previously unexplored sexual territory.

STAND AND DELIVER: You're both so rarin' to go, you sometimes forget the romance factor. So combine your smokin'-hot up-against-the-wall sex with intense eye contact.

THE OPPOSITES

PARTNERSHIPS WITH POWER

There are two sides of every coin. And in astrology, each sign is intimately linked with its opposite, the sign that is located directly across from it on the zodiac wheel, and six months apart, in the calendar.

Opposite signs are the same modality, so they move through life in a similar way. They are concerned about many of the same things in life, so they naturally encourage one another toward their goals and desires.

Another notable aspect of opposite signs is that full moons take place in opposite signs. For example, when the sun is in the sign of Gemini in early June, the full moon that month will always fall in Gemini's opposite sign of Sagittarius. When the sun is in Cancer in early July, the full moon will fall in Cancer's opposite sign of Capricorn, and so on. To find out more about what that means for you, whatever your sun sign may be, see Full Moons on page 172.

Read on to see how these power pairs complement one another and how your opposite-sign BFFs may be some of your best secret weapons.

ARIES & LIBRA

You are both active and ambitious and thrive on the buzz of the win and the new. Aries charges into their endeavors, while Libra likes to consider all the options first. Libra benefits from Aries' make-it-happen mojo. Assertive Aries could learn from Libra's considerable charm.

TAURUS & SCORPIO

These two signs go for the gold, both treasuring money, sex, and satisfaction. But Taurus is drawn to earthy pleasures for their own sake, while Scorpio savors the power it can afford. Scorpio can lead Taurus to be more strategic, while Taurus can help Scorpio relish the moment.

GEMINI & SAGITTARIUS

Gemini and Sagittarius are the seekers of the zodiac. Gemini is cerebral, always sparking new ideas, while Sagittarius's wanderlust is more physical. Gem's intellect stimulates Sag's creativity, and Sag's broad-mindedness helps Gemini structure their thinking into concrete concepts.

CANCER & CAPRICORN

You're both achievers who inspire loyalty. Cancer thrives on nurturing their people and places. Capricorn soars to the top with careful planning and execution. Cap's strategic approach can be a steadying influence for emotional Cancer, while Cancer's warmth helps Cap relax and open up.

LEO & AQUARIUS

Leo and Aquarius both sparkle as independent and innovative leaders. Aquarius's unique creativity and vision inspire Leo. And Leo, as a courageous and magnetic trailblazer, can help make Aquarius's dreams a reality. Leo helps Aquarius put heart and passion into her crusade.

VIRGO & PISCES

Virgo and Pisces are the healers, caretakers, and organizers of the zodiac. Virgo's affinity for details and patience helps her be productive and precise, which can be grounding for whimsical Pisces. Pisces' natural creativity and compassion bring love and lightness to Virgo's structured world.

03.21–04.19

ARIES

ROBERT DOWNEY JR.
04.04.65

PHARELL WILLIAMS
04.05.73

ELEMENT
Fire

MODALITY
Cardinal

LOVE MATCHES
Libra, Leo, Sagittarius

FRIEND MATCHES
Gemini, Aquarius, Capricorn

GOALS
• *To find personal freedom.*
• *To have access to things he wants.*
• *To never feel constricted.*
• *To win.*

KEY WORDS: Direct. Adventurous. Confident. Assertive.

SEX STYLE: This is a man who wants to take you the old-fashioned way—by grabbing you and treating you to a hot and sweaty romp. When he is turned on, his macho confidence shines and he will pursue you ardently. And when you get behind closed doors, he wants to enjoy his victory in the bedroom, over and over again. Don't bother setting a romantic scene with candles and music, he won't even notice. He is there for the main event and he will push you both to new levels of pleasure by keeping things strong and simple.

RELATIONSHIP STYLE: Aries men don't like to be tied down so he needs a lot of room in his relationships. He likes the chase, and he can't resist women who are coquettish or unavailable and present a challenge. If he seems stuck in the game-playing phase, you may decide it's time to move on. He may be a tad on the immature side, but that's the price to pay for his raw enthusiasm and can-do attitude. And once he has decided that you are the one for him, he will pull out all the stops to try and please you. When he finally settles down, he wants to take pride in his partner and have a traditional happy home.

CAREER: He is a bit old-school when it comes to his career path, preferring a slow and steady ascent that will yield a long-term win. He is great at networking and making connections so he is an ace at mixing business with pleasure. If you can help him strategize his climb to the top, all the better. He is ready to put in long hours on the job as long as he can balance this with physical activity and time in the great outdoors.

BEST UNEXPECTED QUALITY: The man is a homebody. For such an assertive manly man, you may think he barely takes a break. But actually, he is quite proud of his home and loves spending time there.

FUN FACT: If he feels like he is integral in the success and victory, he will move mountains to help you achieve your goals.

LOVES: A confident woman who can get along well with his friends and family. A sociable partner who helps him shine and chase his goals.

HATES: Overly emotional mind games. Timid types who aren't game to try new things.

DREAM DATE: Hiking, biking, and boating! He adores being outside. A sports game or amusement park where there is endless adrenaline that follows you home into the bedroom.

WIN HIM OVER: By showing him your spontaneous side and how much you enjoy unexpected escapades. Flatter his healthy ego, and spend lots of time in the bedroom!

04.20–05.21

TAURUS

GEORGE CLOONEY
05.06.61

CHANNING TATUM
04.26.80

ELEMENT
Earth

MODALITY
Fixed

LOVE MATCHES
Scorpio, Virgo, Capricorn

FRIEND MATCHES
Pisces, Cancer, Aquarius

GOALS
- *To create a stable home base.*
- *To move at his own speed.*
- *To see his creative visions brought to life.*
- *To avoid being pressured or influenced.*

KEY WORDS: Reliable. Stable. Loving. Patient.

SEX STYLE: He is a steady and passionate lover. He takes care to set the right ambiance and loves to create a scene that stimulates the senses. You can't rush him. In fact, you may find yourself waiting at a simmer while he whips up a decadent dessert for two or cues up his new favorite playlist. But when he's in the zone, he'll lavish you with hours of bonding and romance. He is especially sensitive to your every touch and loves hot showers and long massages to get him in the mood.

RELATIONSHIP STYLE: While he takes his time warming up, once he has set his sights on you, he will be dogged in his determination to win you over. The constancy of his attention is flattering and once you find your groove you can create your own indestructible bond, in and out of the bedroom. He may even become overly dependent on your time and attention. He dislikes being forced into anything and when you apply pressure, you'll see his hot temper and stubborn streak emerge. Thankfully, these outbursts blow over just as quickly. At heart, he wants to have an easy and functional lifestyle, filled with things that bring him joy and delight his keen senses.

CAREER: His creativity and eye for detail will help him carve out a unique career path. He is very shrewd financially and has a long-term approach to money matters. With his distinctive skills and strengths, he will find an interesting niche within his chosen field. Finance, technology, and humanitarian efforts may catch his attention. The more he is encouraged by others to pursue his own vision, the more likely he is to distinguish himself.

BEST UNEXPECTED QUALITY: The great outdoors is his natural habitat. Even the most refined Taurus man may have a rugged woodsman lurking beneath.

FUN FACT: He has great taste. Expect birthday and holiday presents to be a major jackpot!

LOVES: A passionate and motivated woman who speaks her mind. A determined and reliable partner.

HATES: Flaky and fickle behavior that confuses and distracts him. Manipulative schemers.

DREAM DATE: Listening to music while cooking dinner together, wine in hand. Arouse his passion for culture by going to a concert or gallery exhibit.

WIN HIM OVER: By showing him you are strong and trustworthy. By not coming on too fast. Keep it slow and steady with Mr. Taurus.

147

GEMINI

05.22–06.20

JOHNNY DEPP
06.09.63

BLAKE SHELTON
06.18.76

ELEMENT
Air

MODALITY
Mutable

LOVE MATCHES
Aquarius, Sagittarius, Libra

FRIEND MATCHES
Aries, Pisces, Leo

GOALS
• *To have many diverse experiences.*
• *To do something unique.*
• *To learn.*
• *To have freedom.*

KEY WORDS: Communicative. Intelligent. Whimsical. Open-minded.

SEX STYLE: Gemini can be all over the place. Literally and figuratively. You may have just gotten settled down for a roll in the hay and suddenly he is standing up, checking his phone, getting a drink; then just as suddenly, he's back in bed with you. If you can keep up with his fast pace and sexual acrobatics then you are in for a good time. He is especially adept at using his hands to turn you on. But if he's just not in the mood, he can be one of the most difficult men to tempt into sex.

RELATIONSHIP STYLE: There are two types of Gemini men out there. Ones who have a distinct sense of exactly what they want. And ones who are still sifting through their different interests to find out what they want. If you don't mind an adventure, either can be a good partner—just know that the latter may change direction as often as their shirt. As the most buzzy of mental air signs, he needs to be turned on between the ears before he gets turned on below the belt. Bonding over shared interests, big ideas, and future plans will catch his attention. Once he has his heart set, he will use old-fashioned and gentlemanly tactics to woo you.

CAREER: Geminis tend to have multiple careers to suit their multiple interests. The most organized and capable Gems pull this off with gusto. Gem guys who have not yet honed their organizational skills can deplete their energy, and yours, trying to balance it all or suss out which new opportunity is golden. They need to feel freedom and flexibility in their career so they are likely to do their own thing rather than follow a strict corporate path.

BEST UNEXPECTED QUALITY: He has a nearly photographic memory. So he's the zodiac boyfriend least likely to forget an anniversary.

FUN FACT: Geminis are especially close to their siblings, and if they are only children, they tend to remain very close with their childhood friends.

LOVES: A girl who's up for anything to be his partner in adventure! Curious and inquisitive types who spark his sharp mind.

HATES: Boring Groundhog Day routines that stifle his creativity. Being forced to do things the traditional way.

DREAM DATE: A party with all your friends followed by some intimate alone time. Hours of chatting about anything and everything at his favorite restaurant.

WIN HIM OVER: By letting him teach you about the things he's passionate about. Being game for last-minute travels and changes of plan.

CANCER

BENEDICT CUMBERBATCH
07.19.76

CHRIS PRATT
06.21.79

ELEMENT
Water

MODALITY
Cardinal

LOVE MATCHES
Scorpio, Capricorn, Pisces

FRIEND MATCHES
Taurus, Aries, Virgo

GOALS
• *To be a trailblazer in his career.*
• *To have a happy home life.*
• *To have a personal safe space.*
• *And always... to eat delicious food.*

KEY WORDS: Nurturing. Protective. Hard-working. Cautious.

SEX STYLE: He tends not to be aggressive in courtship nor to want to make the first move, unless he has gotten a clear green light. Yet, once he is in the bedroom and behind closed doors, he can charge full steam into romance. He is quite adoring and reverent of his chosen lover and aims to please. He will keep going until he feels you are satisfied and will happily take cues and instruction as offered. He loves exploring the female body and never tires of lusty, heartfelt lovemaking.

RELATIONSHIP STYLE: Cancers are notoriously sensitive and pick up a lot of their cues about relationships from their parents and early environment. In this sense, the Cancer man can earnestly and without irony expect his partner to play a mother-like role in his life. His sweet and charming personality will win you over, but you may have to assume double duty as his private chef and personal assistant. Yet because he is as gentle and kind-hearted as they come, there's a good chance that you will do it all with a smile, knowing that you are his favorite after-hours play-date.

CAREER: He is considerably more ambitious and hardworking than he may first appear. He takes his time making major decisions and weighs all his options carefully. But he is also quite fearless in terms of what he is willing to take on and he is not afraid to set challenging goals for himself. As traditional as he is in other parts of his life, he can be a bit of a rebel when it comes to work and will disrupt the status quo if he feels there is a better way. His competitive side also shines in his career and he takes great satisfaction in rising to the top.

BEST UNEXPECTED QUALITY: He has cool friends. For all his homey, family-man ways you may assume he just keeps company with his stuffed animals, but really, he has a roster of awesome pals who are loyal for life.

FUN FACT: When they say you can cook your way into a man's heart, that is most definitely true for the Cancer man. Learn to make his favorites and you'll have him hooked.

LOVES: Keeping things mellow and easygoing with old friends. Cozy date nights at home with his sweetheart.

HATES: Overly complicated and melodramatic shenanigans. Loud parties with people he doesn't know.

DREAM DATE: A family-style barbecue in the backyard where everyone is welcome. He loves a classic dinner-and-a-movie date!

WIN HIM OVER: By taking an active interest in his life and being supportive of his dreams and goals. Show that you can hang with his guy pals.

CHRIS HEMSWORTH
08.11.83

07.23–08.22

LEO

JASON MOMOA
08.01.79

ELEMENT
Fire

MODALITY
Fixed

LOVE MATCHES
Aries,
Aquarius,
Sagittarius

FRIEND MATCHES
Gemini,
Taurus,
Libra

GOALS
- *To be a good leader.*
- *To be creative.*
- *To inspire others.*
- *To live up to his potential greatness.*

KEY WORDS: Proud. Magnetic. Creative. Dramatic.

SEX STYLE: He is all about strength and stamina in the bedroom. He doesn't like to be rushed. Instead, he enjoys lavishing his attention on you, expecting the same in return. He loves stroking, full-body contact, and massages. When he is in an amorous mood, he will want to spend a full day lounging in bed and indulging in time together. He also adores it when you play with his hair, which he is deservedly vain about. Being a doting and attentive lover will prompt his roar of approval.

RELATIONSHIP STYLE: He doesn't fall in love very often, but when he does, he gives his whole heart. He needs to feel that he is with a woman who is worthy of being his queen and of whom he can be proud. He is less outgoing and attention-grabbing in public than his female counterpart but he nonetheless requires a great deal of time and energy behind the scenes. He dislikes being questioned or second-guessed, and can take himself a bit seriously, so don't poke this big cat too much. He will worship you like a goddess, but you have to treat him like a king first!

CAREER: A stable career that will yield him a steady, and steadily increasing, income appeals to him. He needs to feel creatively involved in what he does and that his insights are applauded as meaningful and important. He works best in situations where boundaries and expectations are clearly defined. He is willing to give 100% effort when he feels he is being valued and respected by his team. He has a stubborn streak and will retreat and dig in his heels if he believes he has been insulted or wronged.

BEST UNEXPECTED QUALITY: He is extremely generous. He loves lavishing attention and gifts on people and causes he cares about. He knows just how to make you feel special and cherished.

FUN FACTS: He is lucky at gambling. Kids love him. And, of course, like the lion he is, he has the best head of hair in the zodiac.

LOVES: A trailblazing woman who isn't afraid to follow her own path. Receiving praise without tooting his own horn.

HATES: Controlling types who will back him into a corner. Petty bickering and pointless debates.

DREAM DATE: A three-course, gourmet home-cooked meal, followed by hours in the bedroom. An all-day extravaganza that he's planned from start to finish.

WIN HIM OVER: By showing him you are a curious woman with diverse interests and talents. By showing off your silly side and matching his energy on the streets and between the sheets.

VIRGO

JIMMY FALLON
09.19.74

IDRIS ELBA
09.06.72

ELEMENT
Earth

MODALITY
Mutable

LOVE MATCHES
Capricorn, Pisces, Taurus

FRIEND MATCHES
Cancer, Scorpio, Gemini

GOALS
• *To be respected for his work.*
• *To enjoy the rewards of his efforts.*
• *To be his best self.*
• *To spend time in nature.*

KEY WORDS: Observant. Analytical. Considerate. Disciplined.

SEX STYLE: He is all about the details, in life and in bed. Nothing escapes this man's attention, which means that when he is in the mood to please, he will attend to each and every super-sensitive spot on your body. And best of all, he has uncovered clever and innovative ways to access them, so expect a romp with him to be more frisky than you may have imagined from his often reserved demeanor. He is a considerate lover who will remember what pleases you and make sure you are coming back for more.

RELATIONSHIP STYLE: Since sex with him can be a major turn-on, you may just find yourself game for a full-on relationship. But when he's in dating mode, his observant and helpful nature can sometimes veer into the realm of fussiness or full-blown critical-ness. Straddling the line between being mutually supportive and trying to "improve" one another will take some effort, but he is kind and caring at heart, making him a very loyal and loving partner. He revels in time spent together in the great outdoors where his rugged can-do persona shines.

CAREER: He is a hardworking and career-focused person. He has quite a bit of nervous energy, which he needs to direct toward tangible goals. For this reason, he thrives in jobs that require focus and attention to detail. If he can actually build something and see the impressive results, all the better. The Virgo man's keen eye for quality and refinement also help him shine in artistic careers. He is partial to long hours in the office, so be warned that wrangling him to relax and take a chill vacation might be tough.

BEST UNEXPECTED QUALITY: He will take the time to try to figure out things you like and then actually do them! This is close to a miracle in guy-world.

FUN FACT: You can bait him into doing almost anything if you subtly present it as a puzzle or a problem that you just can't solve.

LOVES: A woman who knows who she is and doesn't forget it, no matter where she is. Quality time with thoughtful, creative types who inspire him.

HATES: Chaos that distracts him from being in the moment. Violence and in-your-face energy.

DREAM DATE: Glamping and stargazing: aka an old-school, late-night make-out session. Wine and pillows on hand, obvi.

WIN HIM OVER: With long, witty conversations that reveal your allure is way more than skin deep. By showing him that you get him and understand how important his big life goals are.

LIBRA

09.23–10.22

JOHN KRASINSKI
10.20.79

WILL SMITH
09.25.68

ELEMENT
Air

MODALITY
Cardinal

LOVE MATCHES
Aquarius, Aries, Gemini

FRIEND MATCHES
Leo, Sagittarius, Cancer

GOALS
- *To have beauty in his life.*
- *To be around people he enjoys.*
- *To go to fun parties.*
- *To have lots of friends.*

KEY WORDS: Charming. Attentive. Articulate. Sociable.

SEX STYLE: As a lover, he has a light touch and wants to make sure your bedroom romps are fun and mutually enjoyable. Flirtation and charm are his hallmarks, so he likes to keep the mood light, even when he is in the throes of passion. And he rarely pushes boundaries or gets too experimental. He prefers to put you on a pedestal and treat you like a fairy-tale princess who has captured his attention. He can be very romantic and wants lots of reassurance that you are enjoying his ardent overtures.

RELATIONSHIP STYLE: This is the guy you can hang around with and talk to for hours. In fact, he may as well be one of your best girl-friends with all the fun you two have gabbing together. Unfortunately, other women have caught on to this as well and you will have competition for his attention. He is an expert juggler and has been known to stoke several fires simultaneously. He may well be an incurable commit-ment-phobe. But he could also turn around just as quickly and pledge undying romantic love to someone. At that point, he will want to ride off into the sunset together. On a unicorn.

CAREER: He tends to prioritize his personal and social life more than his career. But he is very creative and needs an outlet for his energy and interests. It is important that he enjoys the people that he works with and his daily routine or he may become deflated. He is apt to work hard when he finds an environment he enjoys and where he feels appre-ciated. He is great at any jobs that involve sales, working with clients, and building relationships.

BEST UNEXPECTED QUALITY: He is hilarious. He has learned exactly how to crack people up and you will be the lucky recipient of his humorous antics.

FUN FACT: He has a very difficult time making up his mind. If you need to stall for 20 minutes, give him two options to choose between and he'll amuse himself by slowly and carefully weighing the pros and cons of each.

LOVES: An articulate and intelligent woman who enjoys brainy banter as much as he does. Spicy sexts that keep him guessing and craving you.

HATES: Time-consuming projects with no immediate payoff. Public fights that make you both look lame.

DREAM DATE: He's romantic to the core, so get ready to be wined, dined, and wooed. The best table, the hottest spot: indulgence plus scene. Score!

WIN HIM OVER: By being the best version of you. He's drawn to strong, independent women, so show him your fierce and loyal side.

SCORPIO

DRAKE
10.24.86

EONARDO DICAPRIO
11.11.74

ELEMENT
Water

MODALITY
Fixed

LOVE MATCHES
Pisces, Taurus, Cancer

FRIEND MATCHES
Virgo, Capricorn, Leo

GOALS
- *To follow his inner path.*
- *To have control over his environment.*
- *To make and maintain strong connections.*
- *To achieve a big dream.*

KEY WORDS: Intense. Passionate. Private. Determined.

SEX STYLE: Scorpios have a reputation for their prowess in the bedroom. And whether he is as feisty, or as downright dirty, as legend would suggest, he is certainly content to allow this glamorous air of mystery and sensuality to surround him. He is a master of the waiting game, stirring his would-be lovers into a frenzy before finally making his move. When he does, the payoff is explosive. And once you have taken a bite of that exotic fruit…

RELATIONSHIP STYLE: Scorpios are known for their extremism. He has an all-or-nothing personality, so you may find yourself either on the lonely side of the equation or by his side 24/7. If he isn't putting in enough effort emotionally, have a firm exit plan, because he may try to maneuver himself back into your heart at the eleventh hour. If he is on the 24/7 end of the spectrum, then you have to decide if his brand of rigorous togetherness is the right fit for you. But when he falls, he falls hard. If you take the leap as a couple, he will move mountains for you.

CAREER: He doesn't commit to things that don't interest him. Instead, he is intent on building a life and career that match his values and priorities. As he plots his moves, he takes even small steps very seriously. As a team,

you can become co conspirators to his master plan. He has a knack for making money, but if he gets power-crazed, he may need you to remind him not to use his seduction skills in any less than reputable schemes. Even if he doesn't always admit it, he cares about success and will work hard to achieve it.

BEST UNEXPECTED QUALITY: Underneath all that smolder, Mr. Scorp can be a total softie. When he is relaxed and comfortable, his tender side comes out. Cue the rom-com movie marathon and get out the tissues.

FUN FACT: He is kind of psychic. He has a sixth sense for knowing exactly what is happening around him and what everyone else is thinking.

LOVES: A determined and grounded woman who is able to make her dreams a reality. Compassionate women who know their own values.

HATES: Flightiness and excessive nervous energy. Scatterbrained antics that waste his time.

DREAM DATE: He loves to be outside so a leisurely walk will spark the romantic in him. An art house play where you can discuss the meaning of life afterward.

WIN HIM OVER: Revealing your emotional depths one layer at a time keeps you constantly on his mind. By making time for long, intense convos and slow, sweet kisses.

SAGITTARIUS

BRAD PITT
12.18.63

JAY Z
12.04.69

ELEMENT
Fire

MODALITY
Mutable

LOVE MATCHES
Leo, Gemini, Aries

FRIEND MATCHES
Libra, Aquarius, Virgo

GOALS
- *To live in the present.*
- *To be free to explore the world.*
- *To experience life as a fun adventure.*
- *To always keep learning.*

KEY WORDS: Adventurous. Optimistic. Free-spirited. Curious.

SEX STYLE: Get ready for a wild ride with the Sagittarius man! He is as laid-back and adventurous in the bedroom as he is in the rest of his life. Embracing a YOLO attitude, this lothario is up for anything, from sex-capades in public places, to fun with toys and even group activities. Being a natural adventurer, sex in transit—anywhere from the backseat to the mile-high club—is a special turn-on for him. He likes variety so he'll want to switch up the action a few different times during any single interlude.

RELATIONSHIP STYLE: When he is ready to settle down, he can be a loyal partner. But if he is still in his free-spirited phase, you may have trouble getting him on the phone—let alone to commit to anything. Once he has found someone as curious and dynamic as he is, he will want to share his life and travel and enjoy new experiences together. You will never be bored in a relationship with him! If you are willing to keep learning together, and give him some space to be spontaneous, the world is your oyster.

CAREER: He needs to feel an emotional connection to his work. He is not likely to enjoy a classic nine-to-five job unless he is very committed to what he is doing. When he is passionate about his job, he is extremely hardworking and capable of gaining a lot of admiration. He is a stickler for details when it comes to projects he puts his creative stamp on. People respect his good humor and positive approach to problem-solving. If he can find a job that allows him to tackle big issues and gives him freedom to travel, then he is very happy.

BEST UNEXPECTED QUALITY: He is knowledgeable and opinion-ated about current affairs and wants to make a difference in the world. If he is spiritual or religious, he is very dedicated to his beliefs and practices.

FUN FACT: He is very lucky. This is the guy who wins the office raffle. Every year.

LOVES: A sophisticated woman who enjoys exploring the world as much as he does. An intelligent and spontaneous partner who is curious to try new things.

HATES: Needy and dramatic antics that reveal superficial tendencies. People who cramp his freedom and make excessive demands.

DREAM DATE: A sporty, outdoorsy day that will get his adrenaline pumping. The more exciting the better for this fiery and fearless dude.

WIN HIM OVER: He loves to teach you new things, so be his most eager pupil. Then turn the tables and teach him a thing or two in bed! Be up for anything, but also show him that you expect to be treated like a lady.

CAPRICORN

LEBRON JAMES
12.30.84

BRADLEY COOPER
01.05.75

ELEMENT
Earth

MODALITY
Cardinal

LOVE MATCHES
Cancer, Taurus, Virgo

FRIEND MATCHES
Scorpio, Pisces, Libra

GOALS
• *To succeed.*
• *To win admiration and respect.*
• *To forge strong personal and professional relationships.*
• *To find time to enjoy nature.*

KEY WORDS: Determined. Ambitious. Loyal. Hardworking.

SEX STYLE: Underneath that somewhat buttoned-up exterior is a guy who loves to throw himself hot and heavy into sex. He is an earthy lover whose somewhat rugged style is a major turn-on. You needn't be delicate or fussy with him, but rather let yourself get swept away by his assertive and determined nature. His confidence shines but he can veer into the realm of bossy from time to time. Sex in the great outdoors, or at the office, is a major turn-on for him, so don't be shy. He may even bring your experimental side out to play.

RELATIONSHIP STYLE: His magnetic allure is an intoxicating mix of rugged and polished qualities. This lends him an air of mystery and he attracts many admirers. He isn't one to rush into relationships and tends to be strategic about who he chooses to settle down with. But once he has committed, he is a very loyal and dedicated partner. His love of the good life is strong, and he will want to hitch up with someone who can help him succeed and who enjoys the same lifestyle. He also needs a nurturing partner who will attend to his softer side and coax him toward achieving his ambitious goals.

CAREER: His career may be largely built on his strong network of relationships. Mixing business with pleasure is second nature to him and he needs a partner who can keep up with him socially. Maintaining strong professional relationships is an important part of his success. He is driven and strategically engages others who can help him achieve his aims and ambitions. He also has a strong eye for quality and may be interested in the arts.

BEST UNEXPECTED QUALITY: He is very considerate. When he wants to, he knows just how to make you feel like the most special person alive!

FUN FACT: Capricorns are said to age the best of all the zodiac signs. Silver fox on the way!

LOVES: A nurturing and supportive mate who can help him navigate his way to the top! Someone who is comfortable in the great outdoors *and* at a posh cocktail party.

HATES: Overly controlling antics that leave him feeling stifled. Public arguments that make him lose face.

DREAM DATE: Dinner at an elegant restaurant where he can indulge his good taste. A long hike followed by a steamy romp on the picnic blanket.

WIN HIM OVER: By showing him you can get along with all of his different friends and colleagues. By being game for some sexy time in the most unexpected of places.

AQUARIUS

CHRISTIAN BALE
01.30.74

MICHAEL B. JORDAN
02.09.87

ELEMENT
Air

MODALITY
Fixed

LOVE MATCHES
Libra, Gemini, Leo

FRIEND MATCHES
Sagittarius, Aries, Scorpio

GOALS
• *To follow his own path.*
• *To inspire others while executing his unique vision.*
• *To find freedom from traditional expectations.*

KEY WORDS: Unique. Independent. Stubborn. Visionary.

SEX STYLE: He is a man who knows what he likes and goes for it. Whether this is swinging upside-down from the rafters or getting down with his favorite tunes on repeat, he knows exactly what he likes when it comes to bedroom activities. Naturally, he puts a lot of time into cultivating his preferences, so if you catch him in the early phase of his sexual exploration, you'll be in for a variety of exciting adventures. But once he is in his groove with what he really likes, you will find you are either a match for his moves in the bedroom or are decidedly not!

RELATIONSHIP STYLE: The Aquarius guy is a difficult one to pin down. True to his own vision and values above all else, he is a unique character who marches to his own drum. He is animated, bright, and curious but does not like to have others' ideas or expectations imposed upon him. If you are fascinated by his perspective and game to join him on his particular ride through life, you can be very happy together in your own bubble. But his mind-set is often "It's the Aquarius way or the highway!" and he is not necessarily skilled at the art of compromise.

CAREER: He is ambitious and determined. But you may never know exactly what his plans are, because he is surprisingly guarded and secretive when it comes to his deepest career goals and passions. Whatever field he pursues, he enjoys exerting power and getting his way. When productively attuned to the service of others, he can be immensely popular and powerful. But his hot-then-cold attitude can make him a controversial figure who can alternately be seen as a visionary leader or a radical rebel.

BEST UNEXPECTED QUALITY: He has a soft underbelly and can be surprisingly romantic. Give him a chance to surprise you!

FUN FACT: He is a technology whisperer. Hand him your broken laptop and watch miracles happen.

LOVES: Curious and thoughtful women who have many hobbies and interests. A confident and courageous woman who isn't afraid to show her true self.

HATES: Boredom and closed-mindedness in others. Pessimistic, flaky types who don't support his grand visions.

DREAM DATE: The quirkier the better! Head to a carnival or an improv show where he can laugh and be goofy with you. But he never tires of his favorite local hangouts.

WIN HIM OVER: By being supportive of his goals and showing him how passionate and committed you are about yours too. By being up for anything! He loves to be spontaneous with his girl.

PISCES

CHRIS MARTIN
03.02.77

ADAM LEVINE
03.18.79

ELEMENT
Water

MODALITY
Mutable

LOVE MATCHES
Scorpio, Cancer, Virgo

FRIEND MATCHES
Taurus, Capricorn, Sagittarius

GOALS
• *To create his own world.*
• *To enjoy an active fantasy life.*
• *To carve out private time.*
• *To execute his creative visions.*

KEY WORDS: Creative. Dreamy. Enigmatic. Romantic.

SEX STYLE: His charm is so subtle and magnetic that before you know it, you may find yourself in bed with the Pisces man. He is an ardent lover who can spend hours and days enthralled with sex, and during those delicious twilight in-between hours, you will find yourself losing all sense of time and place. Then just as quickly, he has vanished and escaped back into the ether. But while you are in each others' arms, you can create and explore magical worlds together. Even if you can't quite remember what was so special about it afterward, you will know in the moment.

RELATIONSHIP STYLE: Pisces are more about the romantic side of love than the practical side of a relationship. You may find him subtly trying to escape from the mundane responsibilities of your life together. And just when you think you have had enough, the wild and unexpected romantic side of him reappears and writes you a song or brings you a ridiculous gift and you are totally charmed. Once you two are in sync and on cruise control, you will conjure a private fantasy land that you both love retreating into, away from the harsh lights of the everyday world.

CAREER: He is a creative soul, and even if he finds himself in the world of business, he brings very original ideas and a fresh perspective. He

sets high and lofty goals for himself and he believes wholeheartedly that he can achieve them. Which of course, he can! In fact, his buoyant and well-founded optimism is one of his most charming qualities. His fertile imagination may lead him to a job that involves travel and distant locations—all the more fun when you set sail together!

BEST UNEXPECTED QUALITY: He is extremely smart. While he may mask these qualities behind a whimsical facade, he will pull through when it really counts.

FUN FACT: He may be from another planet. Spend an hour, a day, a year with him and you will see. There is simply no one else quite like him.

LOVES: A confident but adaptable girl who supports his ambitions. A woman with a quirky sense of humor who'll draw out his softer side.

HATES: A buzzkill pragmatist who doesn't let him dream. People encroaching on his personal space—unless you're his lady, then he'll invite you in!

DREAM DATE: Dancing the night away with his friends, followed by a steamy-hot shower session before bed. An intimate and secluded night at home, away from the city chaos.

WIN HIM OVER: By being whimsical and free-spirited but still open to his ideas and plans. By being a listener when it counts. He needs to vent sometimes.

SEXSCOPES

ARIES
03.21–04.19
Nobody loves a sexy quickie more than an Aries! When they are turned on, they are ready to go, so save your lingering foreplay for another day and jump right into the action. The Aries woman is no shrinking violet, so take cues from her "Me too!" attitude, and don't be afraid to go for what you want. Classic woman-on-top poses and quick-climaxing thrusting romps suit Aries' hot and heavy mood.

TAURUS
04.20–05.21
Not one for acrobatics, Taurus prefers a slow buildup to an earth-shaking orgasm. Famous for their generous foreplay, they escalate the action gradually. Over time, even the slightest movement takes things to a whole new level and they reach great heights in their marathon lovemaking sessions. Keep the action slow, then twist in the most subtle, but effective ways, for the finale fireworks.

GEMINI
05.22–06.20
Geminis are famous multitaskers, so you just never know when the mood may strike. They are quick to get turned on by things that spark their interest, so sex is all about taking that lingering touch to a whole new level or making the most of the preview time during your TV marathon. Everyday props such as chairs are the perfect tools, and keeping the mood playful and light adds to the sauciness.

CANCER
06.21–07.22
As the zodiac's most notorious romantics, Cancers like anything that involves adoring glances, deep kisses, and maximum body-to-body contact. Breasts also feature prominently in Cancer sex so keep the girls front and center! Face-to-face positions that make kissing a priority, and where you can wrap your arms around each other, increase the intimacy. A good old-fashioned cuddle sesh completes the mood.

LEO
07.23–08.22
Leos are a force to be reckoned with. This big-hearted sign gives 100% to everything, so anything less than your best effort just will not do. Their dramatic bedroom escapades tend to feature a star taking center stage and an adoring partner in the supporting role. Take turns in the spotlight and go for maximum stamina and pleasure during high-energy sessions.

VIRGO
08.23–09.22
Virgos are quite a bit friskier in the bedroom than they seem. This sign can get turned on quickly during the course of everyday life and subtle flirtation can turn into sex, even in unlikely places. The desk or kitchen table is a prime location to take this hardworking sign for a joyride. Tune into the same frequency by heating things up in an unexpected, clandestine location.

TWIRL-A-GIRL
This is a special twist on the woman-on-top position, literally. Have him lie down. Instead of straddling, swing your legs over him, so your legs are perpendicular to his. Sitting on his lap, lean back on your arms and open your legs so he can enter you. Then turn up the volume by twisting your hips enthusiastically.

THE BOYS ON-THE-SIDE
Lie down on your side. From behind, have him kneel next to you on the bed, so your bodies are perpendicular. He slides one knee between your legs and then enters you. You take the leg that's on top and extend it out onto the bed, giving him the chance to hold on to your hips as he thrusts inside you.

LAP LIMBO
Have your partner sit back on a couch or chair. Grab a nearby pillow to position under his knees. Straddle his lap and lean back against his thighs. Bend your knees and bring them up to rest on his shoulders. Have him pull you closer with his hands on your hips. Rock back and forth and take turns controlling the pace.

STRADDLE HIS SADDLE
Make this classic move extra sexy by doing it on the floor. On top of a comfy rug, have him sit down cross-legged and straddle him while kneeling. Position yourselves so that you're face-to-face. Have him lean backward on his arms for support. Use your frees hands to fondle your breasts in front of his face.

RIDE OF YOUR LIFE
Begin in the deceptively down-to-earth woman-on-top position. Then subtly curl your feet around the inside of his legs behind your butt. While thrusting, move your chest forward to grab the bedsheets around his head. With your body so tightly wound around him, small, tight thrusts take you both to the max.

SNEAK-A-PEEK
Choose a sturdy, flat surface that hits him at hip level. Then do a striptease and hop onto the surface, with your butt just off the edge. Lie back to give him a special show. Grab a cushion to elevate your hips and then raise your legs to his head. His hands are free to hold your legs or explore the rest of your body.

Just as the seasons change and the weather changes, the cosmic mood also changes as the sun moves through all twelve signs of the zodiac. So when you're looking for a little lovemaking inspiration, check out which sign is celebrating their birthday and let their preferences guide you! In February, frolic like an Aquarius. August? Roar like a Leo! Knowing what it's like to be another sign has never been more fun...or frisky.

LIBRA
09.23–10.22
Libra is the sign of balance, and their bedroom romps carry an air of diplomacy. Making sure you are both getting your jollies is serious business. Finding unique positions that bring you both maximum amounts of pleasure is something this enterprising and active sign enjoys. Practice moves that involve interesting (and symmetrical!) positions until you are both exhausted and oh, so happy.

SCORPIO
10.23–11.21
Scorpios thrive on intimacy and want to get as close as humanly possible when they are taking one of their frequent forays to pleasure town. Full body-to-body spooning contact is a turn-on, as are moves where maximum friction is applied. Making your partner work for their rewards with teasing also hits the jackpot. Keeping contact intense and consistent will take you to a new level.

SAGITTARIUS
11.22–12.21
Throw caution to the wind and try the craziest, kookiest things you have ever dreamed of! Sagittarians tend to be sexually liberated, so leave your hang-ups behind and let out your inner wild child. Role reversal, upside-down positioning—you name it, it's worth trying. Sags are free-spirits and embrace a YOLO attitude so kick-start your experimentation now.

CAPRICORN
12.22–01.19
Capricorns have a strong libido and aren't afraid to go for what they want. Lovers of sensual pleasure, they are capable of turning any experience into a naughty one. Getting carried away in the midst of an unusual (even public!) location may happen and the mood is one of illicit passion and drama. Turn an office visit frisky or do the deed up against the wall before you reach the bedroom.

AQUARIUS
01.20–02.18
Aquarians have a keen imagination and like to use it during sex! Since they are so mentally engaged and stimulated, they enjoy rear-entry positions that leave them open to fantasy. The combination of high-energy action with an imaginative landscape opens the door for a whole new world of experience. Using props, like pillows, also engages the Aquarius sense of fun and adventure.

PISCES
02.19–03.20
A sense of magic and mystery are innate to Pisces and they love bringing those elements into their sex life. They are romantics and when they're near the water, their sexuality kicks into overdrive. Get swept away, Pisces style, when you hear the waves lapping. If you can't make it all the way to the beach for a rendezvous, the pool or shower are perfect stand-ins.

TIME BOMB
Start by having him lie on the bed. He should raise one knee up and leave the other lying down. Instead of mounting him from the front, approach him from the side. Since you are kneeling, you can grind onto his penis and thigh. He will love seeing you cast flirtatious glances over your shoulder.

TIGHT SQUEEZE
Lie on your stomach with him behind you so you're both facing the same direction. His legs are outside of your legs. Part your legs slightly as he enters you. Have him rest his weight on his elbows. Once he is thrusting, pull your legs back together and cross your ankles. Keep your legs squeezed for maximum erotic effect.

PASSION PRETZEL

Kneel on the bed facing one another. Then each of you places the opposite foot flat on the ground. Pull into each others' waists until you have penetration. Then get into a flow of lunging backward and forward, leaning into your planted feet. You may find a whole new erogenous zone with this frisky upright romp!

PLEASURE PICK-ME-UP
With your guy standing with his back up against the edge of a chair or table, have him lift you into his arms. Wrap your legs around his waist and find the surface behind him to balance your feet on. With feet planted, you have more oomph to bounce up and down. Bonus points for a sexy role-play scenario.

MAGIC MOUNTAIN
Arrange a pile of pillows on the floor and relax into it face-first, so your back naturally arches. Your man lies on top of you with both of you facing the same direction, his chest on your back. Using the pillows for support, open your legs so he can kneel between them and enter you from behind.

THE SUBMARINE

Your man sits on the second or third step of the pool or on the hot-tub bench. Straddle him, then lift up your feet so they are behind his shoulders. Lean back so you are floating on the water, and have him grab your thighs to keep you elevated. Rest your elbows on his knees and let yourself float into ecstasy.

3

HOW TO READ YOUR HOROSCOPE

ASTROLOGY 101

Now it's time to demystify this special language as well as how horoscopes are constructed and written. You'll learn about significant astrological concepts like aspects, planets, signs, and houses, and accompanying charts will help you visualize how all these components come together. On page 169 we give you a sneak peek at what goes on behind the scenes every week when your horoscopes are being created. We also explore some of the most important astrological events, including eclipses, Mercury retrograde, and Saturn return, and show you how to use them to your maximum benefit.

What Is the Zodiac, Really?

Western astrology, the kind we practice in this book, is based on the seasons and the earth's rotation around the sun. Season-based astrology is called the Tropical Zodiac and designates your zodiac sign based on when your birthday occurs in relation to the earth's rotation around the sun.

A planet is identified as going through a certain zodiac sign based on where it is in relation to the four solstices and equinox points that occur every year. For example, if your sun sign is Aries, it means you were born in the first 30 days after the spring equinox. If your sun sign is Leo, it means that you were born between 31 and 60 days after the summer solstice, and so on.

The four solstices and equinox points that divide the seasons happen around the same time every year.

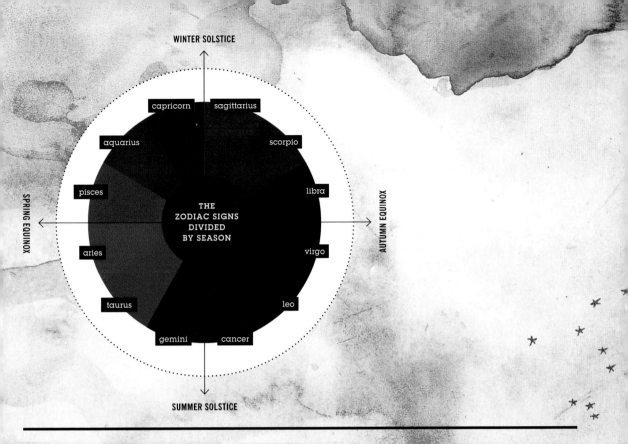

WINTER SOLSTICE

capricorn sagittarius

aquarius   scorpio

pisces   libra

SPRING EQUINOX

THE
ZODIAC SIGNS
DIVIDED
BY SEASON

AUTUMN EQUINOX

aries   virgo

taurus   leo

gemini   cancer

SUMMER SOLSTICE

How to Read Your Horoscope

So how exactly do astrologers know what is going on in the skies? And you've probably wondered...how does this apply to my job, my love life, or my workout routine?

Since the beginning of time, human beings have been curious about the skies. And since the ancient days, they have been drawing maps that keep track of the transiting planets and the corresponding effects of these transits on Earth. These maps are called charts or horoscopes. While we happily make use of computers to create charts in modern times, horoscopes really haven't changed very much. Every chart is calculated for a precise time and location, such as the time and place a person was born or the moment of an important event, like a job interview or a wedding.

Each chart has four basic features: planets, signs, aspects, and houses. We can visualize the way these component pieces relate to one another by using the metaphor of a play on a stage.

• **THE PLANETS** are the actors. They are the creators of action and momentum.

• **THE SIGNS** are the costumes. They clothe each of the actors/planets with certain qualities.

• **THE ASPECTS** are the script. They describe the interaction between the actors at any given time.

• **THE HOUSES** are the set. This is the setting or area of life where all the action takes place.

THE PLANETS

THE WORD *PLANET* DERIVES FROM THE ANCIENT GREEK WORD MEANING "WANDERER."

From the viewpoint of Earth, there are many wanderers in our night sky. In astrology, we give primary importance to ten planets. Although the sun and the moon are luminaries and not planets, they are referred to as planets for the sake of simplicity. Likewise, while astronomers have now determined that Pluto is a dwarf planet, it is still considered an astrological planet, since it is a wanderer with a fixed orbit. An orbit is the amount of time it takes each planet to make a full rotation around the sun.

The earth makes a 365-day orbit around the sun. So from the viewpoint of Earth, it *appears* that the sun has a 365-day orbit going through the twelve signs of the zodiac. The moon has a twenty-eight-day orbit around the earth. Thus, the moon passes through all twelve signs of the zodiac every twenty-eight days.

Here's the duration of orbit for the other eight planets we use in astrology:

MERCURY: 88 days
VENUS: 224 days
MARS: 2 years
JUPITER: 12 years
SATURN: 29 years
URANUS: 84 years
NEPTUNE: 165 years
PLUTO: 248 years

The Personal Planets

Mercury, Mars, and Venus are known as the personal planets, or inner planets, since they orbit

SUN: Energy, confidence, vitality, talents, skills, natural abilities

 MOON: Feelings, needs, desires, instincts, emotional connections

MERCURY: Logic, ideas, communication, correspondence, intellect

VENUS: Attraction, love, beauty, harmony, aesthetics, possessions, ideals

MARS: Action, assertiveness, willpower, stamina, sexual drive

 JUPITER: Abundance, luck, expansion, optimism, benevolence, excess

SATURN: Responsibility, restrictions, rules, time, boundaries, karma

 URANUS: Innovation, rebellion, breakthroughs, egalitarianism, technology

NEPTUNE: Mysticism, inspiration, intuition, compassion, spirituality, dissolution

PLUTO: Power, transformation, energy, destruction, rebirth

the closest to Earth and the sun. They move quickly so they change zodiac signs regularly, like the sun, which changes signs approximately every thirty days. Thus, their position in our birth chart is quite customized, like our sun, moon, and rising signs.

The Social Planets

Jupiter and Saturn are known as the social planets since the majority of people born in a certain year or two-year period will have the same Jupiter and Saturn signs. For example, your classmates at school will likely all have the same Jupiter and Saturn signs, so you are united in your attitude about growth (Jupiter) and responsibility (Saturn). Much of our socialization is done among our peers of the same age group and Saturn and Jupiter play an important role in this socialization.

The Transpersonal Planets

Uranus, Neptune, and Pluto have *long* orbits! Thus, they are often referred to as transpersonal planets and their aspects can be considered generational aspects since they last for such a long time. So while the sun, moon, and rising sign change all the time, everyone born in a certain decade may have the same Pluto sign! Thus, the significance of these planetary positions is seen as affecting an entire generation (see page 176).

THE SIGNS' INFLUENCE ON THE PLANETS

Each planet passes through each of the signs at different times, depending on their orbit. As a planet passes through a zodiac sign, the natural energy of the planet becomes shaded by the qualities and motivations of the sign.

ARIES
A planet in the sign of Aries expresses a drive toward individuality, freedom, and new opportunities.

KEY WORDS
Determined
Competitive
Assertive

TAURUS
A planet in the sign of Taurus expresses itself in subtle ways, by magnetizing its desires, rather than actively pursuing them.

KEY WORDS
Patient
Magnetic
Possessive

GEMINI
A planet in the sign of Gemini expresses itself in a desire to learn, socialize, and share ideas.

KEY WORDS
Diversity
Curiosity
Communication

CANCER
A planet in the sign of Cancer expresses itself in a self-protective way with an instinct to nest and nurture.

KEY WORDS
Domestic
Cautious
Private

LEO
A planet in the sign of Leo expresses itself with confidence and an urge for self-expression.

KEY WORDS
Bold
Demonstrative
Proud

VIRGO
A planet in the sign of Virgo expresses itself with a desire to serve, perfect, and improve.

KEY WORDS
Skill
Dedication
Precision

LIBRA
A planet in the sign of Libra expresses itself through a desire for harmony with others and collaboration.

KEY WORDS
Sociability
Justice
Refinement

SCORPIO
A planet in the sign of Scorpio expresses itself through a desire for intimacy and transformation.

KEY WORDS
Control
Power
Intensity

SAGITTARIUS
A planet in the sign of Sagittarius expresses itself with a need for growth, expansion, and new horizons.

KEY WORDS
Optimism
Learning
Adventure

CAPRICORN
A planet in the sign of Capricorn expresses itself with a desire for achievement, success, and longevity.

KEY WORDS
Durability
Status
Tradition

AQUARIUS
A planet in the sign of Aquarius expresses itself with a need for uniqueness, independence, and equality.

KEY WORDS
Innovative
Unconventional
Group-Oriented

PISCES
A planet in Pisces expresses itself with a need for connection, merging, and inspiration.

KEY WORDS
Sensitive
Intuitive
Giving

ASPECTS

SOME OF THE MOST UNFAMILIAR LANGUAGE YOU MAY ENCOUNTER IN HOROSCOPES IS THE LANGUAGE OF ASPECTS.

An aspect is a geometrical relationship between two planets. Sometimes, planets are "minding their own business" as they go about their orbit. But at other times, they form precise angles to other planets and as such, the two planets engage in a kind of dialogue.

This dialogue may be friendly or hostile, depending on the nature of the two planets involved. This activity between the planets is the primary focus of horoscopes.

Positive Aspects

✴ **SEXTILE (60 DEGREES):** A sextile is a mutually supportive aspect between two planets. Think of this aspect like a cheerleader on the sidelines encouraging you. It isn't *really* doing anything in your favor, but the support makes you feel happy and optimistic. Likewise, a sextile doesn't have a whole lot of oomph behind it, but feels nice nonetheless.

▲ **TRINE (120 DEGREES):** Trines are the golden aspect in astrology, where two planets hook up to bring you the best of both worlds. Trines energize both planets to work in harmony to help you achieve your goals more easily and quickly. Whenever there is a trine in the sky, things are moving smoothly in the areas of life connected by the two planets.

Challenging Aspects

■ **SQUARE (90 DEGREES):** A square is considered the most difficult aspect in astrology. When two planets form a right angle to one another, they are at cross-purposes in terms of their respective goals. Squares force us to resolve a conflict in the two areas of our life where the square is taking place.

Aspects That Can Be Either Positive or Challenging

☌ **CONJUNCTION (0 DEGREES):** When two planets are located in the same place in the zodiac, they are in conjunction. They are "coloring" one another with their own energies so a kind of merging is taking place. If the two planets in question are beneficial (such as Jupiter and Venus), then this can be a very positive aspect. If the two planets are more erratic (such as Mars and Uranus), then the

——	TRINE ▲	between ♆ and ♂
——	OPPOSITION ☍	between ♆ and ♃
——	CONJUNCTION ☌	between ♃ and ♀
——	SEXTILE ✴	between ♃ and ♅
——	SQUARE ■	between ☉ and ♂

conjunction can be a red flag, and it indicates you should be cautious. An astrologer will note in a horoscope whether a specific conjunction is generally seen as beneficial or challenging.

☍ **OPPOSITION (180 DEGREES):** When two planets are exactly opposite one another in the zodiac, they are in opposition. Opposite points are really like two sides of the same coin. A lot of balance and healing can take place in our lives during oppositions. However, if we are not ready to be diplomatic, we can experience oppositions as times of tension and frustration.

HOUSES

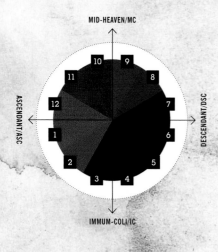

MID-HEAVEN/MC

ASCENDANT/ASC

DESCENDANT/DSC

IMMUM-COLI/IC

THE LOCATIONS WHERE ALL THIS ACTION TAKES PLACE ARE THE TWELVE DIFFERENT HOUSES OF THE CHART.

At any moment, planets are arranged in different houses and from there they will form aspects to one another. For example, oppositions always take place in houses that are directly opposite, or across, from one another.

There are four major angles in a chart, with the eastern horizon (or ascendant) on the left (ASC), and the western horizon (or descendant) on the right (DSC), the mid-heaven at the top (MC), and the nadir (or immum Coli) at the bottom (IC). These four angles divide the chart into four

quadrants. Each of these four quadrants is further divided up into three houses, together comprising the twelve houses of a chart.

ASC / ASCENDANT / CUSP OF THE 1ST HOUSE: Our identity and presentation, how we perceive the world, and how the world perceives us.

IC / IMMUM COLI / NADIR / CUSP OF THE 4TH HOUSE: The most personal part of us, our childhood influences, and the type of environment we want in our private life.

DSC / DESCENDANT / CUSP OF THE 7TH HOUSE: The qualities we seek in others, and the type of relationships we are likely to have, especially in close partnerships such as marriage.

MC / MID-HEAVEN / CUSP OF THE 10TH HOUSE: The influence we seek to have in the world, our career and reputation, the role of authority figures.

The houses in a chart rule certain aspects of our lives. Thus, when a planet is transiting through a certain house, its effect will be to activate that part of our life.

For example, when Mars enters our 6th house, we can expect a horoscope to focus on an increase in activity (Mars) in the area of health, daily routine, and work.

1ST HOUSE
appearance, image, physical body, stamina, presence

2ND HOUSE
income, money, possessions, values, priorities

3RD HOUSE
communication, school, ideas, information, siblings, short trips, neighborhood

4TH HOUSE
home, family, parents, lifestyle, domestic values

5TH HOUSE
love affairs, fun, self-expression, creativity, children, leadership

6TH HOUSE
health, daily routine, everyday job, work, practical skills, employees

7TH HOUSE
relationships, partnerships, marriage, agreements

8TH HOUSE
sex, intimacy, deep feelings, inner psychology, shared resources, transformation

9TH HOUSE
higher education, spirituality and religion, international travel, publishing, legal matters

10TH HOUSE
career, outer success, reputation, VIPs, impact on the world, goals

11TH HOUSE
friends, groups, associations, clubs, technology, humanitarian activities

12TH HOUSE
privacy, intuition, inspiration, connection to the divine, hidden activities

HOW HOROSCOPES ARE WRITTEN

WHEN YOU BRING ALL THESE COMPONENTS TOGETHER—PLANETS, SIGNS, ASPECTS, AND HOUSES— YOU HAVE A HOROSCOPE!

When creating a horoscope, the sign that is being forecast is put on the ASC, or the cusp of the 1st house, on the left side of the chart. That sign is the primary focus of the horoscope so it comes first. Then the rest of the signs follow from there in their usual zodiac order in a counterclockwise direction.

Here is a sample horoscope, where we examine the aspects—the geometrical relationship between the planets—during the week of September 13, 2015 and how they affected Leo and Pisces.

You can see how the planets and aspects fall in different houses for each sign. And from there we can anticipate where they are likely to make an impact in Pisces' and Leo's lives. That translates into the two different corresponding horoscopes, at right.

LEO: You could get some very exciting financial news around Sunday's new moon solar eclipse. The next few weeks are the perfect time to ask for a raise! Especially since lucky Jupiter in your 2nd house forms an opposition to Neptune on Thursday. And even though verbal Mercury also goes retrograde on Thursday, which is bad for signing new paperwork, it is good for renegotiating existing deals. So let your business-savvy side take over. If there has been drama with your family for ages, things will get easier now, thanks to stubborn Saturn finally moving out of your 4th house of home. Breathe a sigh of relief and get back to your upbeat self!

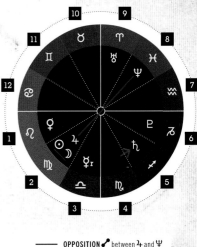

—— **OPPOSITION** ⚹ between ♃ and ♆
—— **CONJUNCTION** ☌ between ☉ and ☽

PISCES: This is a very important week for your relationships, Pisces! Sunday's new moon solar eclipse falls in your 7th house of marriage and close partnerships. You could meet some very important people right now! Pay attention to your instincts since lucky Jupiter is opposing your ruler, intuitive Neptune, in your sign on Thursday. Verbal Mercury also goes retrograde on Thursday and could mess with your communications, especially in financial matters. Practical Saturn moves into your 10th house of fame and success on Thursday where it will reside for the next two years. Great opportunities are coming, but they will require a lot of hard work and stamina to materialize. You have it in you, Pisces!

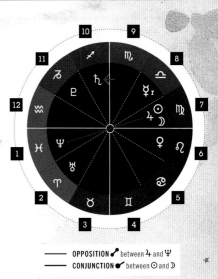

—— **OPPOSITION** ⚹ between ♃ and ♆
—— **CONJUNCTION** ☌ between ☉ and ☽

WHAT ARE RETROGRADES?

SINCE ASTROLOGY IS BASED ON THE APPARENT PATH OF THE PLANETS FROM THE PERSPECTIVE OF EARTH, THERE ARE PERIODS OF THE YEAR WHEN CERTAIN PLANETS *SEEM* TO BE GOING BACKWARD.

No planets actually ever move backward, but because of our vantage point on Earth, it appears as though they do. All planets have retrograde periods, with the exception of the luminaries—the sun and moon—which never appear to go backward.

When planets are retrograde, they are not acting at their full capacity and their function is dimmed. However, this does not have to be a negative thing. Retrogrades are an excellent time for us to reappraise the part of our life related to that planet. For example, when Venus, the planet of love and beauty, is retrograde, it is a good time to reflect on the state of our relationships, partnerships, and finances.

However, it is advisable to wait before taking important actions related to these things until after the retrograde period, when the planet is returned to its full strength.

Here we describe the frequency and duration of retrogrades as well as beneficial reflections and activities to undertake during these times.

The Social and Transpersonal Planets
JUPITER, SATURN, URANUS, NEPTUNE, AND PLUTO
Planets with slower orbits have longer and more frequent retrogrades. Many of the outer planets are retrograde for several months each year. For this reason, their retrogrades have a less significant influence and we won't be including them here.

Personal Planets
MERCURY, VENUS, AND MARS
These planets have a significant impact on the functioning of our day-to-day lives so when they are retrograde it's important to take notice.

Mercury
FREQUENCY: Three times a year.
DURATION: Three weeks each time.
REFLECT ON: Reading, writing, school, correspondence, people we interact with in our everyday lives, neighbors, entrepreneurship, siblings, news, ideas, information, the internet, social media, trips. Mercury Retrograde is extremely influential in our lives and a full exploration on its effect is on the next page.

Venus
FREQUENCY: Once every eighteen months.
DURATION: Forty days.
REFLECT ON: Love, relationships, harmony, agreements, balance, money, friendships, pleasure, art, leisure, possessions.
WAIT UNTIL AFTER TO: Get engaged, get married, sign important partnerships or contracts, redecorate, get a makeover, buy art, buy a home, make major investments.

Mars
FREQUENCY: Once every twenty-six months.
DURATION: Ten weeks.
REFLECT ON: Goals, achievement, action, competitors, risks, energy, health.
WAIT UNTIL AFTER TO: Start a new job, enter a competition, start a new fitness regime, take a big risk, start a business.

THE POWER OF MERCURY RETROGRADE

HAVE YOU EVER NOTICED HOW EVERYONE FREAKS OUT WHEN MERCURY IS RETROGRADE?!

This is the planet that rules our daily communication so it is no surprise that when it goes retrograde, everyone wants to talk about it. It's also because the effects of this planet are very tangible so we can feel the disruption that Mercury retrograde causes more acutely than some of the other retrogrades.

When Mercury is retrograde we are being asked to slow down the high-speed technical activities of our lives. This includes not only the gadgets that we love so dearly, but also the old-fashioned ways of communicating: our words, both written and spoken. Now is the time to pause and see if we are really getting our message across to others and, perhaps even more important, that our message is in line with our true beliefs and goals. So while it is easy to freak out about e-mails misfiring and software meltdowns, save yourself some stress right now and consider this an opportunity to take a breather and reflect.

Mercury Retrograde Activities

Journaling, clearing your Spam folder, responding to old e-mails, reaching out to people you haven't spoken to in ages, cleaning out old paperwork, rewriting your statement of purpose for your business or any other big projects.

WAIT UNTIL AFTER TO: Sign a contract, buy any kind of technology, invest in new software, make a business agreement, buy travel tickets, initiate an important conversation.

The essence of Mercury retrograde is that anything that is *started* during that time will need to be reworked, revised, or redone at a later time. So it's not a good time to start things for that reason—unless you feel like it would be advantageous to agree to something, or begin something, knowing that it will be revised later. Since we want our computers and tech gadgets to be working A-OK from the moment we unwrap their shiny box, we should not invest in new technology during this time.

But Mercury retrograde is a great time to hit the refresh button on lots of things in your life including old friendships, so have fun reaching out and reconnecting.

NEW MOONS, FULL MOONS & ECLIPSES

EVERY 28 TO 29 DAYS, THE SUN AND THE MOON FORM A CONJUNCTION, WHICH IS A NEW MOON.

The moon appears dark because the location of the moon is between the sun and Earth, which means that from Earth we cannot see the sun's light reflected on the moon (the light is reflected only on the backside of the moon).

Two weeks later, the sun and the moon form an opposition, which is a full moon. The moon is fully illuminated because the earth is between the sun and the moon and thus the full face of the moon that is visible from Earth is illuminated by the sun.

There is a new moon, and a full moon, in each zodiac sign every year.

New Moons

The new moon is a time of fresh starts. With the sun and moon united in the same zodiac sign, there is a concentration of purpose and energy. New moons are the perfect time to set intentions that are related to the priorities of that particular sign. So whatever your sun sign may be, you can use the energy of every new moon to channel your focus onto new goals in certain areas of life.

To set an intention, simply write down, within ten hours after the new moon, a list of up to ten goals or desires related to the area of your life that the new moon corresponds with. These goals can be specific or general, depending on your desires.

Consider the following areas when setting your New Moon intentions each month:

NEW MOON IN ARIES: new goals, new projects, stamina, winning

NEW MOON IN TAURUS: income, security, values, stability

NEW MOON IN GEMINI: education, learning, siblings, communication, writing

NEW MOON IN CANCER: parents, home, family, emotional stability

NEW MOON IN LEO: creativity, confidence, leadership, love, children

NEW MOON IN VIRGO: health, efficiency, work, skills, employment, coworkers, employees

NEW MOON IN LIBRA: relationships, partnerships, contracts, harmony, social life

NEW MOON IN SCORPIO: sex, intimacy, transformation, power, money

NEW MOON IN SAGITTARIUS: travel, religion, spirituality, international affairs, law, publishing

NEW MOON IN CAPRICORN: career, status, achievement, fame, recognition, VIPs

NEW MOON IN AQUARIUS: friends, groups, clubs, technology, innovation

NEW MOON IN PISCES: privacy, intuition, inspiration, philanthropy

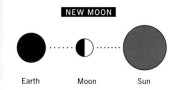

NEW MOON

Earth   Moon   Sun

Full Moons

Full moons occur when the sun and moon are in opposite signs. As such, full moons emphasize harmony and balance. This means two parts of our life need to be brought into alignment. For example, a full moon that connects the opposite signs of Gemini and Sagittarius always offers an opportunity to bridge our big-picture goals with the learning and activities we undertake in our daily lives. We already looked at opposite signs in terms of our relationships on page 144. Here, we are looking at opposite signs in terms of how they interact with one another during our monthly full moon cycle.

Each of these pairs of signs shares the spotlight twice a year. For example, when the sun is in Aries and the full moon is in Libra, and then again six months later when the sun is in Libra and the full moon is in Aries.

Regardless of our own sun sign, the energy during each of these full moons invites us all to explore the following themes:

ARIES/LIBRA: Balancing our own interests with the needs and wants of others.

TAURUS/SCORPIO: Being conscious of our desire for stability and intimacy while paying attention to financial matters.

GEMINI/SAGITTARIUS: Ideas, travel, education, and the quest for growth and expansion.

CANCER/CAPRICORN: Celebrating tradition, family, and career achievement.

LEO/AQUARIUS: Personal versus collective goals, self-expression, and innovation.

VIRGO/PISCES: Compassion, dedication, and our ability to be of service to ourselves and others.

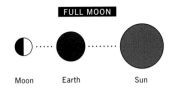

FULL MOON

Moon   Earth   Sun

Eclipses

The earth is engaged in two cycles that are happening simultaneously at all times. There is the moon's orbit around the earth and the earth's orbit around the sun. When the moon's orbit around the earth lines up with the earth's orbit around the sun, an eclipse occurs.

Eclipses happen four times a year, in two pairs. Each pair is a new moon and a full moon spaced two weeks apart. So, for example, we may have two eclipses that are two weeks apart in March and then two eclipses two weeks apart in September. The weeks surrounding eclipses are some of the most sensitive times of the year, when major changes in our lives are likely to happen.

Eclipses are turbo-charged new and full moons.

• **A SOLAR ECLIPSE** is a very powerful new moon.

• **A LUNAR ECLIPSE** is a very powerful full moon.

With two solar eclipses and two lunar eclipses each year, we have four opportunities for major change and growth. The areas where this change and growth are likely to occur are in the houses where the eclipses take place.

1ST AND 7TH HOUSES: Changes in relationships, partnerships, meeting important new people, self-direction, image

2ND AND 8TH HOUSES: Changes in income, finances, intimacy, sex, values and priorities

3RD AND 9TH HOUSES: Changes in travel plans, journeys, information, ideas, communication style, education

4TH AND 10TH HOUSES: Changes in home, career, goals, real estate, parental relationships, work opportunities

5TH AND 11TH HOUSES: Changes in creative projects, group dynamics, leadership, children, technology projects

6TH AND 12TH HOUSES: Changes in private matters, health, health care, fitness, coworkers, daily routine

We don't need to be pushy or force matters around an eclipse. For example, if your horoscope alerts you that there will be an eclipse in your 10th house of career, you needn't charge into your boss's office and demand a promotion. Important events and changes will flow of their own accord. But if we are feeling like we need to make a significant adjustment in our lives, the energy of an eclipse can help us find clarity.

JUPITER RETURN

WHENEVER JUPITER INFLUENCES YOUR CHART, IT'S A GOOD THING!

Jupiter is associated with abundance, luck, expansion, optimism, benevolence, and excess.

Jupiter has a twelve-year orbit. What that means is that every twelve years, Jupiter returns to the same sign it was in when you were born. This is known as your Jupiter return.

When a planet returns to the same sign it was in when we were born, we have an opportunity to tap into its resources. Thus, the benefits of Jupiter become a major focus for us during the years of our Jupiter return. Each of us has a Jupiter return at the same ages.

AGE 12: We start to become confident in our own identity, develop a sense of our personal interests, and exert our will to explore them.

AGE 24: We have finished most of our education and have a sense of freedom and optimism about what big goals we want to conquer as adults.

AGE 36: We have developed and stabilized our adult lives and new opportunities present themselves more readily.

AGE 48: We have established recognition in our field and life feels effortless and satisfying.

AGE 60: We have made some important changes in our lives and now live more authentically according to what we truly desire.

AGE 72: We no longer seek the approval of others to enjoy our lives.

AGE 84: We truly take great satisfaction from the small joys in life.

AGE 96: Congratulations! You're ninety-six. You win.

Each of these different ages comes with many blessings and opportunities, delivered courtesy of Jupiter. Important people come into our lives and there is an effortless flow of optimism. However, just because opportunities arrive doesn't mean that we will be able to reap all of their rewards. During the years of our Jupiter returns, we can suffer from foolhardiness and excess. So in order to reap the true, long-term rewards of Jupiter, we have to temper any proclivity for overindulgence with discipline and hard work.

Speaking of hard work…

SATURN RETURN

SATURN RETURN HAS A REPUTATION AS ONE OF THE MOST CHALLENGING ASTROLOGICAL EVENTS FOR GOOD REASON.

Saturn is associated with responsibility, restrictions, rules, time, boundaries, and karma.

Saturn's orbit is twenty-nine years. So each of us has our first Saturn return when we are twenty-nine years old, and again when we are fifty-eight.

AGE 29: We are now adults and have weathered many different kinds of experiences, both positive and negative. Saturn places great emphasis on stability and durability, so now our resilience is tested. We can reap wonderful rewards for all of the discipline and effort we have put into certain areas of our lives. In other areas, where we have not been as thorough or practical, we will face challenges. This is Saturn's way of showing us the lessons we need to learn. The commitments we make at this time have extra weight so we may feel overwhelmed. This is a reminder that our decisions have a long-term impact so we should weigh our choices wisely.

AGE 58: Many of us have raised families at this point, but with grown children out of the home, we are now reappraising our lives. For example, people who have felt like they were suffering through a bad marriage may now find the stress of living this way unbearable and decide to make a major life change. Even people who have been quite satisfied may no longer want to abide by certain rules and decide to drastically change their lives. Saturn continuously reminds us that we have to live with the results of our choices, so this is another critical time when we may decide to reject certain responsibilities or take on different ones.

Saturn is not a bad planet. There is no such thing as a bad planet. But Saturn represents realism and as such has the important role of reminding us that we have responsibilities in life and that we should make decisions carefully.

What is Karma?

Karma is a word that seems cute and mystical, but what does it mean? And what on earth does it have to do with strict Saturn?

Karma is an idea that is based on a worldview of interconnection—the belief that all of life is energetically intertwined. This belief supports a universe where the planets are in sync in beautiful and mysterious ways (astrology), and where all action creates an energetic ripple effect (karma).

We can think of karma as a spiritual checking account. When our actions are pure and in line with our own good and the good of others, we have a robust account, with frequent deposits arriving from the universe. We are creating good karma by sending out positive ripples. When our actions derive from less-than-noble motivations, or we cut corners to get to where we want to go, we send out negative ripples and drain our account. There is a direct proportionality between what we think and do, and the karma we accrue. And since Saturn is such a stickler for logistics and practicality, he is the one who oversees this very clear and precise energetic exchange. "What you sow, so you shall reap" is the great explanation of karma, and we all get our karmic bank statement in the mail each time we have a Saturn Return.

GENERATIONAL ASPECTS

WHILE OUR SUN, MOON, AND RISING SIGNS HAVE THE MOST INTIMATE EFFECT ON OUR PERSONALITIES, WE ARE ALSO VERY CONNECTED TO OUR PEERS BY VIRTUE OF THE FACT THAT OUR TRANSPERSONAL OUTER PLANETS ARE IN THE SAME SIGNS.

For example, your best friend may have a different sun, moon, and rising sign than you do, but if you were born the same year, you will share many of the same generational aspects that define the larger groups and tribes you are part of.

Since we each have all of the outer planets in our chart, we are members of several different generational tribes that influence our interests and the types of communities we are likely to identify with.

Below are the dates of today's major generational aspects. Since outer planets change signs erratically by retrograding back into the previous sign at least once before fully moving forward, there are certain "cusp" years that are listed twice since that is a year when the planet moved back and forth between two signs. Even though the planet was only in one sign when you were born, which you can find out by calculating your exact birth chart, you may identify with both generations and have many friends in each group. For more on cusps, see page 180.

Look for the year that you were born under each Transpersonal Planet to find out which tribes you belong to and how you and your peers are changing the world!

⛢ Uranus
INNOVATION, REBELLION, BREAKTHROUGHS, EGALITARIANISM, TECHNOLOGY

1962–1968: **URANUS IN VIRGO GENERATION:** They are visionaries in the realm of health and wellness, responsible for contributing to a better, more thorough understanding of the mind-body connection.

1968–1975: **URANUS IN LIBRA GENERATION:** They are breaking the mold when it comes to relationships and setting their own standards for the modern partnership.

1975–1981: **URANUS IN SCORPIO GENERATION:** They are pioneers who are changing the access to power through information and technology.

1981–1988: **URANUS IN SAGITTARIUS GENERATION:** They are responsible for collapsing boundaries around the world through travel, education, and the internet.

1988–1995: **URANUS IN CAPRICORN GENERATION:** They are changing the face of business. They are ambitious and are updating procedures and rewriting the rules within many major industries.

1995–2003: **URANUS IN AQUARIUS GENERATION:** They have brilliant technical and scientific skills. They are committed to human rights and care about leveling the playing field for success.

2003–2010: **URANUS IN PISCES GENERATION:** They are extremely creative and compassionate. They will find innovative ways to help others and be of service.

2010–2018: **URANUS IN ARIES GENERATION:** They are original and independent. They will charge into uncharted territory, setting many new standards and insisting on doing things their own way.

2018–2025: **URANUS IN TAURUS GENERATION:** They will adopt a new set of values. They will alter traditional financial structures and have an important influence on the way money is earned, invested, and distributed.

♆ Neptune

MYSTICISM, INSPIRATION,
INTUITION, COMPASSION,
SPIRITUALITY, DISSOLUTION

**1956–1970: NEPTUNE IN SCORPIO
GENERATION:** They have redefined
their own connection with their
personal power, rather than
following the mold of society or
authority figures. They reject
doing things based purely on the
status quo and instead trust
their own instincts and personal
moral and spiritual compass.

**1970–1984: NEPTUNE IN SAGITTARIUS
GENERATION:** They are global
dreamers and adventurers. The
world is their oyster and they
seek inspiration in the exotic and
the unusual. They are naturally
inclusive of many types of people
and desire to connect and share
experiences either through
traveling or exploring the world
in school or online.

**1984–1999: NEPTUNE IN CAPRICORN
GENERATION:** They seek a
personal, almost spiritual,
connection to their work.
Not content with a ho-hum
nine-to-five job, they see their
career as an extension of their
identity and want to feel a sense
of purpose behind their efforts.
They will seek to integrate
philanthropy and sustainable
practices into their business.

**1999–2012: NEPTUNE IN AQUARIUS
GENERATION:** They are intimately

connected to science and
technology. With an intuitive
understanding of the tech world,
they will invent many of this
century's great breakthroughs.
They are also fiercely egalitarian
and care about equal rights for
all and have a collaborative and
group-centric lifestyle.

**2012–2025: NEPTUNE IN PISCES
GENERATION:** They are very
sensitive and artistic. Deeply
connected to nature and to their
feelings, they will seek to serve
the world through conservation,
philanthropy, and humble service.
They reject purely materialistic
values and seek a return to
nature and creative pursuits.

♇ Pluto

POWER, TRANSFORMATION,
ENERGY, DESTRUCTION, REBIRTH

**1957–1972: PLUTO IN VIRGO
GENERATION:** They are focused
on transforming their
relationships with themselves
and their bodies. Keenly aware
of the mind-body connection
and the value of self-care, they
are bringing increased education
to this area. They are leading
through example and inspiring
others to improve their well-being.

**1972–1984: PLUTO IN LIBRA
GENERATION:** They are
transforming the way we view
relationships. Pioneers of
equality for all types of

partnerships, including same-sex
marriage, they are throwing
away the old script about what
it means to have a marriage
or business partnership, and
they are creating their own
relationship rules.

**1984–1995: PLUTO IN SCORPIO
GENERATION:** They reject a lot of
the status quo and expectations
of earlier generations. They
believe in doing things their own
way rather than following a
traditional path. They are very
aware of the inner workings of
people and systems and are
quick to look for revolutionary
solutions, especially in the realm
of power, energy, and finances.

**1995–2008: PLUTO IN SAGITTARIUS
GENERATION:** They have a global
focus. With access to information
from around the world, they
are interested in building
bridges of communication and
understanding. They will
transform global legal structures
to support human rights and
aim to strengthen religious
understanding and tolerance.

**2008–2024: PLUTO IN CAPRICORN
GENERATION:** They will change the
power structure in government
and big business. Through their
efforts, outdated bureaucracies
and corrupt industries
will be transformed by more
meritocratic and transparent
ideals. They desire to be
leaders and have the patience
to take on major projects.

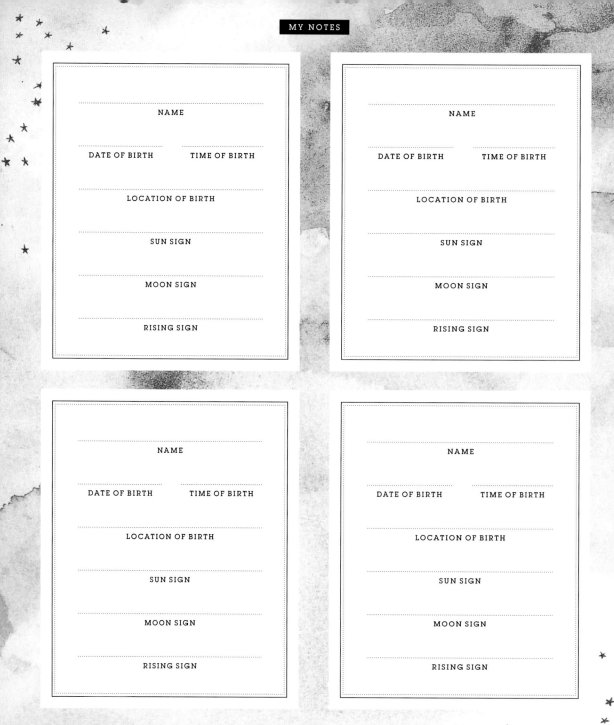

NAME

DATE OF BIRTH   TIME OF BIRTH

LOCATION OF BIRTH

SUN SIGN

MOON SIGN

RISING SIGN

NAME

DATE OF BIRTH   TIME OF BIRTH

LOCATION OF BIRTH

SUN SIGN

MOON SIGN

RISING SIGN

NAME

DATE OF BIRTH   TIME OF BIRTH

LOCATION OF BIRTH

SUN SIGN

MOON SIGN

RISING SIGN

NAME

DATE OF BIRTH   TIME OF BIRTH

LOCATION OF BIRTH

SUN SIGN

MOON SIGN

RISING SIGN

NAME

DATE OF BIRTH   TIME OF BIRTH

LOCATION OF BIRTH

SUN SIGN

MOON SIGN

RISING SIGN

NAME

DATE OF BIRTH   TIME OF BIRTH

LOCATION OF BIRTH

SUN SIGN

MOON SIGN

RISING SIGN

NAME

DATE OF BIRTH   TIME OF BIRTH

LOCATION OF BIRTH

SUN SIGN

MOON SIGN

RISING SIGN

NAME

DATE OF BIRTH   TIME OF BIRTH

LOCATION OF BIRTH

SUN SIGN

MOON SIGN

RISING SIGN

EPHEMERIS

FIND YOUR MOON SIGN AND RISING SIGN

An ephemeris is a table that lists the position of the moon and planets from the earth's viewpoint. Use the moon sign tables that start on page 182 to look up your birthday and find out your moon sign. Then, applying the time of your birth, use the rising sign charts on page 200 to determine your rising sign.

A NOTE ABOUT CUSPS: A cusp is the borderline between one sign and the next. If your moon sign or rising sign is near a cusp then you should read descriptions of both and see which one suits you best. You cannot have more than one sun sign, moon sign, or rising sign, so do some soul-searching to see which describes you better. When in doubt, ask your friends which one they think suits you!

DOUBLES AND TRIPLES: Have you ever heard someone say they are a "double Pisces"? What this means is that two out of three of their signs are Pisces. If your moon sign or rising sign is the same sign as your sun sign, then this sign is emphasized more strongly in your personality. Likewise, if your sun, moon, and rising signs are all the same sign, this is called a triple, which is very rare. Being a double or a triple helps you express the best qualities of your sun sign in many different ways, and gives you a lot of conviction about what you want. However, it may also give you a tendency to take things personally, since you are so attached to your way of seeing things.

Find Your Moon Sign

The moon changes signs every few days and your moon sign influences your needs and emotions.

1. Turn to page 182 to find moon sign tables from 1960 to 2031.
2. Look up the year that you are interested in, whether the year of your birth or your friends' and family's. (Remember: You

can make notes on these signs on page 178.)

3. Look up the month and day. Next to the day, you'll see a sign. For example, if you look up May 8, 1966, you'll see CAP next to May 8. (This is an abbreviation for Capricorn.) That means that the moon moved from the sign of Sagittarius into the sign of Capricorn on May 8, 1966. Since that's what we call a cusp day, you should read the pages titled "If Sagittarius Is Your Moon Sign" on page 102 and "If Capricorn Is Your Moon Sign" on page 112 and see which one suits you more.

Don't worry if the day you are looking for is not listed. For example, if you are looking for June 10, 2001, but in the June 2001 table, it lists only June 9 and June 11, that simply means your moon sign is listed before the day you are looking for. Since the chart says AQU next to June 9, then the moon was in Aquarius from June 9 until June 11. So your moon sign is Aquarius. No guess work involved!

Find Your Rising Sign

The rising sign, also called the ascendant, is the sign that was rising over the eastern horizon at the time you were born. Our rising sign influences our external personality. All twelve signs of the zodiac rise over the eastern horizon at some point each day.

1. Turn to the chart on page 200.

2. Look up the month and date of your birth. For example, if your birthday is March 24, look under the column that says March 15. This is because you were born between March 15 and April 1. For rising signs, it does not matter which year you were born in.

3. Look up the time of day you were born. If you were born at 7:34 p.m., look for the time listed right before your birth time. You will see that 7:25 p.m. has the sign Libra written next to it. This means that at around 7:25 pm, Libra became the sign on the horizon, so your rising sign is Libra.

Note: If your time of birth is very close to one of the cusps (the time period when the signs change from one to another), then read both signs and see which one suits you the best. In this example, you may want to read about the rising sign of Virgo as well as the rising sign of Libra since 7:34 p.m. is close to the cusp.

If you do not know the precise time you were born, try to find out if you were born in the morning, afternoon, evening, or night. Then read the rising sign sections for the signs that correspond to that general time of day to see if their characteristics apply to you.

If you were born in a location far away from the equator, where the hours of sunlight are very different seasonally (Alaska, for example), it may be worth consulting a free online computer program, like Astro.com, to confirm your rising sign, since these areas have atypical daily cycles.

1960

	JAN	FEB	MAR	APR	MAY	JUN	JUL	AUG	SEP	OCT	NOV	DEC
	2 PIS	3 TAU	1 TAU	2 CAN	2 LEO	1 VIR	1 LIB	1 SAG	2 AQU	1 PIS	2 TAU	2 GEM
	4 ARI	5 GEM	4 GEM	5 LEO	5 VIR	3 LIB	3 SCO	3 CAP	4 PIS	3 ARI	4 GEM	4 CAN
	6 TAU	8 CAN	6 CAN	7 VIR	7 LIB	6 SCO	5 SAG	5 AQU	6 ARI	6 TAU	7 CAN	7 LEO
	9 GEM	10 LEO	9 LEO	10 LIB	9 SCO	8 SAG	7 CAP	7 PIS	8 TAU	8 GEM	9 LEO	9 VIR
	11 CAN	13 VIR	11 VIR	12 SCO	11 SAG	10 CAP	9 AQU	10 ARI	11 GEM	10 CAN	12 VIR	12 LIB
	14 LEO	15 LIB	13 LIB	14 SAG	13 CAP	12 AQU	11 PIS	12 TAU	13 CAN	13 LEO	14 LIB	14 SCO
	16 VIR	17 SCO	15 SCO	16 CAP	15 AQU	14 PIS	13 ARI	14 GEM	16 LEO	15 VIR	16 SCO	16 SAG
	19 LIB	19 SAG	17 SAG	18 AQU	17 PIS	16 ARI	15 TAU	17 CAN	18 VIR	18 LIB	19 SAG	18 CAP
	21 SCO	21 CAP	20 CAP	20 PIS	20 ARI	18 TAU	18 GEM	19 LEO	20 LIB	20 SCO	21 CAP	20 AQU
	23 SAG	23 AQU	22 AQU	22 ARI	22 TAU	21 GEM	20 CAN	22 VIR	23 SCO	22 SAG	23 AQU	22 PIS
	25 CAP	26 PIS	24 PIS	25 TAU	24 GEM	23 CAN	23 LEO	24 LIB	25 SAG	24 CAP	25 PIS	24 ARI
	27 AQU	28 ARI	26 ARI	27 GEM	27 CAN	26 LEO	25 VIR	26 SCO	27 CAP	26 AQU	27 ARI	26 TAU
	29 PIS		28 TAU	30 CAN	29 LEO	28 VIR	28 LIB	29 SAG	29 AQU	28 PIS	29 TAU	29 GEM
	31 ARI		31 GEM				30 SCO	31 CAP		31 ARI		31 CAN

1961

	JAN	FEB	MAR	APR	MAY	JUN	JUL	AUG	SEP	OCT	NOV	DEC
	3 LEO	2 VIR	1 VIR	2 SCO	2 SAG	2 AQU	1 PIS	2 TAU	1 GEM	3 LEO	2 VIR	1 LIB
	5 VIR	4 LIB	3 LIB	4 SAG	4 CAP	4 PIS	4 ARI	4 GEM	3 CAN	5 VIR	4 LIB	4 SCO
	8 LIB	6 SCO	6 SCO	6 CAP	6 AQU	6 ARI	6 TAU	7 CAN	5 LEO	8 LIB	6 SCO	6 SAG
	10 SCO	9 SAG	8 SAG	9 AQU	8 PIS	8 TAU	8 GEM	9 LEO	8 VIR	10 SCO	9 SAG	8 CAP
	12 SAG	11 CAP	10 CAP	11 PIS	10 ARI	11 GEM	11 CAN	12 VIR	10 LIB	13 SAG	11 CAP	10 AQU
	14 CAP	13 AQU	12 AQU	13 ARI	12 TAU	13 CAN	13 LEO	14 LIB	13 SCO	15 CAP	13 AQU	13 PIS
	16 AQU	15 PIS	14 PIS	15 TAU	14 GEM	16 LEO	15 VIR	17 SCO	15 SAG	17 AQU	15 PIS	15 ARI
	18 PIS	17 ARI	16 ARI	17 GEM	17 CAN	18 VIR	18 LIB	19 SAG	17 CAP	19 PIS	17 ARI	17 TAU
	20 ARI	19 TAU	18 TAU	19 CAN	19 LEO	21 LIB	20 SCO	21 CAP	20 AQU	21 ARI	20 TAU	19 GEM
	23 TAU	21 GEM	21 GEM	22 LEO	22 VIR	23 SCO	23 SAG	23 AQU	22 PIS	23 TAU	22 GEM	21 CAN
	25 GEM	24 CAN	23 CAN	25 VIR	24 LIB	25 SAG	25 CAP	25 PIS	24 ARI	25 GEM	24 CAN	24 LEO
	28 CAN	26 LEO	26 LEO	27 LIB	27 SCO	27 CAP	27 AQU	27 ARI	26 TAU	28 CAN	26 LEO	26 VIR
	30 LEO		28 VIR	29 SCO	29 SAG	29 AQU	29 PIS	29 TAU	28 GEM	30 LEO	29 VIR	29 LIB
			31 LIB		31 CAP		31 ARI		30 CAN			31 SCO

1962

	JAN	FEB	MAR	APR	MAY	JUN	JUL	AUG	SEP	OCT	NOV	DEC
	3 SAG	1 CAP	1 CAP	1 PIS	1 ARI	1 GEM	1 CAN	2 VIR	3 SCO	3 SAG	1 CAP	1 AQU
	5 CAP	3 AQU	3 AQU	3 ARI	3 TAU	3 CAN	3 LEO	4 LIB	5 SAG	5 CAP	4 AQU	3 PIS
	7 AQU	5 PIS	5 PIS	5 TAU	5 GEM	6 LEO	5 VIR	7 SCO	8 CAP	7 AQU	6 PIS	5 ARI
	9 PIS	7 ARI	7 ARI	7 GEM	7 CAN	8 VIR	8 LIB	9 SAG	10 AQU	10 PIS	8 ARI	7 TAU
	11 ARI	9 TAU	9 TAU	9 CAN	9 LEO	10 LIB	10 SCO	11 CAP	12 PIS	12 ARI	10 TAU	9 GEM
	13 TAU	12 GEM	11 GEM	12 LEO	12 VIR	13 SCO	13 SAG	14 AQU	14 ARI	14 TAU	12 GEM	11 CAN
	15 GEM	14 CAN	13 CAN	14 VIR	14 LIB	15 SAG	15 CAP	16 PIS	16 TAU	16 GEM	14 CAN	14 LEO
	18 CAN	16 LEO	16 LEO	17 LIB	17 SCO	18 CAP	17 AQU	18 ARI	18 GEM	18 CAN	16 LEO	16 VIR
	20 LEO	19 VIR	18 VIR	19 SCO	19 SAG	20 AQU	19 PIS	20 TAU	20 CAN	20 LEO	19 VIR	19 LIB
	23 VIR	21 LIB	21 LIB	22 SAG	22 CAP	22 PIS	21 ARI	22 GEM	23 LEO	22 VIR	21 LIB	21 SCO
	25 LIB	24 SCO	23 SCO	24 CAP	24 AQU	24 ARI	23 TAU	24 CAN	25 VIR	25 LIB	24 SCO	24 SAG
	28 SCO	26 SAG	26 SAG	26 AQU	26 PIS	26 TAU	26 GEM	26 LEO	28 LIB	27 SCO	26 SAG	26 CAP
	30 SAG		28 CAP	28 PIS	28 ARI	28 GEM	28 CAN	29 VIR	30 SCO	30 SAG	29 CAP	28 AQU
			30 AQU		30 TAU		30 LEO	31 LIB				30 PIS

1963

	JAN	FEB	MAR	APR	MAY	JUN	JUL	AUG	SEP	OCT	NOV	DEC
	1 ARI	2 GEM	1 GEM	2 LEO	2 VIR	3 SCO	3 SAG	1 CAP	2 PIS	2 ARI	2 GEM	2 CAN
	4 TAU	4 CAN	3 CAN	4 VIR	4 LIB	5 SAG	5 CAP	4 AQU	4 ARI	4 TAU	4 CAN	4 LEO
	6 GEM	6 LEO	6 LEO	7 LIB	7 SCO	8 CAP	7 AQU	6 PIS	7 TAU	6 GEM	6 LEO	6 VIR
	8 CAN	9 VIR	8 VIR	9 SCO	9 SAG	10 AQU	10 PIS	8 ARI	9 GEM	8 CAN	9 VIR	8 LIB
	10 LEO	11 LIB	11 LIB	12 SAG	12 CAP	12 PIS	12 ARI	10 TAU	11 CAN	10 LEO	11 LIB	11 SCO
	12 VIR	14 SCO	13 SCO	14 CAP	14 AQU	15 ARI	14 TAU	12 GEM	13 LEO	12 VIR	14 SCO	13 SAG
	15 LIB	16 SAG	16 SAG	17 AQU	16 PIS	17 TAU	16 GEM	14 CAN	15 VIR	15 LIB	16 SAG	16 CAP
	17 SCO	19 CAP	18 CAP	19 PIS	18 ARI	19 GEM	18 CAN	17 LEO	18 LIB	17 SCO	19 CAP	18 AQU
	20 SAG	21 AQU	20 AQU	21 ARI	20 TAU	21 CAN	20 LEO	19 VIR	20 SCO	20 SAG	21 AQU	21 PIS
	22 CAP	23 PIS	23 PIS	23 TAU	22 GEM	23 LEO	23 VIR	21 LIB	23 SAG	22 CAP	24 PIS	23 ARI
	25 AQU	25 ARI	25 ARI	25 GEM	24 CAN	25 VIR	25 LIB	24 SCO	25 CAP	25 AQU	26 ARI	25 TAU
	27 PIS	27 TAU	27 TAU	27 CAN	27 LEO	28 LIB	27 SCO	26 SAG	28 AQU	27 PIS	28 TAU	27 GEM
	29 ARI		29 GEM	29 LEO	29 VIR	30 SCO	30 SAG	29 CAP	30 PIS	29 ARI	30 GEM	29 CAN
	31 TAU		31 CAN		31 LIB			31 AQU		31 TAU		31 LEO

1964

JAN	FEB	MAR	APR	MAY	JUN	JUL	AUG	SEP	OCT	NOV	DEC
2 VIR	1 LIB	2 SCO	1 SAG	1 CAP	2 PIS	1 ARI	2 GEM	2 LEO	2 VIR	3 SCO	2 SAG
5 LIB	4 SCO	4 SAG	3 CAP	3 AQU	4 ARI	4 TAU	4 CAN	5 VIR	4 LIB	5 SAG	5 CAP
7 SCO	6 SAG	7 CAP	6 AQU	5 PIS	6 TAU	6 GEM	6 LEO	7 LIB	6 SCO	8 CAP	7 AQU
10 SAG	9 CAP	9 AQU	8 PIS	8 ARI	8 GEM	8 CAN	8 VIR	9 SCO	9 SAG	10 AQU	10 PIS
12 CAP	11 AQU	12 PIS	10 ARI	10 TAU	10 CAN	10 LEO	10 LIB	11 SAG	11 CAP	13 PIS	12 ARI
15 AQU	13 PIS	14 ARI	12 TAU	12 GEM	12 LEO	12 VIR	13 SCO	14 CAP	14 AQU	15 ARI	15 TAU
17 PIS	16 ARI	16 TAU	14 GEM	14 CAN	14 VIR	14 LIB	15 SAG	16 AQU	16 PIS	17 TAU	17 GEM
19 ARI	18 TAU	18 GEM	16 CAN	16 LEO	17 LIB	16 SCO	18 CAP	19 PIS	19 ARI	19 GEM	19 CAN
21 TAU	20 GEM	20 CAN	19 LEO	18 VIR	19 SCO	19 SAG	20 AQU	21 ARI	21 TAU	21 CAN	21 LEO
24 GEM	22 CAN	22 LEO	21 VIR	20 LIB	22 SAG	21 CAP	23 PIS	23 TAU	23 GEM	23 LEO	23 VIR
26 CAN	24 LEO	25 VIR	23 LIB	23 SCO	24 CAP	24 AQU	25 ARI	25 GEM	25 CAN	25 VIR	25 LIB
28 LEO	26 VIR	27 LIB	26 SCO	25 SAG	27 AQU	26 PIS	27 TAU	28 CAN	27 LEO	28 LIB	27 SCO
30 VIR	28 LIB	29 SCO	28 SAG	28 CAP	29 PIS	29 ARI	29 GEM	30 LEO	29 VIR	30 SCO	30 SAG
				30 AQU		31 TAU	31 CAN		31 LIB		

1965

JAN	FEB	MAR	APR	MAY	JUN	JUL	AUG	SEP	OCT	NOV	DEC
1 CAP	2 PIS	2 PIS	3 TAU	2 GEM	1 CAN	2 VIR	3 SCO	1 SAG	1 CAP	2 PIS	2 ARI
4 AQU	5 ARI	4 ARI	5 GEM	4 CAN	3 LEO	4 LIB	5 SAG	4 CAP	4 AQU	5 ARI	5 TAU
6 PIS	7 TAU	6 TAU	7 CAN	6 LEO	5 VIR	6 SCO	7 CAP	6 AQU	6 PIS	7 TAU	7 GEM
9 ARI	9 GEM	9 GEM	9 LEO	8 VIR	7 LIB	9 SAG	10 AQU	9 PIS	9 ARI	9 GEM	9 CAN
11 TAU	11 CAN	11 CAN	11 VIR	11 LIB	9 SCO	11 CAP	13 PIS	11 ARI	11 TAU	12 CAN	11 LEO
13 GEM	13 LEO	13 LEO	13 LIB	13 SCO	12 SAG	14 AQU	15 ARI	14 TAU	13 GEM	14 LEO	13 VIR
15 CAN	16 VIR	15 VIR	16 SCO	15 SAG	14 CAP	16 PIS	17 TAU	16 GEM	15 CAN	16 VIR	15 LIB
17 LEO	18 LIB	17 LIB	18 SAG	18 CAP	16 AQU	19 ARI	20 GEM	18 CAN	17 LEO	18 LIB	17 SCO
19 VIR	20 SCO	19 SCO	20 CAP	20 AQU	19 PIS	21 TAU	22 CAN	20 LEO	20 VIR	20 SCO	20 SAG
21 LIB	22 SAG	22 SAG	23 AQU	23 PIS	21 ARI	23 GEM	24 LEO	22 VIR	22 LIB	22 SAG	22 CAP
23 SCO	25 CAP	24 CAP	25 PIS	25 ARI	24 TAU	25 CAN	26 VIR	24 LIB	24 SCO	25 CAP	25 AQU
26 SAG	27 AQU	27 AQU	28 ARI	27 TAU	26 GEM	27 LEO	28 LIB	26 SCO	26 SAG	27 AQU	27 PIS
28 CAP		29 PIS	30 TAU	30 GEM	28 CAN	29 VIR	30 SCO	29 SAG	28 CAP	30 PIS	30 ARI
31 AQU		31 ARI			30 LEO	31 LIB			31 AQU		

1966

JAN	FEB	MAR	APR	MAY	JUN	JUL	AUG	SEP	OCT	NOV	DEC
1 TAU	2 CAN	1 CAN	2 VIR	1 LIB	2 SAG	1 CAP	2 PIS	1 ARI	1 TAU	2 CAN	2 LEO
3 GEM	4 LEO	3 LEO	4 LIB	3 SCO	4 CAP	4 AQU	5 ARI	4 TAU	3 GEM	4 LEO	4 VIR
5 CAN	6 VIR	5 VIR	6 SCO	5 SAG	6 AQU	6 PIS	7 TAU	6 GEM	6 CAN	6 VIR	6 LIB
7 LEO	8 LIB	7 LIB	8 SAG	8 CAP	9 PIS	9 ARI	10 GEM	9 CAN	8 LEO	8 LIB	8 SCO
9 VIR	10 SCO	9 SCO	10 CAP	10 AQU	11 ARI	11 TAU	12 CAN	11 LEO	10 VIR	11 SCO	10 SAG
11 LIB	12 SAG	12 SAG	13 AQU	12 PIS	14 TAU	14 GEM	14 LEO	13 VIR	12 LIB	13 SAG	12 CAP
14 SCO	15 CAP	14 CAP	15 PIS	15 ARI	16 GEM	16 CAN	16 VIR	15 LIB	14 SCO	15 CAP	14 AQU
16 SAG	17 AQU	16 AQU	18 ARI	17 TAU	18 CAN	18 LEO	18 LIB	17 SCO	16 SAG	17 AQU	17 PIS
18 CAP	20 PIS	19 PIS	20 TAU	20 GEM	20 LEO	20 VIR	20 SCO	19 SAG	18 CAP	20 PIS	19 ARI
21 AQU	22 ARI	21 ARI	22 GEM	22 CAN	23 VIR	22 LIB	22 SAG	21 CAP	21 AQU	22 ARI	22 TAU
23 PIS	25 TAU	24 TAU	25 CAN	24 LEO	25 LIB	24 SCO	25 CAP	23 AQU	23 PIS	25 TAU	24 GEM
26 ARI	27 GEM	26 GEM	27 LEO	26 VIR	27 SCO	26 SAG	27 AQU	26 PIS	26 ARI	27 GEM	27 CAN
28 TAU		29 CAN	29 VIR	28 LIB	29 SAG	29 CAP	30 PIS	28 ARI	28 TAU	29 CAN	29 LEO
31 GEM		31 LEO		31 SCO		31 AQU			31 GEM		31 VIR

1967

JAN	FEB	MAR	APR	MAY	JUN	JUL	AUG	SEP	OCT	NOV	DEC
2 LIB	3 SAG	2 SAG	3 AQU	2 PIS	1 ARI	1 TAU	2 CAN	1 LEO	2 LIB	1 SCO	2 CAP
4 SCO	5 CAP	4 CAP	5 PIS	5 ARI	4 TAU	3 GEM	4 LEO	3 VIR	4 SCO	3 SAG	4 AQU
6 SAG	7 AQU	6 AQU	8 ARI	7 TAU	6 GEM	6 CAN	7 VIR	5 LIB	6 SAG	5 CAP	7 PIS
9 CAP	10 PIS	9 PIS	10 TAU	10 GEM	9 CAN	8 LEO	9 LIB	7 SCO	9 CAP	7 AQU	9 ARI
11 AQU	12 ARI	11 ARI	13 GEM	12 CAN	11 LEO	10 VIR	11 SCO	9 SAG	11 AQU	9 PIS	12 TAU
13 PIS	15 TAU	14 TAU	15 CAN	15 LEO	13 VIR	12 LIB	13 SAG	11 CAP	13 PIS	12 ARI	14 GEM
16 ARI	17 GEM	16 GEM	17 LEO	17 VIR	15 LIB	15 SCO	15 CAP	14 AQU	16 ARI	14 TAU	17 CAN
18 TAU	19 CAN	19 CAN	20 VIR	19 LIB	17 SCO	17 SAG	17 AQU	16 PIS	18 TAU	17 GEM	19 LEO
21 GEM	22 LEO	21 LEO	22 LIB	21 SCO	19 SAG	19 CAP	20 PIS	18 ARI	21 GEM	19 CAN	21 VIR
23 CAN	24 VIR	23 VIR	24 SCO	23 SAG	21 CAP	21 AQU	22 ARI	21 TAU	23 CAN	22 LEO	24 LIB
25 LEO	26 LIB	25 LIB	26 SAG	25 CAP	24 AQU	23 PIS	25 TAU	23 GEM	26 LEO	24 VIR	26 SCO
27 VIR	28 SCO	27 SCO	28 CAP	27 AQU	26 PIS	26 ARI	27 GEM	26 CAN	28 VIR	26 LIB	28 SAG
29 LIB		29 SAG	30 AQU	30 PIS	28 ARI	28 TAU	30 CAN	28 LEO	30 LIB	28 SCO	30 CAP
31 SCO		31 CAP				31 GEM		30 VIR		30 SAG	

1968

JAN	FEB	MAR	APR	MAY	JUN	JUL	AUG	SEP	OCT	NOV	DEC
1 AQU	2 ARI	3 TAU	2 GEM	1 CAN	2 VIR	2 LIB	3 SAG	1 CAP	2 PIS	1 ARI	1 TAU
3 PIS	4 TAU	5 GEM	4 CAN	4 LEO	5 LIB	4 SCO	5 CAP	3 AQU	5 ARI	3 TAU	3 GEM
6 ARI	7 GEM	8 CAN	7 LEO	6 VIR	7 SCO	6 SAG	7 AQU	5 PIS	7 TAU	6 GEM	6 CAN
8 TAU	9 CAN	10 LEO	9 VIR	8 LIB	9 SAG	8 CAP	9 PIS	7 ARI	10 GEM	8 CAN	8 LEO
11 GEM	12 LEO	12 VIR	11 LIB	10 SCO	11 CAP	10 AQU	11 ARI	10 TAU	12 CAN	11 LEO	11 VIR
13 CAN	14 VIR	14 LIB	13 SCO	12 SAG	13 AQU	12 PIS	13 TAU	12 GEM	15 LEO	13 VIR	13 LIB
15 LEO	16 LIB	17 SCO	15 SAG	14 CAP	15 PIS	15 ARI	16 GEM	15 CAN	17 VIR	16 LIB	15 SCO
18 VIR	18 SCO	19 SAG	17 CAP	16 AQU	17 ARI	17 TAU	18 CAN	17 LEO	19 LIB	18 SCO	17 SAG
20 LIB	20 SAG	21 CAP	19 AQU	19 PIS	20 TAU	19 GEM	21 LEO	20 VIR	21 SCO	20 SAG	19 CAP
22 SCO	22 CAP	23 AQU	21 PIS	21 ARI	22 GEM	22 CAN	23 VIR	22 LIB	23 SAG	22 CAP	21 AQU
24 SAG	25 AQU	25 PIS	24 ARI	24 TAU	25 CAN	25 LEO	25 LIB	24 SCO	25 CAP	24 AQU	23 PIS
26 CAP	27 PIS	28 ARI	26 TAU	26 GEM	27 LEO	27 VIR	28 SCO	26 SAG	27 AQU	26 PIS	26 ARI
28 AQU	29 ARI	30 TAU	29 GEM	29 CAN	30 VIR	29 LIB	30 SAG	28 CAP	30 PIS	28 ARI	28 TAU
31 PIS				31 LEO		31 SCO		30 AQU			30 GEM

1969

JAN	FEB	MAR	APR	MAY	JUN	JUL	AUG	SEP	OCT	NOV	DEC
2 CAN	1 LEO	2 VIR	1 LIB	1 SCO	1 CAP	1 AQU	1 ARI	2 GEM	2 CAN	1 LEO	1 VIR
4 LEO	3 VIR	5 LIB	3 SCO	3 SAG	3 AQU	3 PIS	3 TAU	5 CAN	4 LEO	3 VIR	3 LIB
7 VIR	6 LIB	7 SCO	5 SAG	5 CAP	5 PIS	5 ARI	6 GEM	7 LEO	7 VIR	6 LIB	5 SCO
9 LIB	8 SCO	9 SAG	8 CAP	7 AQU	7 ARI	7 TAU	8 CAN	10 VIR	9 LIB	8 SCO	8 SAG
12 SCO	10 SAG	11 CAP	10 AQU	9 PIS	10 TAU	10 GEM	11 LEO	12 LIB	12 SCO	10 SAG	10 CAP
14 SAG	12 CAP	13 AQU	12 PIS	11 ARI	12 GEM	12 CAN	13 VIR	14 SCO	14 SAG	12 CAP	12 AQU
16 CAP	14 AQU	16 PIS	14 ARI	14 TAU	15 CAN	15 LEO	16 LIB	17 SAG	16 CAP	14 AQU	14 PIS
18 AQU	16 PIS	18 ARI	16 TAU	16 GEM	17 LEO	17 VIR	18 SCO	19 CAP	18 AQU	16 PIS	16 ARI
20 PIS	18 ARI	20 TAU	19 GEM	19 CAN	20 VIR	20 LIB	20 SAG	21 AQU	20 PIS	19 ARI	18 TAU
22 ARI	21 TAU	22 GEM	21 CAN	21 LEO	22 LIB	22 SCO	22 CAP	23 PIS	22 ARI	21 TAU	20 GEM
24 TAU	23 GEM	25 CAN	24 LEO	24 VIR	25 SCO	24 SAG	24 AQU	25 ARI	25 TAU	23 GEM	23 CAN
27 GEM	26 CAN	27 LEO	26 VIR	26 LIB	27 SAG	26 CAP	26 PIS	27 TAU	27 GEM	26 CAN	25 LEO
29 CAN	28 LEO	30 VIR	29 LIB	28 SCO	29 CAP	28 AQU	29 ARI	29 GEM	29 CAN	28 LEO	28 VIR
				30 SAG		30 PIS	31 TAU				30 LIB

1970

JAN	FEB	MAR	APR	MAY	JUN	JUL	AUG	SEP	OCT	NOV	DEC
2 SCO	2 CAP	2 CAP	2 PIS	2 ARI	2 GEM	2 CAN	1 LEO	2 LIB	2 SCO	3 CAP	2 AQU
4 SAG	4 AQU	4 AQU	4 ARI	4 TAU	5 CAN	4 LEO	3 VIR	5 SCO	4 SAG	5 AQU	4 PIS
6 CAP	6 PIS	6 PIS	6 TAU	6 GEM	7 LEO	7 VIR	6 LIB	7 SAG	6 CAP	7 PIS	6 ARI
8 AQU	8 ARI	8 ARI	9 GEM	8 CAN	10 VIR	10 LIB	8 SCO	9 CAP	9 AQU	9 ARI	8 TAU
10 PIS	11 TAU	10 TAU	11 CAN	11 LEO	12 LIB	12 SCO	11 SAG	11 AQU	11 PIS	11 TAU	11 GEM
12 ARI	13 GEM	12 GEM	14 LEO	13 VIR	15 SCO	15 SAG	13 CAP	13 PIS	13 ARI	13 GEM	13 CAN
14 TAU	15 CAN	15 CAN	16 VIR	16 LIB	17 SAG	17 CAP	15 AQU	15 ARI	15 TAU	16 CAN	15 LEO
17 GEM	18 LEO	17 LEO	19 LIB	18 SCO	19 CAP	19 AQU	17 PIS	17 TAU	17 GEM	18 LEO	18 VIR
19 CAN	20 VIR	20 VIR	21 SCO	20 SAG	21 AQU	21 PIS	19 ARI	19 GEM	19 CAN	20 VIR	20 LIB
22 LEO	23 LIB	22 LIB	23 SAG	22 CAP	23 PIS	23 ARI	21 TAU	22 CAN	22 LEO	23 LIB	23 SCO
24 VIR	25 SCO	25 SCO	25 CAP	25 AQU	25 ARI	25 TAU	23 GEM	24 LEO	24 VIR	25 SCO	25 SAG
27 LIB	28 SAG	27 SAG	27 AQU	27 PIS	27 TAU	27 GEM	25 CAN	27 VIR	27 LIB	28 SAG	27 CAP
29 SCO		29 CAP	30 PIS	29 ARI	29 GEM	30 CAN	28 LEO	29 LIB	29 SCO	30 CAP	29 AQU
31 SAG		31 AQU		31 TAU			31 VIR		31 SAG		31 PIS

1971

JAN	FEB	MAR	APR	MAY	JUN	JUL	AUG	SEP	OCT	NOV	DEC
3 ARI	1 TAU	2 GEM	1 CAN	1 LEO	2 LIB	2 SCO	1 SAG	2 AQU	1 PIS	2 TAU	1 GEM
5 TAU	3 GEM	5 CAN	3 LEO	3 VIR	5 SCO	4 SAG	3 CAP	4 PIS	3 ARI	4 GEM	3 CAN
7 GEM	5 CAN	7 LEO	6 VIR	6 LIB	7 SAG	7 CAP	5 AQU	6 ARI	5 TAU	6 CAN	5 LEO
9 CAN	8 LEO	10 VIR	8 LIB	8 SCO	9 CAP	9 AQU	7 PIS	8 TAU	7 GEM	8 LEO	8 VIR
12 LEO	10 VIR	12 LIB	11 SCO	11 SAG	11 AQU	11 PIS	9 ARI	10 GEM	9 CAN	10 VIR	10 LIB
14 VIR	13 LIB	15 SCO	13 SAG	13 CAP	14 PIS	13 ARI	11 TAU	12 CAN	12 LEO	13 LIB	13 SCO
17 LIB	15 SCO	17 SAG	16 CAP	15 AQU	16 ARI	15 TAU	13 GEM	14 LEO	14 VIR	15 SCO	15 SAG
19 SCO	18 SAG	19 CAP	18 AQU	17 PIS	18 TAU	17 GEM	16 CAN	17 VIR	16 LIB	18 SAG	17 CAP
22 SAG	20 CAP	22 AQU	20 PIS	20 ARI	20 GEM	19 CAN	18 LEO	19 LIB	19 SCO	20 CAP	20 AQU
24 CAP	22 AQU	24 PIS	22 ARI	22 TAU	22 CAN	22 LEO	20 VIR	22 SCO	22 SAG	23 AQU	22 PIS
26 AQU	24 PIS	26 ARI	24 TAU	24 GEM	24 LEO	24 VIR	23 LIB	24 SAG	24 CAP	25 PIS	24 ARI
28 PIS	26 ARI	28 TAU	26 GEM	26 CAN	27 VIR	27 LIB	26 SCO	27 CAP	26 AQU	27 ARI	26 TAU
30 ARI	28 TAU	30 GEM	28 CAN	28 LEO	29 LIB	29 SCO	28 SAG	29 AQU	28 PIS	29 TAU	28 GEM
				30 VIR			30 CAP		31 ARI		30 CAN

1972

JAN	FEB	MAR	APR	MAY	JUN	JUL	AUG	SEP	OCT	NOV	DEC
2 LEO	3 LIB	1 LIB	2 SAG	2 CAP	1 AQU	3 ARI	1 TAU	1 CAN	1 LEO	2 LIB	1 SCO
4 VIR	5 SCO	4 SCO	5 CAP	5 AQU	3 PIS	5 TAU	3 GEM	4 LEO	3 VIR	4 SCO	4 SAG
6 LIB	8 SAG	6 SAG	7 AQU	7 PIS	5 ARI	7 GEM	5 CAN	6 VIR	5 LIB	7 SAG	7 CAP
9 SCO	10 CAP	9 CAP	9 PIS	9 ARI	7 TAU	9 CAN	7 LEO	8 LIB	8 SCO	9 CAP	9 AQU
11 SAG	12 AQU	11 AQU	12 ARI	11 TAU	9 GEM	11 LEO	10 VIR	11 SCO	10 SAG	12 AQU	11 PIS
14 CAP	15 PIS	13 PIS	14 TAU	13 GEM	11 CAN	13 VIR	12 LIB	13 SAG	13 CAP	14 PIS	14 ARI
16 AQU	17 ARI	15 ARI	16 GEM	15 CAN	14 LEO	15 LIB	14 SCO	16 CAP	15 AQU	16 ARI	16 TAU
18 PIS	19 TAU	17 TAU	18 CAN	17 LEO	16 VIR	18 SCO	17 SAG	18 AQU	18 PIS	18 TAU	18 GEM
20 ARI	21 GEM	19 GEM	20 LEO	19 VIR	18 LIB	20 SAG	19 CAP	20 PIS	20 ARI	20 GEM	20 CAN
23 TAU	23 CAN	21 CAN	22 VIR	22 LIB	21 SCO	23 CAP	22 AQU	22 ARI	22 TAU	22 CAN	22 LEO
25 GEM	25 LEO	24 LEO	25 LIB	24 SCO	23 SAG	25 AQU	24 PIS	24 TAU	24 GEM	24 LEO	24 VIR
27 CAN	28 VIR	26 VIR	27 SCO	27 SAG	26 CAP	28 PIS	26 ARI	27 GEM	26 CAN	27 VIR	26 LIB
29 LEO		28 LIB	30 SAG	29 CAP	28 AQU	30 ARI	28 TAU	29 CAN	28 LEO	29 LIB	29 SCO
31 VIR		31 SCO			30 PIS		30 GEM		30 VIR		31 SAG

1973

JAN	FEB	MAR	APR	MAY	JUN	JUL	AUG	SEP	OCT	NOV	DEC
3 CAP	2 AQU	1 AQU	2 ARI	1 TAU	2 CAN	1 LEO	2 LIB	1 SCO	3 CAP	2 AQU	1 PIS
5 AQU	4 PIS	3 PIS	4 TAU	3 GEM	4 LEO	3 VIR	4 SCO	3 SAG	5 AQU	4 PIS	4 ARI
8 PIS	6 ARI	5 ARI	6 GEM	5 CAN	6 VIR	5 LIB	7 SAG	5 CAP	8 PIS	6 ARI	6 TAU
10 ARI	8 TAU	8 TAU	8 CAN	7 LEO	8 LIB	8 SCO	9 CAP	8 AQU	10 ARI	9 TAU	8 GEM
12 TAU	10 GEM	10 GEM	10 LEO	10 VIR	11 SCO	10 SAG	12 AQU	10 PIS	12 TAU	11 GEM	10 CAN
14 GEM	13 CAN	12 CAN	12 VIR	12 LIB	13 SAG	13 CAP	14 PIS	13 ARI	14 GEM	13 CAN	12 LEO
16 CAN	15 LEO	14 LEO	15 LIB	14 SCO	16 CAP	15 AQU	16 ARI	15 TAU	16 CAN	15 LEO	14 VIR
18 LEO	17 VIR	16 VIR	17 SCO	17 SAG	18 AQU	18 PIS	19 TAU	17 GEM	19 LEO	17 VIR	16 LIB
20 VIR	19 LIB	18 LIB	20 SAG	19 CAP	21 PIS	20 ARI	21 GEM	19 CAN	21 VIR	19 LIB	19 SCO
23 LIB	21 SCO	21 SCO	22 CAP	22 AQU	23 ARI	22 TAU	23 CAN	21 LEO	23 LIB	22 SCO	21 SAG
25 SCO	24 SAG	23 SAG	25 AQU	24 PIS	25 TAU	25 GEM	25 LEO	23 VIR	25 SCO	24 SAG	24 CAP
28 SAG	26 CAP	26 CAP	27 PIS	27 ARI	27 GEM	27 CAN	27 VIR	26 LIB	28 SAG	26 CAP	26 AQU
30 CAP		28 AQU	29 ARI	29 TAU	29 CAN	29 LEO	29 LIB	28 SCO	30 CAP	29 AQU	29 PIS
		31 PIS		31 GEM		31 VIR		30 SAG			31 ARI

1974

JAN	FEB	MAR	APR	MAY	JUN	JUL	AUG	SEP	OCT	NOV	DEC
2 TAU	1 GEM	2 CAN	1 LEO	2 LIB	1 SCO	3 CAP	2 AQU	3 ARI	2 TAU	1 GEM	1 CAN
5 GEM	3 CAN	4 LEO	3 VIR	4 SCO	3 SAG	5 AQU	4 PIS	5 TAU	5 GEM	3 CAN	3 LEO
7 CAN	5 LEO	7 VIR	5 LIB	7 SAG	6 CAP	8 PIS	7 ARI	8 GEM	7 CAN	5 LEO	5 VIR
9 LEO	7 VIR	9 LIB	7 SCO	9 CAP	8 AQU	10 ARI	9 TAU	10 CAN	9 LEO	8 VIR	7 LIB
11 VIR	9 LIB	11 SCO	9 SAG	12 AQU	11 PIS	13 TAU	11 GEM	12 LEO	11 VIR	10 LIB	9 SCO
13 LIB	11 SCO	13 SAG	12 CAP	14 PIS	13 ARI	15 GEM	13 CAN	14 VIR	13 LIB	12 SCO	11 SAG
15 SCO	14 SAG	16 CAP	14 AQU	17 ARI	15 TAU	17 CAN	15 LEO	16 LIB	15 SCO	14 SAG	14 CAP
17 SAG	16 CAP	18 AQU	17 PIS	19 TAU	18 GEM	19 LEO	17 VIR	18 SCO	18 SAG	16 CAP	16 AQU
20 CAP	19 AQU	21 PIS	19 ARI	21 GEM	20 CAN	21 VIR	19 LIB	20 SAG	20 CAP	19 AQU	19 PIS
22 AQU	21 PIS	23 ARI	22 TAU	23 CAN	22 LEO	23 LIB	22 SCO	23 CAP	22 AQU	21 PIS	21 ARI
25 PIS	24 ARI	25 TAU	24 GEM	25 LEO	24 VIR	25 SCO	24 SAG	25 AQU	25 PIS	24 ARI	24 TAU
27 ARI	26 TAU	27 GEM	26 CAN	27 VIR	26 LIB	28 SAG	26 CAP	28 PIS	27 ARI	26 TAU	26 GEM
30 TAU	28 GEM	30 CAN	28 LEO	30 LIB	28 SCO	30 CAP	29 AQU	30 ARI	30 TAU	30 TAU	28 CAN
			30 VIR		30 SAG		31 PIS				30 LEO

1975

JAN	FEB	MAR	APR	MAY	JUN	JUL	AUG	SEP	OCT	NOV	DEC
1 VIR	2 SCO	1 SCO	2 CAP	2 AQU	3 ARI	3 TAU	1 GEM	2 LEO	2 VIR	2 SCO	2 SAG
3 LIB	4 SAG	3 SAG	4 AQU	4 PIS	5 TAU	5 GEM	4 CAN	4 VIR	4 LIB	4 SAG	4 CAP
5 SCO	6 CAP	5 CAP	7 PIS	7 ARI	8 GEM	7 CAN	6 LEO	6 LIB	6 SCO	6 CAP	6 AQU
8 SAG	9 AQU	8 AQU	9 ARI	9 TAU	10 CAN	9 LEO	8 VIR	8 SCO	8 SAG	9 AQU	8 PIS
10 CAP	11 PIS	10 PIS	12 TAU	11 GEM	12 LEO	11 VIR	10 LIB	10 SAG	10 CAP	11 PIS	11 ARI
12 AQU	14 ARI	13 ARI	14 GEM	14 CAN	14 VIR	14 LIB	12 SCO	13 CAP	12 AQU	14 ARI	13 TAU
15 PIS	16 TAU	15 TAU	16 CAN	16 LEO	16 LIB	16 SCO	14 SAG	15 AQU	15 PIS	16 TAU	16 GEM
17 ARI	19 GEM	18 GEM	19 LEO	18 VIR	18 SCO	18 SAG	16 CAP	18 PIS	17 ARI	19 GEM	18 CAN
20 TAU	21 CAN	20 CAN	21 VIR	20 LIB	21 SAG	20 CAP	19 AQU	20 ARI	20 TAU	21 CAN	20 LEO
22 GEM	23 LEO	22 LEO	23 LIB	22 SCO	23 CAP	23 AQU	21 PIS	23 TAU	22 GEM	23 LEO	23 VIR
24 CAN	25 VIR	24 VIR	25 SAG	24 SAG	25 AQU	25 PIS	24 ARI	25 GEM	25 CAN	25 VIR	25 LIB
26 LEO	27 LIB	26 LIB	27 SCO	27 CAP	28 PIS	28 ARI	26 TAU	27 CAN	27 LEO	27 LIB	27 SCO
28 VIR		28 SCO	29 CAP	29 AQU	30 ARI	30 TAU	29 GEM	30 LEO	29 VIR	30 SCO	29 SAG
30 LIB		30 SAG		31 PIS			31 CAN		31 LIB		31 CAP

1976

JAN	FEB	MAR	APR	MAY	JUN	JUL	AUG	SEP	OCT	NOV	DEC
2 AQU	1 PIS	2 ARI	1 TAU	3 CAN	1 LEO	1 VIR	1 SCO	2 CAP	1 AQU	2 ARI	2 TAU
5 PIS	4 ARI	4 TAU	3 GEM	5 LEO	4 VIR	3 LIB	4 SAG	4 AQU	4 PIS	5 TAU	5 GEM
7 ARI	6 TAU	7 GEM	6 CAN	7 VIR	6 LIB	5 SCO	6 CAP	7 PIS	6 ARI	8 GEM	7 CAN
10 TAU	9 GEM	9 CAN	8 LEO	10 LIB	8 SCO	7 SAG	8 AQU	9 ARI	9 TAU	10 CAN	10 LEO
12 GEM	11 CAN	12 LEO	10 VIR	12 SCO	10 SAG	9 CAP	10 PIS	11 TAU	11 GEM	12 LEO	12 VIR
15 CAN	13 LEO	14 VIR	12 LIB	14 SAG	12 CAP	12 AQU	13 ARI	14 GEM	14 CAN	15 VIR	14 LIB
17 LEO	15 VIR	16 LIB	14 SCO	16 CAP	14 AQU	14 PIS	15 TAU	17 CAN	16 LEO	17 LIB	16 SCO
19 VIR	17 LIB	18 SCO	16 SAG	18 AQU	17 PIS	16 ARI	18 GEM	19 LEO	18 VIR	19 SCO	18 SAG
21 LIB	19 SCO	20 SAG	18 CAP	20 PIS	19 ARI	19 TAU	20 CAN	21 VIR	21 LIB	21 SAG	20 CAP
23 SCO	21 SAG	22 CAP	20 AQU	23 ARI	22 TAU	21 GEM	22 LEO	23 LIB	23 SCO	23 CAP	22 AQU
25 SAG	24 CAP	24 AQU	23 PIS	25 TAU	24 GEM	24 CAN	25 VIR	25 SCO	25 SAG	25 AQU	25 PIS
27 CAP	26 AQU	27 PIS	25 ARI	28 GEM	26 CAN	26 LEO	27 LIB	27 SAG	27 CAP	27 PIC	27 ARI
30 AQU	28 PIS	29 ARI	28 TAU	30 CAN	29 LEO	28 VIR	29 SCO	29 CAP	29 AQU	30 ARI	30 TAU
			30 GEM			30 LIB	31 SAG		31 PIS		

1977

JAN	FEB	MAR	APR	MAY	JUN	JUL	AUG	SEP	OCT	NOV	DEC
1 GEM	2 LEO	2 LEO	2 LIB	2 SCO	2 CAP	2 AQU	3 ARI	1 TAU	1 GEM	3 LEO	2 VIR
4 CAN	5 VIR	4 VIR	5 SCO	4 SAG	4 AQU	4 PIS	5 TAU	4 GEM	4 CAN	5 VIR	5 LIB
6 LEO	7 LIB	6 LIB	7 SAG	6 CAP	7 PIS	6 ARI	7 GEM	6 CAN	6 LEO	7 LIB	7 SCO
8 VIR	9 SCO	8 SCO	9 CAP	8 AQU	9 ARI	9 TAU	10 CAN	9 LEO	9 VIR	9 SCO	9 SAG
10 LIB	11 SAG	10 SAG	11 AQU	10 PIS	11 TAU	11 GEM	12 LEO	11 VIR	11 LIB	11 SAG	11 CAP
13 SCO	13 CAP	12 CAP	13 PIS	13 ARI	14 GEM	14 CAN	15 VIR	13 LIB	13 SCO	13 CAP	13 AQU
15 SAG	15 AQU	15 AQU	15 ARI	16 TAU	16 CAN	16 LEO	17 LIB	16 SCO	15 SAG	15 AQU	15 PIS
17 CAP	17 PIS	17 PIS	18 TAU	18 GEM	19 LEO	19 VIR	19 SCO	18 SAG	17 CAP	18 PIS	17 ARI
19 AQU	20 ARI	19 ARI	20 GEM	20 CAN	21 VIR	21 LIB	21 SAG	20 CAP	19 AQU	20 ARI	19 TAU
21 PIS	22 TAU	22 TAU	23 CAN	23 LEO	23 LIB	23 SCO	24 CAP	22 AQU	21 PIS	22 TAU	22 GEM
23 ARI	25 GEM	24 GEM	25 LEO	25 VIR	26 SCO	26 SAG	26 AQU	24 PIS	24 ARI	25 GEM	25 CAN
26 TAU	27 CAN	27 CAN	28 VIR	27 LIB	28 SAG	28 CAP	28 PIS	26 ARI	26 TAU	27 CAN	27 LEO
28 GEM		29 LEO	30 LIB	29 SCO	30 CAP	31 PIS	30 ARI	29 TAU	28 GEM	30 LEO	30 VIR
31 CAN		31 VIR		31 SAG					31 CAN		

1978

JAN	FEB	MAR	APR	MAY	JUN	JUL	AUG	SEP	OCT	NOV	DEC
1 LIB	2 SAG	1 SAG	1 AQU	1 PIS	1 TAU	1 GEM	2 LEO	1 VIR	1 LIB	2 SAG	1 CAP
3 SCO	4 CAP	3 CAP	3 PIS	3 ARI	4 GEM	4 CAN	5 VIR	4 LIB	3 SCO	4 CAP	3 AQU
5 SAG	6 AQU	5 AQU	6 ARI	5 TAU	6 CAN	6 LEO	7 LIB	6 SCO	5 SAG	6 AQU	5 PIS
7 CAP	8 PIS	7 PIS	8 TAU	8 GEM	9 LEO	9 VIR	10 SCO	8 SAG	8 CAP	8 PIS	7 ARI
9 AQU	10 ARI	9 ARI	10 GEM	10 CAN	11 VIR	11 LIB	12 SAG	10 CAP	10 AQU	10 ARI	10 TAU
11 PIS	12 TAU	12 TAU	13 CAN	13 LEO	14 LIB	13 SCO	14 CAP	12 AQU	12 PIS	12 TAU	12 GEM
13 ARI	15 GEM	14 GEM	15 LEO	15 VIR	16 SCO	16 SAG	16 AQU	14 PIS	14 ARI	15 GEM	14 CAN
16 TAU	17 CAN	16 CAN	18 VIR	17 LIB	18 SAG	18 CAP	18 PIS	17 ARI	16 TAU	17 CAN	17 LEO
18 GEM	20 LEO	19 LEO	20 LIB	20 SCO	20 CAP	20 AQU	20 ARI	19 TAU	18 GEM	20 LEO	19 VIR
21 CAN	22 VIR	21 VIR	22 SCO	22 SAG	22 AQU	22 PIS	22 TAU	21 GEM	21 CAN	22 VIR	22 LIB
23 LEO	24 LIB	24 LIB	24 SAG	24 CAP	24 PIS	24 ARI	25 GEM	23 CAN	23 LEO	25 LIB	24 SCO
26 VIR	27 SCO	26 SCO	26 CAP	26 AQU	26 ARI	26 TAU	27 CAN	26 LEO	26 VIR	27 SCO	27 SAG
28 LIB		28 SAG	29 AQU	28 PIS	29 TAU	28 GEM	30 LEO	28 VIR	28 LIB	29 SAG	29 CAP
30 SCO		30 CAP		30 ARI		31 CAN			31 SCO		31 AQU

1979

JAN	FEB	MAR	APR	MAY	JUN	JUL	AUG	SEP	OCT	NOV	DEC
2 PIS	2 TAU	2 TAU	3 CAN	2 LEO	1 VIR	1 LIB	2 SAG	1 CAP	2 PIS	1 ARI	2 GEM
4 ARI	5 GEM	4 GEM	5 LEO	5 VIR	4 LIB	4 SCO	4 CAP	3 AQU	4 ARI	3 TAU	4 CAN
6 TAU	7 CAN	6 CAN	8 VIR	7 LIB	6 SCO	6 SAG	6 AQU	5 PIS	6 TAU	5 GEM	7 LEO
8 GEM	9 LEO	9 LEO	10 LIB	10 SCO	9 SAG	8 CAP	8 PIS	7 ARI	8 GEM	7 CAN	9 VIR
11 CAN	12 VIR	11 VIR	12 SCO	12 SAG	11 CAP	10 AQU	10 ARI	9 TAU	11 CAN	9 LEO	12 LIB
13 LEO	15 LIB	14 LIB	15 SAG	14 CAP	13 AQU	12 PIS	13 TAU	11 GEM	13 LEO	12 VIR	14 SCO
16 VIR	17 SCO	16 SCO	17 CAP	16 AQU	15 PIS	14 ARI	15 GEM	13 CAN	16 VIR	14 LIB	17 SAG
18 LIB	19 SAG	19 SAG	19 AQU	18 PIS	17 ARI	16 TAU	17 CAN	16 LEO	18 LIB	17 SCO	19 CAP
21 SCO	21 CAP	21 CAP	21 PIS	21 ARI	19 TAU	18 GEM	20 LEO	18 VIR	21 SCO	19 SAG	21 AQU
23 SAG	24 AQU	23 AQU	23 ARI	23 TAU	21 GEM	21 CAN	22 VIR	21 LIB	23 SAG	22 CAP	23 PIS
25 CAP	25 PIS	25 PIS	25 TAU	25 GEM	24 CAN	23 LEO	25 LIB	23 SCO	25 CAP	24 AQU	25 ARI
27 AQU	27 ARI	27 ARI	28 GEM	27 CAN	26 LEO	26 VIR	27 SCO	26 SAG	28 AQU	26 PIS	27 TAU
29 PIS		29 TAU	30 CAN	30 LEO	29 VIR	28 LIB	30 SAG	28 CAP	30 PIS	28 ARI	30 GEM
31 ARI		31 GEM				31 SCO		30 AQU		30 TAU	

1980

JAN	FEB	MAR	APR	MAY	JUN	JUL	AUG	SEP	OCT	NOV	DEC
1 CAN	2 VIR	3 LIB	2 SCO	1 SAG	2 AQU	2 PIS	2 TAU	3 CAN	2 LEO	1 VIR	1 LIB
3 LEO	4 LIB	5 SCO	4 SAG	4 CAP	4 PIS	4 ARI	4 GEM	5 LEO	5 VIR	3 LIB	3 SCO
6 VIR	7 SCO	8 SAG	6 CAP	6 AQU	6 ARI	6 TAU	6 CAN	7 VIR	7 LIB	6 SCO	6 SAG
8 LIB	9 SAG	10 CAP	9 AQU	8 PIS	9 TAU	8 GEM	9 LEO	10 LIB	10 SCO	8 SAG	8 CAP
11 SCO	12 CAP	12 AQU	11 PIS	10 ARI	11 GEM	10 CAN	11 VIR	12 SCO	12 SAG	11 CAP	10 AQU
13 SAG	14 AQU	14 PIS	13 ARI	12 TAU	13 CAN	12 LEO	14 LIB	15 SAG	15 CAP	13 AQU	13 PIS
15 CAP	16 PIS	16 ARI	15 TAU	14 GEM	15 LEO	15 VIR	16 SCO	17 CAP	17 AQU	15 PIS	15 ARI
17 AQU	18 ARI	18 TAU	17 GEM	16 CAN	17 VIR	17 LIB	19 SAG	20 AQU	19 PIS	18 ARI	17 TAU
19 PIS	20 TAU	20 GEM	19 CAN	19 LEO	20 LIB	20 SCO	21 CAP	22 PIS	21 ARI	20 TAU	19 GEM
21 ARI	22 GEM	23 CAN	21 LEO	21 VIR	22 SCO	22 SAG	23 AQU	23 ARI	23 TAU	22 GEM	21 CAN
24 TAU	24 CAN	25 LEO	24 VIR	24 LIB	25 SAG	25 CAP	25 PIS	26 TAU	25 GEM	24 CAN	23 LEO
26 GEM	27 LEO	27 VIR	26 LIB	26 SCO	27 CAP	27 AQU	27 ARI	28 GEM	27 CAN	26 LEO	25 VIR
28 CAN	29 VIR	30 LIB	29 SCO	29 SAG	29 AQU	29 PIS	29 TAU	30 CAN	29 LEO	28 VIR	28 LIB
30 LEO				31 CAP		31 ARI	31 GEM				30 SCO

1981

JAN	FEB	MAR	APR	MAY	JUN	JUL	AUG	SEP	OCT	NOV	DEC
2 SAG	1 CAP	2 AQU	1 PIS	1 ARI	1 GEM	2 LEO	1 VIR	2 SCO	2 SAG	1 CAP	1 AQU
4 CAP	3 AQU	5 PIS	3 ARI	3 TAU	3 CAN	5 VIR	3 LIB	5 SAG	5 CAP	3 AQU	3 PIS
7 AQU	5 PIS	7 ARI	5 TAU	5 GEM	5 LEO	7 LIB	6 SCO	7 CAP	7 AQU	6 PIS	5 ARI
9 PIS	7 ARI	9 TAU	7 GEM	7 CAN	7 VIR	10 SCO	8 SAG	10 AQU	9 PIS	8 ARI	7 TAU
11 ARI	9 TAU	11 GEM	9 CAN	9 LEO	10 LIB	12 SAG	11 CAP	12 PIS	11 ARI	10 TAU	9 GEM
13 TAU	12 GEM	13 CAN	11 LEO	11 VIR	12 SCO	15 CAP	13 AQU	14 ARI	13 TAU	12 GEM	11 CAN
15 GEM	14 CAN	15 LEO	14 VIR	13 LIB	15 SAG	17 AQU	16 PIS	16 TAU	15 GEM	14 CAN	13 LEO
17 CAN	16 LEO	18 VIR	16 LIB	16 SCO	17 CAP	19 PIS	18 ARI	18 GEM	18 CAN	16 LEO	16 VIR
20 LEO	18 VIR	20 LIB	19 SCO	18 SAG	20 AQU	21 ARI	20 TAU	20 CAN	20 LEO	18 VIR	18 LIB
22 VIR	21 LIB	22 SCO	21 SAG	21 CAP	22 PIS	24 TAU	22 GEM	22 LEO	22 VIR	21 LIB	20 SCO
24 LIB	23 SCO	25 SAG	24 CAP	23 AQU	24 ARI	26 GEM	24 CAN	25 VIR	24 LIB	23 SCO	23 SAG
27 SCO	26 SAG	27 CAP	26 AQU	25 PIS	26 TAU	28 CAN	26 LEO	27 LIB	27 SCO	26 SAG	25 CAP
29 SAG	28 CAP	30 AQU	28 PIS	28 ARI	28 GEM	30 LEO	28 VIR	29 SCO	29 SAG	28 CAP	28 AQU
				30 TAU	30 CAN		31 LIB				30 PIS

1982

JAN	FEB	MAR	APR	MAY	JUN	JUL	AUG	SEP	OCT	NOV	DEC
2 ARI	2 GEM	1 GEM	2 LEO	1 VIR	2 SCO	2 SAG	1 CAP	2 PIS	2 ARI	2 GEM	2 CAN
4 TAU	4 CAN	3 CAN	4 VIR	4 LIB	5 SAG	4 CAP	3 AQU	4 ARI	4 TAU	4 CAN	4 LEO
6 GEM	6 LEO	6 LEO	6 LIB	6 SCO	7 CAP	7 AQU	6 PIS	7 TAU	6 GEM	6 LEO	6 VIR
8 CAN	8 VIR	8 VIR	9 SCO	8 SAG	10 AQU	9 PIS	8 ARI	9 GEM	8 CAN	9 VIR	8 LIB
10 LEO	11 LIB	10 LIB	11 SAG	11 CAP	12 PIS	12 ARI	10 TAU	11 CAN	10 LEO	11 LIB	10 SCO
12 VIR	13 SCO	12 SCO	14 CAP	13 AQU	15 ARI	14 TAU	13 GEM	13 LEO	12 VIR	13 SCO	13 SAG
14 LIB	15 SAG	15 SAG	16 AQU	16 PIS	17 TAU	16 GEM	15 CAN	15 VIR	15 LIB	15 SAG	15 CAP
17 SCO	18 CAP	17 CAP	19 PIS	18 ARI	19 GEM	18 CAN	17 LEO	17 LIB	17 SCO	18 CAP	18 AQU
19 SAG	20 AQU	20 AQU	21 ARI	20 TAU	21 CAN	20 LEO	19 VIR	19 SCO	19 SAG	21 AQU	20 PIS
22 CAP	23 PIS	22 PIS	23 TAU	22 GEM	23 LEO	22 VIR	21 LIB	22 SAG	22 CAP	23 PIS	23 ARI
24 AQU	25 ARI	24 ARI	25 GEM	24 CAN	25 VIR	24 LIB	23 SCO	24 CAP	24 AQU	25 ARI	25 TAU
26 PIS	27 TAU	27 TAU	27 CAN	26 LEO	27 LIB	27 SCO	25 SAG	27 AQU	27 PIS	28 TAU	27 GEM
29 ARI		29 GEM	29 LEO	29 VIR	29 SCO	29 SAG	28 CAP	29 PIS	29 ARI	30 GEM	29 CAN
31 TAU		31 CAN		31 LIB			31 AQU		31 TAU		31 LEO

1983

JAN	FEB	MAR	APR	MAY	JUN	JUL	AUG	SEP	OCT	NOV	DEC
2 VIR	1 LIB	2 SCO	1 SAG	1 CAP	2 PIS	2 ARI	1 TAU	1 CAN	1 LEO	1 LIB	1 SCO
4 LIB	3 SCO	5 SAG	3 CAP	3 AQU	5 ARI	4 TAU	3 GEM	3 LEO	3 VIR	3 SCO	3 SAG
7 SCO	5 SAG	7 CAP	6 AQU	6 PIS	7 TAU	7 GEM	5 CAN	5 VIR	5 LIB	6 SAG	5 CAP
9 SAG	8 CAP	10 AQU	8 PIS	8 ARI	9 GEM	9 CAN	7 LEO	7 LIB	7 SCO	8 CAP	8 AQU
12 CAP	10 AQU	12 PIS	11 ARI	11 TAU	11 CAN	11 LEO	9 VIR	10 SCO	9 SAG	10 AQU	10 PIS
14 AQU	13 PIS	15 ARI	13 TAU	13 GEM	13 LEO	13 VIR	11 LIB	12 SAG	11 CAP	13 PIS	13 ARI
17 PIS	15 ARI	17 TAU	15 GEM	15 CAN	15 VIR	15 LIB	13 SCO	14 CAP	14 AQU	15 ARI	15 TAU
19 ARI	17 TAU	19 GEM	18 CAN	17 LEO	17 LIB	17 SCO	15 SAG	17 AQU	16 PIS	18 TAU	17 GEM
21 TAU	20 GEM	21 CAN	20 LEO	19 VIR	20 SCO	20 SAG	18 CAP	19 PIS	19 ARI	20 GEM	20 CAN
24 GEM	22 CAN	23 LEO	22 VIR	21 LIB	22 SAG	22 CAP	20 AQU	22 ARI	21 TAU	22 CAN	22 LEO
26 CAN	24 LEO	26 VIR	24 LIB	23 SCO	24 CAP	24 AQU	23 PIS	24 TAU	24 GEM	24 LEO	24 VIR
28 LEO	26 VIR	28 LIB	26 SCO	26 SAG	27 AQU	27 PIS	25 ARI	26 GEM	26 CAN	26 VIR	26 LIB
30 VIR	28 LIB	30 SCO	28 SAG	28 CAP	29 PIS	29 ARI	28 TAU	29 CAN	28 LEO	29 LIB	28 SCO
				31 AQU			30 GEM		30 VIR		30 SAG

187

1984

JAN	FEB	MAR	APR	MAY	JUN	JUL	AUG	SEP	OCT	NOV	DEC
2 CAP	3 PIS	1 PIS	2 TAU	2 GEM	1 CAN	2 VIR	3 SCO	1 SAG	1 CAP	2 PIS	1 ARI
4 AQU	5 ARI	4 ARI	5 GEM	4 CAN	3 LEO	4 LIB	5 SAG	3 CAP	3 AQU	4 ARI	4 TAU
6 PIS	8 TAU	6 TAU	7 CAN	6 LEO	5 VIR	6 SCO	7 CAP	6 AQU	5 PIS	7 TAU	6 GEM
9 ARI	10 GEM	8 GEM	9 LEO	9 VIR	7 LIB	9 SAG	9 AQU	8 PIS	8 ARI	9 GEM	9 CAN
11 TAU	12 CAN	11 CAN	11 VIR	11 LIB	9 SCO	11 CAP	11 PIS	11 ARI	10 TAU	12 CAN	11 LEO
14 GEM	15 LEO	13 LEO	13 LIB	13 SCO	11 SAG	13 AQU	14 ARI	13 TAU	13 GEM	14 LEO	13 VIR
16 CAN	16 VIR	15 VIR	15 SCO	15 SAG	13 CAP	16 PIS	17 TAU	16 GEM	15 CAN	16 VIR	15 LIB
18 LEO	18 LIB	17 LIB	17 SAG	17 CAP	16 AQU	18 ARI	19 GEM	18 CAN	18 LEO	18 LIB	17 SCO
20 VIR	20 SCO	19 SCO	20 CAP	19 AQU	18 PIS	21 TAU	22 CAN	20 LEO	20 VIR	20 SCO	19 SAG
22 LIB	23 SAG	21 SAG	22 AQU	22 PIS	21 ARI	23 GEM	25 LEO	22 VIR	22 LIB	22 SAG	22 CAP
24 SCO	25 CAP	23 CAP	25 PIS	24 ARI	23 TAU	25 CAN	27 VIR	24 LIB	24 SCO	24 CAP	24 AQU
26 SAG	28 AQU	26 AQU	27 ARI	27 TAU	26 GEM	27 LEO	28 LIB	26 SCO	26 SAG	27 AQU	26 PIS
29 CAP		28 PIS	30 TAU	29 GEM	28 CAN	29 VIR	30 SCO	28 SAG	28 CAP	29 PIS	29 ARI
31 AQU		31 ARI			30 LEO	31 LIB			30 AQU		31 TAU

1985

JAN	FEB	MAR	APR	MAY	JUN	JUL	AUG	SEP	OCT	NOV	DEC
3 GEM	2 CAN	1 CAN	2 VIR	1 LIB	2 SAG	1 CAP	2 PIS	1 ARI	3 GEM	2 CAN	1 LEO
5 CAN	4 LEO	3 LEO	4 LIB	3 SCO	4 CAP	3 AQU	4 ARI	3 TAU	5 CAN	4 LEO	4 VIR
7 LEO	6 VIR	5 VIR	6 SCO	5 SAG	6 AQU	5 PIS	7 TAU	6 GEM	8 LEO	6 VIR	6 LIB
9 VIR	8 LIB	7 LIB	8 SAG	7 CAP	8 PIS	8 ARI	9 GEM	8 CAN	10 VIR	9 LIB	8 SCO
12 LIB	10 SCO	9 SCO	10 CAP	9 AQU	11 ARI	10 TAU	12 CAN	10 LEO	12 LIB	11 SCO	10 SAG
14 SCO	12 SAG	11 SAG	12 AQU	12 PIS	13 TAU	13 GEM	14 LEO	13 VIR	14 SCO	13 SAG	12 CAP
16 SAG	14 CAP	14 CAP	14 PIS	14 ARI	16 GEM	16 CAN	16 VIR	15 LIB	16 SAG	15 CAP	14 AQU
18 CAP	17 AQU	16 AQU	17 ARI	17 TAU	18 CAN	18 LEO	18 LIB	17 SCO	18 CAP	17 AQU	16 PIS
20 AQU	19 PIS	18 PIS	20 TAU	19 GEM	20 LEO	20 VIR	20 SCO	19 SAG	20 AQU	19 PIS	19 ARI
23 PIS	21 ARI	21 ARI	22 GEM	22 CAN	23 VIR	22 LIB	22 SAG	21 CAP	23 PIS	21 ARI	21 TAU
25 ARI	24 TAU	23 TAU	25 CAN	24 LEO	25 LIB	25 SCO	24 CAP	23 AQU	25 ARI	24 TAU	24 GEM
28 TAU	27 GEM	26 GEM	27 LEO	26 VIR	27 SCO	27 SAG	26 AQU	25 PIS	28 TAU	26 GEM	26 CAN
30 GEM		28 CAN	29 VIR	29 LIB	29 SAG	29 CAP	29 PIS	28 ARI	30 GEM	29 CAN	29 LEO
		31 LEO		31 SCO		31 AQU		30 TAU			31 VIR

1986

JAN	FEB	MAR	APR	MAY	JUN	JUL	AUG	SEP	OCT	NOV	DEC
2 LIB	1 SCO	2 SAG	2 AQU	2 PIS	3 TAU	3 GEM	2 CAN	3 VIR	2 LIB	1 SCO	2 CAP
4 SCO	3 SAG	4 CAP	5 PIS	4 ARI	5 GEM	5 CAN	4 LEO	5 LIB	4 SCO	3 SAG	4 AQU
6 SAG	5 CAP	6 AQU	7 ARI	7 TAU	8 CAN	8 LEO	6 VIR	7 SCO	7 SAG	5 CAP	6 PIS
8 CAP	7 AQU	8 PIS	9 TAU	9 GEM	11 LEO	10 VIR	9 LIB	9 SAG	9 CAP	7 AQU	9 ARI
11 AQU	9 PIS	11 ARI	12 GEM	12 CAN	13 VIR	13 LIB	11 SCO	11 CAP	11 AQU	9 PIS	11 TAU
13 PIS	11 ARI	13 TAU	14 CAN	14 LEO	15 LIB	15 SCO	13 SAG	14 AQU	13 PIS	11 ARI	14 GEM
15 ARI	14 TAU	16 GEM	17 LEO	17 VIR	17 SCO	17 SAG	15 CAP	16 PIS	15 ARI	14 TAU	16 CAN
17 TAU	16 GEM	18 CAN	19 VIR	19 LIB	19 SAG	19 CAP	17 AQU	18 ARI	18 TAU	16 GEM	19 LEO
20 GEM	19 CAN	21 LEO	21 LIB	21 SCO	21 CAP	21 AQU	19 PIS	20 TAU	20 GEM	19 CAN	21 VIR
22 CAN	21 LEO	23 VIR	24 SCO	23 SAG	23 AQU	23 PIS	22 ARI	23 GEM	23 CAN	21 LEO	23 LIB
25 LEO	23 VIR	25 LIB	26 SAG	25 CAP	26 PIS	25 ARI	24 TAU	25 CAN	25 LEO	24 VIR	26 SCO
27 VIR	26 LIB	27 SCO	28 CAP	27 AQU	28 ARI	28 TAU	26 GEM	28 LEO	27 VIR	26 LIB	28 SAG
29 LIB	28 SCO	29 SAG	30 AQU	29 PIS	30 TAU	30 GEM	29 CAN	30 VIR	30 LIB	28 SCO	30 CAP
		31 CAP		31 ARI			31 LEO			30 SAG	

1987

JAN	FEB	MAR	APR	MAY	JUN	JUL	AUG	SEP	OCT	NOV	DEC
1 AQU	1 ARI	1 ARI	2 GEM	2 CAN	3 VIR	3 LIB	1 SCO	2 CAP	1 AQU	2 ARI	1 TAU
3 PIS	4 TAU	3 TAU	4 CAN	4 LEO	5 LIB	5 SCO	4 SAG	4 AQU	3 PIS	4 TAU	4 GEM
5 ARI	6 GEM	5 GEM	7 LEO	7 VIR	8 SCO	7 SAG	6 CAP	6 PIS	6 ARI	6 GEM	6 CAN
7 TAU	9 CAN	8 CAN	9 VIR	9 LIB	10 SAG	9 CAP	8 AQU	8 ARI	8 TAU	9 CAN	8 LEO
10 GEM	11 LEO	10 LEO	12 LIB	11 SCO	12 CAP	11 AQU	10 PIS	10 TAU	10 GEM	11 LEO	11 VIR
12 CAN	14 VIR	13 VIR	14 SCO	13 SAG	14 AQU	13 PIS	12 ARI	13 GEM	12 CAN	14 VIR	14 LIB
15 LEO	16 LIB	15 LIB	16 SAG	15 CAP	16 PIS	15 ARI	14 TAU	15 CAN	15 LEO	16 LIB	16 SCO
17 VIR	18 SCO	18 SCO	18 CAP	17 AQU	18 ARI	18 TAU	16 GEM	17 LEO	17 VIR	18 SCO	18 SAG
20 LIB	21 SAG	20 SAG	20 AQU	20 PIS	21 TAU	20 GEM	19 CAN	20 VIR	20 LIB	21 SAG	20 CAP
22 SCO	23 CAP	22 CAP	22 PIS	22 ARI	23 GEM	23 CAN	21 LEO	22 LIB	22 SCO	23 CAP	22 AQU
24 SAG	27 PIS	24 AQU	25 ARI	24 TAU	25 CAN	25 LEO	24 VIR	25 SCO	24 SAG	25 AQU	24 PIS
26 CAP		26 PIS	27 TAU	26 GEM	28 LEO	27 VIR	26 LIB	27 SAG	26 CAP	27 PIS	26 ARI
28 AQU		28 ARI	29 GEM	29 CAN	30 VIR	30 LIB	29 SCO	29 CAP	29 AQU	29 ARI	29 TAU
30 PIS		30 TAU		31 LEO			31 SAG		31 PIS		31 GEM

1988

JAN	FEB	MAR	APR	MAY	JUN	JUL	AUG	SEP	OCT	NOV	DEC
2 CAN	1 LEO	2 VIR	1 LIB	3 SAG	1 CAP	1 AQU	1 ARI	2 GEM	1 CAN	2 VIR	2 LIB
5 LEO	4 VIR	4 LIB	3 SCO	5 CAP	3 AQU	3 PIS	3 TAU	4 CAN	4 LEO	5 LIB	5 SCO
7 VIR	6 LIB	7 SCO	5 SAG	7 AQU	5 PIS	5 ARI	5 GEM	6 LEO	6 VIR	7 SCO	7 SAG
10 LIB	9 SCO	9 SAG	8 CAP	9 PIS	8 ARI	7 TAU	8 CAN	9 VIR	9 LIB	10 SAG	9 CAP
12 SCO	11 SAG	11 CAP	10 AQU	11 ARI	10 TAU	9 GEM	10 LEO	11 LIB	11 SCO	12 CAP	12 AQU
15 SAG	13 CAP	14 AQU	12 PIS	13 TAU	12 GEM	11 CAN	13 VIR	14 SCO	14 SAG	14 AQU	14 PIS
17 CAP	15 AQU	16 PIS	14 ARI	16 GEM	14 CAN	14 LEO	15 LIB	16 SAG	16 CAP	17 PIS	16 ARI
19 AQU	17 PIS	18 ARI	16 TAU	18 CAN	17 LEO	16 VIR	18 SCO	19 CAP	18 AQU	19 ARI	18 TAU
21 PIS	19 ARI	20 TAU	18 GEM	20 LEO	19 VIR	19 LIB	20 SAG	21 AQU	20 PIS	21 TAU	20 GEM
23 ARI	21 TAU	22 GEM	20 CAN	23 VIR	22 LIB	21 SCO	22 CAP	23 PIS	22 ARI	23 GEM	22 CAN
25 TAU	23 GEM	24 CAN	23 LEO	25 LIB	24 SCO	24 SAG	24 AQU	25 ARI	24 TAU	25 CAN	25 LEO
27 GEM	26 CAN	27 LEO	25 VIR	28 SCO	26 SAG	26 CAP	26 PIS	27 TAU	26 GEM	27 LEO	27 VIR
30 CAN	28 LEO	29 VIR	28 LIB	30 SAG	29 CAP	28 AQU	28 ARI	29 GEM	29 CAN	30 VIR	30 LIB
			30 SCO			30 PIS	30 TAU		31 LEO		

1989

JAN	FEB	MAR	APR	MAY	JUN	JUL	AUG	SEP	OCT	NOV	DEC
1 SCO	2 CAP	2 CAP	2 PIS	2 ARI	2 GEM	2 CAN	3 VIR	1 LIB	1 SCO	2 CAP	2 AQU
4 SAG	4 AQU	4 AQU	4 ARI	4 TAU	4 CAN	4 LEO	5 LIB	4 SCO	3 SAG	5 AQU	4 PIS
6 CAP	6 PIS	6 PIS	6 TAU	6 GEM	7 LEO	6 VIR	8 SCO	6 SAG	6 CAP	7 PIS	7 ARI
8 AQU	8 ARI	8 ARI	8 GEM	8 CAN	9 VIR	9 LIB	10 SAG	9 CAP	9 AQU	9 ARI	9 TAU
10 PIS	11 TAU	10 TAU	10 CAN	10 LEO	11 LIB	11 SCO	12 CAP	11 AQU	11 PIS	11 TAU	11 GEM
12 ARI	13 GEM	12 GEM	13 LEO	13 VIR	14 SCO	14 SAG	15 AQU	13 PIS	13 ARI	13 GEM	13 CAN
14 TAU	15 CAN	14 CAN	15 VIR	15 LIB	16 SAG	16 CAP	17 PIS	15 ARI	15 TAU	15 CAN	15 LEO
16 GEM	17 LEO	17 LEO	18 LIB	18 SCO	19 CAP	18 AQU	19 ARI	17 TAU	17 GEM	17 LEO	17 VIR
19 CAN	20 VIR	19 VIR	20 SCO	20 SAG	21 AQU	20 PIS	21 TAU	19 GEM	19 CAN	20 VIR	19 LIB
21 LEO	22 LIB	22 LIB	23 SAG	22 CAP	23 PIS	23 ARI	23 GEM	21 CAN	21 LEO	22 LIB	22 SCO
23 VIR	25 SCO	24 SCO	25 CAP	25 AQU	25 ARI	25 TAU	25 CAN	24 LEO	23 VIR	25 SCO	24 SAG
26 LIB	27 SAG	27 SAG	28 AQU	27 PIS	27 TAU	27 GEM	27 LEO	26 VIR	26 LIB	27 SAG	27 CAP
29 SCO		29 CAP	30 PIS	29 ARI	30 GEM	29 CAN	30 VIR	29 LIB	28 SCO	30 CAP	29 AQU
31 SAG		31 AQU		31 TAU		31 LEO			31 SAG		

1990

JAN	FEB	MAR	APR	MAY	JUN	JUL	AUG	SEP	OCT	NOV	DEC
1 PIS	1 TAU	2 GEM	1 CAN	3 VIR	1 LIB	1 SCO	2 CAP	1 AQU	1 PIS	2 TAU	1 GEM
3 ARI	3 GEM	5 CAN	3 LEO	5 LIB	4 SCO	4 SAG	5 AQU	3 PIS	3 ARI	4 GEM	3 CAN
5 TAU	5 CAN	7 LEO	5 VIR	8 SCO	6 SAG	6 CAP	7 PIS	6 ARI	5 TAU	6 CAN	5 LEO
7 GEM	8 LEO	9 VIR	8 LIB	10 SAG	9 CAP	9 AQU	9 ARI	8 TAU	7 GEM	8 LEO	7 VIR
9 CAN	10 VIR	12 LIB	10 SCO	13 CAP	11 AQU	11 PIS	11 TAU	10 GEM	9 CAN	10 VIR	9 LIB
11 LEO	12 LIB	14 SCO	13 SAG	15 AQU	14 PIS	13 ARI	14 GEM	12 CAN	11 LEO	12 LIB	12 SCO
13 VIR	15 SCO	16 SAG	15 CAP	17 PIS	16 ARI	15 TAU	16 CAN	14 LEO	14 VIR	15 SCO	14 SAG
16 LIB	17 SAG	19 CAP	18 AQU	20 ARI	18 TAU	17 GEM	18 LEO	16 VIR	16 LIB	17 SAG	17 CAP
18 SCO	20 CAP	21 AQU	20 PIS	22 TAU	20 GEM	19 CAN	20 VIR	18 LIB	18 SCO	20 CAP	19 AQU
21 SAG	22 AQU	24 PIS	22 ARI	24 GEM	22 CAN	21 LEO	22 LIB	21 SCO	21 SAG	22 AQU	22 PIS
23 CAP	24 PIS	26 ARI	24 TAU	26 CAN	24 LEO	24 VIR	25 SCO	23 SAG	23 CAP	25 PIS	24 ARI
26 AQU	26 ARI	28 TAU	26 GEM	28 LEO	26 VIR	26 LIB	27 SAG	26 CAP	26 AQU	27 ARI	26 TAU
28 PIS	28 TAU	30 GEM	28 CAN	30 VIR	29 LIB	28 SCO	30 CAP	29 AQU	28 PIS	29 TAU	28 GEM
30 ARI			30 LEO			31 SAG			30 ARI		30 CAN

1991

JAN	FEB	MAR	APR	MAY	JUN	JUL	AUG	SEP	OCT	NOV	DEC
1 LEO	2 LIB	2 LIB	3 SAG	2 CAP	1 AQU	1 PIS	2 TAU	3 CAN	2 LEO	2 LIB	2 SCO
3 VIR	4 SCO	4 SCO	5 CAP	5 AQU	4 PIS	3 ARI	4 GEM	5 LEO	4 VIR	5 SCO	4 SAG
6 LIB	7 SAG	6 SAG	8 AQU	7 PIS	6 ARI	6 TAU	6 CAN	7 VIR	6 LIB	7 SAG	7 CAP
8 SCO	9 CAP	9 CAP	10 PIS	10 ARI	8 TAU	8 GEM	8 LEO	9 LIB	8 SCO	10 CAP	9 AQU
11 SAG	12 AQU	11 AQU	12 ARI	12 TAU	10 GEM	10 CAN	10 VIR	11 SCO	11 SAG	12 AQU	12 PIS
13 CAP	14 PIS	14 PIS	15 TAU	14 GEM	12 CAN	12 LEO	12 LIB	13 SAG	13 CAP	15 PIS	14 ARI
16 AQU	17 ARI	16 ARI	17 GEM	16 CAN	14 LEO	14 VIR	15 SCO	16 CAP	16 AQU	17 ARI	17 TAU
18 PIS	19 TAU	18 TAU	19 CAN	18 LEO	16 VIR	16 LIB	17 SAG	18 AQU	18 PIS	19 TAU	19 GEM
20 ARI	21 GEM	20 GEM	21 LEO	20 VIR	19 LIB	18 SCO	20 CAP	21 PIS	21 ARI	21 GEM	21 CAN
23 TAU	23 CAN	22 CAN	23 VIR	23 LIB	21 SCO	21 SAG	22 AQU	23 ARI	23 TAU	23 CAN	23 LEO
25 GEM	25 LEO	25 LEO	25 LIB	25 SCO	23 SAG	23 CAP	25 PIS	25 TAU	25 GEM	25 LEO	25 VIR
27 CAN	27 VIR	27 VIR	28 SCO	27 SAG	26 CAP	26 AQU	27 ARI	28 GEM	27 CAN	28 VIR	27 LIB
29 LEO		29 LIB	30 SAG	30 CAP	29 AQU	28 PIS		30 CAN	29 LEO	30 LIB	29 SCO
31 VIR		31 SCO				31 ARI	31 GEM		31 VIR		

1992

JAN	FEB	MAR	APR	MAY	JUN	JUL	AUG	SEP	OCT	NOV	DEC
1 SAG	2 AQU	3 PIS	1 ARI	1 TAU	2 CAN	1 LEO	2 LIB	2 SAG	2 CAP	1 AQU	1 PIS
3 CAP	4 PIS	5 ARI	4 TAU	3 GEM	4 LEO	3 VIR	4 SCO	5 CAP	4 AQU	3 PIS	3 ARI
6 AQU	7 ARI	8 TAU	6 GEM	5 CAN	6 VIR	5 LIB	6 SAG	7 AQU	7 PIS	6 ARI	6 TAU
8 PIS	9 TAU	10 GEM	8 CAN	8 LEO	8 LIB	7 SCO	8 CAP	10 PIS	10 ARI	8 TAU	8 GEM
11 ARI	12 GEM	12 CAN	10 LEO	10 VIR	10 SCO	10 SAG	11 AQU	12 ARI	12 TAU	11 GEM	10 CAN
13 TAU	14 CAN	14 LEO	12 VIR	12 LIB	13 SAG	12 CAP	13 PIS	15 TAU	14 GEM	13 CAN	12 LEO
15 GEM	18 VIR	16 VIR	15 LIB	14 SCO	15 CAP	15 AQU	16 ARI	17 GEM	17 CAN	15 LEO	14 VIR
17 CAN	20 LIB	18 LIB	17 SCO	16 SAG	17 AQU	17 PIS	18 TAU	19 CAN	19 LEO	16 VIR	16 LIB
19 LEO	22 SCO	20 SCO	19 SAG	19 CAP	20 PIS	20 ARI	21 GEM	21 LEO	21 VIR	19 LIB	19 SCO
21 VIR	24 SAG	23 SAG	21 CAP	21 AQU	22 ARI	22 TAU	23 CAN	24 VIR	23 LIB	21 SCO	21 SAG
23 LIB	27 CAP	25 CAP	24 AQU	24 PIS	25 TAU	24 GEM	25 LEO	25 LIB	25 SCO	24 SAG	23 CAP
25 SCO	29 AQU	27 AQU	26 PIS	26 ARI	27 GEM	27 CAN	27 VIR	28 SCO	27 SAG	26 CAP	26 AQU
28 SAG		30 PIS	29 ARI	28 TAU	29 CAN	29 LEO	29 LIB	30 SAG	29 CAP	28 AQU	28 PIS
30 CAP				31 GEM		31 VIR	31 SCO				31 ARI

1993

JAN	FEB	MAR	APR	MAY	JUN	JUL	AUG	SEP	OCT	NOV	DEC
2 TAU	1 GEM	2 CAN	1 LEO	2 LIB	1 SCO	2 CAP	1 AQU	2 ARI	2 TAU	1 GEM	3 LEO
4 GEM	3 CAN	5 LEO	3 VIR	4 SCO	3 SAG	5 AQU	3 PIS	5 TAU	4 GEM	3 CAN	5 VIR
7 CAN	5 LEO	7 VIR	5 LIB	6 SAG	5 CAP	7 PIS	6 ARI	7 GEM	7 CAN	5 LEO	7 LIB
9 LEO	7 VIR	8 LIB	7 SCO	9 CAP	7 AQU	10 ARI	8 TAU	10 CAN	9 LEO	8 VIR	9 SCO
11 VIR	9 LIB	10 SCO	9 SAG	11 AQU	10 PIS	12 TAU	11 GEM	12 LEO	11 VIR	10 LIB	11 SAG
13 LIB	11 SCO	13 SAG	11 CAP	13 PIS	12 ARI	15 GEM	13 CAN	14 VIR	13 LIB	12 SCO	13 CAP
15 SCO	13 SAG	15 CAP	14 AQU	16 ARI	14 TAU	17 CAN	15 LEO	16 LIB	15 SCO	14 SAG	15 AQU
17 SAG	16 CAP	17 AQU	16 PIS	18 TAU	17 GEM	19 LEO	17 VIR	18 SCO	17 SAG	16 CAP	18 PIS
19 CAP	18 AQU	20 PIS	19 ARI	21 GEM	19 CAN	21 VIR	19 LIB	20 SAG	20 CAP	18 AQU	20 ARI
22 AQU	21 PIS	22 ARI	21 TAU	23 CAN	22 LEO	23 LIB	21 SCO	22 CAP	22 AQU	20 PIS	23 TAU
24 PIS	23 ARI	25 TAU	24 GEM	25 LEO	24 VIR	25 SCO	24 SAG	24 AQU	24 PIS	23 ARI	25 GEM
27 ARI	26 TAU	27 GEM	26 CAN	28 VIR	26 LIB	27 SAG	26 CAP	27 PIS	27 ARI	26 TAU	28 CAN
29 TAU	28 GEM	30 CAN	28 LEO	30 LIB	28 SCO	30 CAP	28 AQU	29 ARI	29 TAU	28 GEM	30 LEO
			30 VIR		30 SAG		31 PIS			30 CAN	

1994

JAN	FEB	MAR	APR	MAY	JUN	JUL	AUG	SEP	OCT	NOV	DEC
1 VIR	2 SCO	1 SCO	1 CAP	1 AQU	2 ARI	2 TAU	1 GEM	2 LEO	2 VIR	2 SCO	2 SAG
3 LIB	4 SAG	3 SAG	4 AQU	3 PIS	5 TAU	4 GEM	3 CAN	4 VIR	4 LIB	4 SAG	4 CAP
5 SCO	6 CAP	5 CAP	6 PIS	6 ARI	7 GEM	7 CAN	6 LEO	6 LIB	6 SCO	6 CAP	6 AQU
8 SAG	8 AQU	7 AQU	9 ARI	8 TAU	10 CAN	9 LEO	8 VIR	8 SCO	8 SAG	8 AQU	8 PIS
10 CAP	11 PIS	10 PIS	11 TAU	11 GEM	12 LEO	11 VIR	10 LIB	10 SAG	10 CAP	11 PIS	10 ARI
12 AQU	13 ARI	12 ARI	14 GEM	13 CAN	14 VIR	14 LIB	12 SCO	13 CAP	12 AQU	13 ARI	13 TAU
14 PIS	16 TAU	15 TAU	16 CAN	16 LEO	16 LIB	16 SCO	14 SAG	15 AQU	15 PIS	16 TAU	15 GEM
17 ARI	18 GEM	17 GEM	18 LEO	18 VIR	19 SCO	18 SAG	16 CAP	17 PIS	17 ARI	18 GEM	18 CAN
19 TAU	20 CAN	20 CAN	21 VIR	20 LIB	21 SAG	20 CAP	18 AQU	19 ARI	19 TAU	20 CAN	20 LEO
22 GEM	23 LEO	22 LEO	23 LIB	22 SCO	23 CAP	22 AQU	21 PIS	22 TAU	22 GEM	23 LEO	23 VIR
24 CAN	25 VIR	24 VIR	25 SCO	24 SAG	25 AQU	24 PIS	23 ARI	24 GEM	24 CAN	25 VIR	25 LIB
26 LEO	27 LIB	26 LIB	27 SAG	26 CAP	27 PIS	27 ARI	26 TAU	27 CAN	27 LEO	28 LIB	27 SCO
28 VIR		28 SCO	29 CAP	28 AQU	29 ARI	29 TAU	28 GEM	29 LEO	29 VIR	30 SCO	29 SAG
31 LIB		30 SAG		31 PIS			31 CAN		31 LIB		31 CAP

1995

JAN	FEB	MAR	APR	MAY	JUN	JUL	AUG	SEP	OCT	NOV	DEC
2 AQU	1 PIS	2 ARI	1 TAU	1 GEM	2 LEO	2 VIR	3 SCO	1 SAG	2 AQU	1 PIS	3 TAU
4 PIS	3 ARI	5 TAU	3 GEM	3 CAN	5 VIR	4 LIB	5 SAG	3 CAP	5 PIS	3 ARI	5 GEM
6 ARI	5 TAU	7 GEM	6 CAN	6 LEO	7 LIB	6 SCO	7 CAP	5 AQU	7 ARI	5 TAU	8 CAN
9 TAU	8 GEM	10 CAN	9 LEO	8 VIR	9 SCO	8 SAG	9 AQU	7 PIS	9 TAU	8 GEM	10 LEO
11 GEM	10 CAN	12 LEO	11 VIR	10 LIB	11 SAG	10 CAP	11 PIS	9 ARI	12 GEM	10 CAN	13 VIR
14 CAN	13 LEO	14 VIR	13 LIB	13 SCO	13 CAP	12 AQU	13 ARI	12 TAU	14 CAN	13 LEO	15 LIB
16 LEO	15 VIR	17 LIB	15 SCO	15 SAG	15 AQU	15 PIS	15 TAU	14 GEM	17 LEO	15 VIR	17 SCO
19 VIR	17 LIB	19 SCO	17 SAG	17 CAP	17 PIS	17 ARI	18 GEM	17 CAN	19 VIR	18 LIB	19 SAG
21 LIB	19 SCO	21 SAG	19 CAP	19 AQU	19 ARI	19 TAU	20 CAN	19 LEO	21 LIB	20 SCO	21 CAP
23 SCO	22 SAG	23 CAP	21 AQU	21 PIS	22 TAU	22 GEM	23 LEO	22 VIR	23 SCO	22 SAG	23 AQU
25 SAG	24 CAP	25 AQU	24 PIS	23 ARI	24 GEM	24 CAN	25 VIR	24 LIB	26 SAG	24 CAP	25 PIS
27 CAP	26 AQU	27 PIS	26 ARI	26 TAU	27 CAN	27 LEO	28 LIB	26 SCO	28 CAP	26 AQU	28 ARI
30 AQU	28 PIS	30 ARI	28 TAU	28 GEM	29 LEO	29 VIR	30 SCO	28 SAG	30 AQU	28 PIS	30 TAU
				31 CAN		31 LIB		30 CAP		30 ARI	

1996

JAN: 1 GEM · 4 CAN · 6 LEO · 9 VIR · 11 LIB · 14 SCO · 16 SAG · 18 CAP · 20 AQU · 22 PIS · 24 ARI · 26 TAU · 29 GEM · 31 CAN

FEB: 3 LEO · 5 VIR · 8 LIB · 10 SCO · 12 SAG · 14 CAP · 16 AQU · 18 PIS · 20 ARI · 23 TAU · 25 GEM · 27 CAN

MAR: 1 LEO · 3 VIR · 6 LIB · 8 SCO · 10 SAG · 13 CAP · 15 AQU · 17 PIS · 19 ARI · 21 TAU · 23 GEM · 26 CAN · 28 LEO · 31 VIR

APR: 2 LIB · 4 SCO · 7 SAG · 9 CAP · 11 AQU · 13 PIS · 15 ARI · 17 TAU · 20 GEM · 22 CAN · 25 LEO · 27 VIR · 30 LIB

MAY: 2 SCO · 4 SAG · 6 CAP · 8 AQU · 10 PIS · 12 ARI · 15 TAU · 17 GEM · 19 CAN · 22 LEO · 24 VIR · 27 LIB · 29 SCO · 31 SAG

JUN: 2 CAP · 4 AQU · 6 PIS · 9 ARI · 11 TAU · 13 GEM · 16 CAN · 18 LEO · 21 VIR · 23 LIB · 26 SCO · 28 SAG · 30 CAP

JUL: 2 AQU · 4 PIS · 6 ARI · 8 TAU · 11 GEM · 13 CAN · 16 LEO · 18 VIR · 21 LIB · 23 SCO · 25 SAG · 27 CAP · 29 AQU · 31 PIS

AUG: 2 ARI · 4 TAU · 7 GEM · 9 CAN · 12 LEO · 14 VIR · 17 LIB · 19 SCO · 21 SAG · 24 CAP · 26 AQU · 28 PIS · 30 ARI

SEP: 1 TAU · 3 GEM · 6 CAN · 8 LEO · 11 VIR · 13 LIB · 15 SCO · 18 SAG · 20 CAP · 22 AQU · 24 PIS · 26 ARI · 28 TAU · 30 GEM

OCT: 3 CAN · 5 LEO · 8 VIR · 10 LIB · 13 SCO · 15 SAG · 17 CAP · 19 AQU · 21 PIS · 23 ARI · 26 TAU · 28 GEM · 30 CAN

NOV: 2 LEO · 4 VIR · 7 LIB · 9 SCO · 11 SAG · 13 CAP · 16 AQU · 18 PIS · 20 ARI · 22 TAU · 24 GEM · 27 CAN · 29 LEO

DEC: 2 VIR · 4 LIB · 6 SCO · 9 SAG · 11 CAP · 13 AQU · 15 PIS · 17 ARI · 19 TAU · 22 GEM · 24 CAN · 26 LEO · 29 VIR · 31 LIB

1997

JAN: 3 SCO · 5 SAG · 7 CAP · 9 AQU · 11 PIS · 13 ARI · 15 TAU · 18 GEM · 20 CAN · 23 LEO · 25 VIR · 28 LIB · 30 SCO

FEB: 1 SAG · 4 CAP · 6 AQU · 8 PIS · 10 ARI · 12 TAU · 14 GEM · 16 CAN · 19 LEO · 21 VIR · 24 LIB · 26 SCO

MAR: 1 SAG · 3 CAP · 5 AQU · 7 PIS · 9 ARI · 11 TAU · 13 GEM · 16 CAN · 18 LEO · 21 VIR · 23 LIB · 26 SCO · 28 SAG · 30 CAP

APR: 1 AQU · 4 PIS · 6 ARI · 8 TAU · 10 GEM · 12 CAN · 14 LEO · 17 VIR · 19 LIB · 22 SCO · 24 SAG · 27 CAP · 29 AQU

MAY: 1 PIS · 3 ARI · 5 TAU · 7 GEM · 9 CAN · 12 LEO · 14 VIR · 17 LIB · 19 SCO · 22 SAG · 24 CAP · 26 AQU · 28 PIS · 30 ARI

JUN: 1 TAU · 3 GEM · 6 CAN · 8 LEO · 11 VIR · 13 LIB · 16 SCO · 18 SAG · 20 CAP · 22 AQU · 24 PIS · 26 ARI · 29 TAU

JUL: 1 GEM · 3 CAN · 5 LEO · 8 VIR · 11 LIB · 13 SCO · 15 SAG · 18 CAP · 20 AQU · 22 PIS · 24 ARI · 26 TAU · 28 GEM · 30 CAN

AUG: 2 LEO · 4 VIR · 7 LIB · 9 SCO · 12 SAG · 14 CAP · 16 AQU · 18 PIS · 20 ARI · 22 TAU · 24 GEM · 27 CAN · 29 LEO · 31 VIR

SEP: 3 LIB · 6 SCO · 8 SAG · 10 CAP · 13 AQU · 15 PIS · 16 ARI · 18 TAU · 21 GEM · 23 CAN · 25 LEO · 28 VIR · 30 LIB

OCT: 3 SCO · 5 SAG · 8 CAP · 10 AQU · 12 PIS · 14 ARI · 16 TAU · 18 GEM · 20 CAN · 23 LEO · 25 VIR · 28 LIB · 30 SCO

NOV: 1 SAG · 4 CAP · 6 AQU · 8 PIS · 10 ARI · 12 TAU · 14 GEM · 17 CAN · 19 LEO · 21 VIR · 24 LIB · 26 SCO · 29 SAG

DEC: 1 CAP · 3 AQU · 5 PIS · 8 ARI · 10 TAU · 12 GEM · 14 CAN · 16 LEO · 19 VIR · 21 LIB · 24 SCO · 26 SAG · 28 CAP · 31 AQU

1998

JAN: 2 PIS · 4 ARI · 6 TAU · 8 GEM · 10 CAN · 13 LEO · 15 VIR · 18 LIB · 20 SCO · 23 SAG · 25 CAP · 27 AQU · 29 PIS · 31 ARI

FEB: 2 TAU · 4 GEM · 7 CAN · 9 LEO · 11 VIR · 14 LIB · 16 SCO · 19 SAG · 21 CAP · 23 AQU · 25 PIS · 27 ARI

MAR: 2 TAU · 4 GEM · 6 CAN · 8 LEO · 11 VIR · 13 LIB · 16 SCO · 18 SAG · 21 CAP · 23 AQU · 25 PIS · 27 ARI · 29 TAU · 31 GEM

APR: 2 CAN · 4 LEO · 7 VIR · 9 LIB · 12 SCO · 14 SAG · 17 CAP · 19 AQU · 21 PIS · 23 ARI · 25 TAU · 27 GEM · 29 CAN

MAY: 2 LEO · 4 VIR · 7 LIB · 9 SCO · 12 SAG · 14 CAP · 16 AQU · 19 PIS · 21 ARI · 23 TAU · 25 GEM · 27 CAN · 29 LEO · 31 VIR

JUN: 3 LIB · 5 SCO · 8 SAG · 10 CAP · 13 AQU · 15 PIS · 17 ARI · 19 TAU · 21 GEM · 23 CAN · 25 LEO · 28 VIR · 30 LIB

JUL: 3 SCO · 5 SAG · 8 CAP · 10 AQU · 12 PIS · 14 ARI · 16 TAU · 18 GEM · 21 CAN · 23 LEO · 25 VIR · 28 LIB · 30 SCO

AUG: 2 SAG · 4 CAP · 6 AQU · 8 PIS · 11 ARI · 13 TAU · 15 GEM · 17 CAN · 19 LEO · 21 VIR · 24 LIB · 26 SCO · 29 SAG · 31 CAP

SEP: 3 AQU · 5 PIS · 7 ARI · 9 TAU · 11 GEM · 13 CAN · 15 LEO · 18 VIR · 20 LIB · 23 SCO · 25 SAG · 28 CAP · 30 AQU

OCT: 2 PIS · 4 ARI · 6 TAU · 8 GEM · 10 CAN · 13 LEO · 15 VIR · 17 LIB · 20 SCO · 23 SAG · 25 CAP · 27 AQU · 30 PIS

NOV: 1 ARI · 3 TAU · 5 GEM · 7 CAN · 9 LEO · 11 VIR · 14 LIB · 16 SCO · 19 SAG · 21 CAP · 24 AQU · 26 PIS · 28 ARI · 30 TAU

DEC: 2 GEM · 4 CAN · 6 LEO · 9 VIR · 11 LIB · 14 SCO · 16 SAG · 18 CAP · 21 AQU · 23 PIS · 25 ARI · 28 TAU · 30 GEM

1999

JAN: 1 CAN · 3 LEO · 5 VIR · 7 LIB · 10 SCO · 12 SAG · 15 CAP · 17 AQU · 19 PIS · 22 ARI · 24 TAU · 26 GEM · 28 CAN · 30 LEO

FEB: 1 VIR · 4 LIB · 6 SCO · 9 SAG · 11 CAP · 14 AQU · 16 PIS · 18 ARI · 20 TAU · 22 GEM · 24 CAN · 26 LEO

MAR: 1 VIR · 3 LIB · 6 SCO · 8 SAG · 11 CAP · 13 AQU · 15 PIS · 17 ARI · 19 TAU · 21 GEM · 23 CAN · 26 LEO · 28 VIR · 30 LIB

APR: 2 SCO · 4 SAG · 7 CAP · 9 AQU · 12 PIS · 14 ARI · 16 TAU · 18 GEM · 20 CAN · 22 LEO · 24 VIR · 27 LIB · 29 SCO

MAY: 2 SAG · 4 CAP · 7 AQU · 9 PIS · 11 ARI · 13 TAU · 15 GEM · 17 CAN · 19 LEO · 21 VIR · 24 LIB · 26 SCO · 29 SAG · 31 CAP

JUN: 3 AQU · 5 PIS · 8 ARI · 10 TAU · 12 GEM · 14 CAN · 16 LEO · 18 VIR · 21 LIB · 23 SCO · 25 SAG · 28 CAP · 30 AQU

JUL: 2 PIS · 5 ARI · 7 TAU · 9 GEM · 11 CAN · 13 LEO · 15 VIR · 17 LIB · 20 SCO · 22 SAG · 25 CAP · 27 AQU · 30 PIS

AUG: 1 ARI · 3 TAU · 5 GEM · 7 CAN · 9 LEO · 12 VIR · 14 LIB · 16 SCO · 19 SAG · 21 CAP · 24 AQU · 26 PIS · 28 ARI · 30 TAU

SEP: 2 GEM · 4 CAN · 6 LEO · 8 VIR · 10 LIB · 13 SCO · 15 SAG · 18 CAP · 20 AQU · 22 PIS · 25 ARI · 27 TAU · 29 GEM

OCT: 1 CAN · 3 LEO · 6 VIR · 8 LIB · 10 SCO · 12 SAG · 15 CAP · 17 AQU · 20 PIS · 22 ARI · 24 TAU · 26 GEM · 28 CAN · 30 LEO

NOV: 1 VIR · 4 LIB · 6 SCO · 9 SAG · 11 CAP · 14 AQU · 16 PIS · 18 ARI · 21 TAU · 23 GEM · 25 CAN · 27 LEO · 29 VIR

DEC: 1 LIB · 3 SCO · 6 SAG · 8 CAP · 11 AQU · 13 PIS · 16 ARI · 18 TAU · 20 GEM · 22 CAN · 24 LEO · 26 VIR · 28 LIB · 31 SCO

2000

JAN	FEB	MAR	APR	MAY	JUN	JUL	AUG	SEP	OCT	NOV	DEC
2 SAG	1 CAP	2 AQU	1 PIS	2 TAU	1 GEM	2 LEO	1 VIR	2 SCO	1 SAG	3 AQU	2 PIS
5 CAP	4 AQU	4 PIS	3 ARI	5 GEM	3 CAN	4 VIR	3 LIB	4 SAG	4 CAP	5 PIS	5 ARI
7 AQU	6 PIS	7 ARI	5 TAU	7 CAN	5 LEO	7 LIB	5 SCO	6 CAP	6 AQU	8 ARI	7 TAU
10 PIS	8 ARI	9 TAU	7 GEM	9 LEO	7 VIR	9 SCO	8 SAG	9 AQU	9 PIS	10 TAU	9 GEM
12 ARI	11 TAU	11 GEM	9 CAN	11 VIR	9 LIB	11 SAG	10 CAP	11 PIS	11 ARI	12 GEM	11 CAN
14 TAU	13 GEM	13 CAN	11 LEO	13 LIB	12 SCO	14 CAP	13 AQU	14 ARI	13 TAU	14 CAN	13 LEO
16 GEM	15 CAN	15 LEO	14 VIR	15 SCO	14 SAG	16 AQU	15 PIS	16 TAU	16 GEM	16 LEO	15 VIR
18 CAN	17 LEO	17 VIR	16 LIB	18 SAG	17 CAP	19 PIS	18 ARI	18 GEM	18 CAN	18 VIR	18 LIB
20 LEO	19 VIR	19 LIB	18 SCO	20 CAP	19 AQU	21 ARI	20 TAU	20 CAN	20 LEO	20 LIB	20 SCO
23 VIR	21 LIB	22 SCO	20 SAG	23 AQU	22 PIS	24 TAU	22 GEM	23 LEO	22 VIR	23 SCO	22 SAG
25 LIB	23 SCO	24 SAG	23 CAP	25 PIS	24 ARI	26 GEM	24 CAN	25 VIR	24 LIB	25 SAG	25 CAP
27 SCO	26 SAG	27 CAP	25 AQU	28 ARI	26 TAU	28 CAN	26 LEO	27 LIB	26 SCO	27 CAP	27 AQU
29 SAG	28 CAP	29 AQU	28 PIS	30 TAU	28 GEM	30 LEO	28 VIR	29 SCO	29 SAG	30 AQU	30 PIS
			30 ARI		30 CAN		30 LIB		31 CAP		

2001

JAN	FEB	MAR	APR	MAY	JUN	JUL	AUG	SEP	OCT	NOV	DEC
1 ARI	2 GEM	1 GEM	2 LEO	1 VIR	2 SCO	1 SAG	3 AQU	1 PIS	1 ARI	2 GEM	2 CAN
4 TAU	4 CAN	4 CAN	4 VIR	3 LIB	4 SAG	4 CAP	5 PIS	4 ARI	4 TAU	4 CAN	4 LEO
6 GEM	6 LEO	6 LEO	6 LIB	6 SCO	7 CAP	6 AQU	8 ARI	6 TAU	6 GEM	7 LEO	6 VIR
8 CAN	8 VIR	8 VIR	8 SCO	8 SAG	9 AQU	9 PIS	10 TAU	9 GEM	8 CAN	9 VIR	8 LIB
10 LEO	10 LIB	10 LIB	10 SAG	10 CAP	11 PIS	11 ARI	12 GEM	11 CAN	10 LEO	11 LIB	10 SCO
12 VIR	12 SCO	12 SCO	13 CAP	13 AQU	14 ARI	14 TAU	15 CAN	13 LEO	12 VIR	13 SCO	12 SAG
14 LIB	15 SAG	14 SAG	15 AQU	15 PIS	16 TAU	16 GEM	17 LEO	15 VIR	14 LIB	15 SAG	15 CAP
16 SCO	17 CAP	16 CAP	18 PIS	18 ARI	19 GEM	18 CAN	19 VIR	17 LIB	17 SCO	17 CAP	17 AQU
18 SAG	20 AQU	19 AQU	20 ARI	20 TAU	21 CAN	20 LEO	21 LIB	19 SCO	19 SAG	20 AQU	20 PIS
21 CAP	22 PIS	22 PIS	23 TAU	22 GEM	23 LEO	22 VIR	23 SCO	21 SAG	21 CAP	22 PIS	22 ARI
23 AQU	25 ARI	24 ARI	25 GEM	24 CAN	25 VIR	24 LIB	25 SAG	24 CAP	24 AQU	25 ARI	25 TAU
26 PIS	27 TAU	26 TAU	27 CAN	27 LEO	27 LIB	26 SCO	27 CAP	26 AQU	26 PIS	27 TAU	27 GEM
28 ARI		29 GEM	29 LEO	29 VIR	29 SCO	29 SAG	30 AQU	29 PIS	28 ARI	30 GEM	29 CAN
31 TAU		31 CAN		31 LIB		31 CAP			31 TAU		31 LEO

2002

JAN	FEB	MAR	APR	MAY	JUN	JUL	AUG	SEP	OCT	NOV	DEC
2 VIR	1 LIB	2 SCO	1 SAG	2 AQU	1 PIS	1 ARI	2 GEM	1 CAN	1 LEO	1 LIB	1 SCO
4 LIB	3 SCO	4 SAG	3 CAP	5 PIS	4 ARI	4 TAU	5 CAN	3 LEO	3 VIR	3 SCO	3 SAG
6 SCO	5 SAG	6 CAP	5 AQU	7 ARI	6 TAU	6 GEM	7 LEO	5 VIR	5 LIB	5 SAG	5 CAP
9 SAG	7 CAP	9 AQU	8 PIS	10 TAU	9 GEM	8 CAN	9 VIR	7 LIB	7 SCO	7 CAP	7 AQU
11 CAP	10 AQU	11 PIS	10 ARI	12 GEM	11 CAN	11 LEO	11 LIB	9 SCO	9 SAG	10 AQU	9 PIS
13 AQU	12 PIS	14 ARI	13 TAU	15 CAN	13 LEO	13 VIR	13 SCO	12 SAG	11 CAP	12 PIS	12 ARI
16 PIS	15 ARI	16 TAU	15 GEM	17 LEO	15 VIR	15 LIB	15 SAG	14 CAP	13 AQU	15 ARI	14 TAU
18 ARI	17 TAU	19 GEM	18 CAN	19 VIR	18 LIB	17 SCO	18 CAP	16 AQU	16 PIS	17 TAU	17 GEM
21 TAU	20 GEM	21 CAN	20 LEO	21 LIB	20 SCO	19 SAG	20 AQU	18 PIS	18 ARI	20 GEM	19 CAN
23 GEM	22 CAN	24 LEO	22 VIR	23 SCO	22 SAG	21 CAP	22 PIS	21 ARI	21 TAU	22 CAN	22 LEO
26 CAN	24 LEO	26 VIR	24 LIB	25 SAG	24 CAP	24 AQU	25 ARI	23 TAU	23 GEM	24 LEO	24 VIR
28 LEO	26 VIR	28 LIB	26 SCO	28 CAP	26 AQU	26 PIS	27 TAU	26 GEM	26 CAN	27 VIR	26 LIB
30 VIR	28 LIB	30 SCO	28 SAG	30 AQU	29 PIS	28 ARI	30 GEM	29 CAN	28 LEO	29 LIB	28 SCO
			30 CAP			31 TAU			30 VIR		30 SAG

2003

JAN	FEB	MAR	APR	MAY	JUN	JUL	AUG	SEP	OCT	NOV	DEC
1 CAP	2 PIS	1 PIS	3 TAU	2 GEM	1 CAN	1 LEO	2 LIB	2 SAG	1 CAP	2 PIS	2 ARI
3 AQU	5 ARI	4 ARI	5 GEM	5 CAN	4 LEO	3 VIR	4 SCO	4 CAP	4 AQU	5 ARI	4 TAU
6 PIS	7 TAU	6 TAU	8 CAN	7 LEO	6 VIR	5 LIB	6 SAG	6 AQU	6 PIS	7 TAU	7 GEM
8 ARI	10 GEM	9 GEM	10 LEO	10 VIR	8 LIB	7 SCO	8 CAP	9 PIS	8 ARI	10 GEM	9 CAN
11 TAU	12 CAN	11 CAN	12 VIR	12 LIB	10 SCO	10 SAG	10 AQU	11 ARI	11 TAU	12 CAN	12 LEO
13 GEM	14 LEO	14 LEO	14 LIB	14 SCO	12 SAG	12 CAP	12 PIS	13 TAU	13 GEM	15 LEO	14 VIR
16 CAN	16 VIR	16 VIR	16 SCO	16 SAG	14 CAP	14 AQU	15 ARI	16 GEM	16 CAN	17 VIR	16 LIB
18 LEO	18 LIB	18 LIB	18 SAG	18 CAP	16 AQU	16 PIS	17 TAU	18 CAN	18 LEO	19 LIB	19 SCO
20 VIR	21 SCO	20 SCO	20 CAP	20 AQU	19 PIS	18 ARI	20 GEM	21 LEO	21 VIR	21 SCO	21 SAG
22 LIB	23 SAG	22 SAG	23 AQU	22 PIS	21 ARI	21 TAU	22 CAN	23 VIR	23 LIB	23 SAG	23 CAP
24 SCO	25 CAP	24 CAP	25 PIS	25 ARI	23 TAU	23 GEM	24 LEO	25 LIB	25 SCO	25 CAP	25 AQU
26 SAG	27 AQU	26 AQU	27 ARI	27 TAU	26 GEM	26 CAN	27 VIR	27 SCO	27 SAG	27 AQU	27 PIS
29 CAP		29 PIS	30 TAU	30 GEM	28 CAN	28 LEO	29 LIB	29 SAG	29 CAP	29 PIS	29 ARI
31 AQU		31 ARI				30 VIR	31 SCO		31 AQU		

2004

	JAN	FEB	MAR	APR	MAY	JUN	JUL	AUG	SEP	OCT	NOV	DEC
	1 TAU	2 CAN	3 LEO	1 VIR	1 LIB	2 SAG	1 CAP	1 PIS	2 TAU	2 GEM	1 CAN	1 LEO
	3 GEM	4 LEO	5 VIR	4 LIB	3 SCO	4 CAP	3 AQU	4 ARI	5 GEM	5 CAN	3 LEO	3 VIR
	6 CAN	7 VIR	7 LIB	6 SCO	5 SAG	6 AQU	5 PIS	6 TAU	7 CAN	7 LEO	6 VIR	5 LIB
	8 LEO	9 LIB	9 SCO	8 SAG	7 CAP	8 PIS	7 ARI	8 GEM	10 LEO	10 VIR	8 LIB	8 SCO
	10 VIR	11 SCO	11 SAG	10 CAP	9 AQU	10 ARI	10 TAU	11 CAN	12 VIR	12 LIB	10 SCO	10 SAG
	13 LIB	13 SAG	14 CAP	12 AQU	11 PIS	12 TAU	12 GEM	13 LEO	14 LIB	14 SCO	13 SAG	12 CAP
	15 SCO	15 CAP	16 AQU	14 PIS	14 ARI	15 GEM	15 CAN	16 VIR	17 SCO	16 SAG	15 CAP	14 AQU
	17 SAG	17 AQU	18 PIS	16 ARI	16 TAU	17 CAN	17 LEO	18 LIB	19 SAG	18 CAP	17 AQU	16 PIS
	19 CAP	20 PIS	20 ARI	19 TAU	19 GEM	20 LEO	20 VIR	20 SCO	21 CAP	20 AQU	19 PIS	18 ARI
	21 AQU	22 ARI	23 TAU	21 GEM	21 CAN	22 VIR	22 LIB	23 SAG	23 AQU	23 PIS	21 ARI	21 TAU
	23 PIS	24 TAU	25 GEM	24 CAN	24 LEO	25 LIB	24 SCO	25 CAP	25 PIS	25 ARI	23 TAU	23 GEM
	25 ARI	27 GEM	28 CAN	26 LEO	26 VIR	27 SCO	26 SAG	27 AQU	27 ARI	27 TAU	26 GEM	25 CAN
	28 TAU	29 CAN	30 LEO	29 VIR	28 LIB	29 SAG	28 CAP	29 PIS	30 TAU	29 GEM	28 CAN	28 LEO
	30 GEM				31 SCO		30 AQU	31 ARI				31 VIR

2005

	JAN	FEB	MAR	APR	MAY	JUN	JUL	AUG	SEP	OCT	NOV	DEC
	2 LIB	1 SCO	2 SAG	3 AQU	2 PIS	3 TAU	2 GEM	1 CAN	2 VIR	2 LIB	1 SCO	2 CAP
	4 SCO	3 SAG	4 CAP	5 PIS	4 ARI	5 GEM	5 CAN	3 LEO	5 LIB	4 SCO	3 SAG	4 AQU
	6 SAG	5 CAP	6 AQU	7 ARI	6 TAU	7 CAN	7 LEO	6 VIR	7 SCO	7 SAG	5 CAP	7 PIS
	8 CAP	7 AQU	8 PIS	9 TAU	9 GEM	9 LEO	10 VIR	8 LIB	9 SAG	9 CAP	7 AQU	9 ARI
	10 AQU	9 PIS	10 ARI	11 GEM	11 CAN	12 VIR	12 LIB	11 SCO	12 CAP	11 AQU	9 PIS	11 TAU
	12 PIS	11 ARI	13 TAU	14 CAN	14 LEO	15 LIB	15 SCO	13 SAG	14 AQU	13 PIS	11 ARI	13 GEM
	15 ARI	13 TAU	15 GEM	16 LEO	16 VIR	17 SCO	17 SAG	15 CAP	16 PIS	15 ARI	14 TAU	15 CAN
	17 TAU	16 GEM	17 CAN	19 VIR	18 LIB	19 SAG	19 CAP	17 AQU	18 ARI	17 TAU	16 GEM	18 LEO
	19 GEM	18 CAN	20 LEO	21 LIB	21 SCO	21 CAP	21 AQU	19 PIS	20 TAU	19 GEM	18 CAN	20 VIR
	22 CAN	21 LEO	22 VIR	23 SCO	23 SAG	23 AQU	23 PIS	21 ARI	22 GEM	22 CAN	21 LEO	23 LIB
	24 LEO	23 VIR	25 LIB	26 SAG	25 PIS	25 PIS	25 ARI	23 TAU	24 CAN	24 LEO	23 VIR	25 SCO
	27 VIR	25 LIB	27 SCO	28 CAP	27 AQU	28 ARI	27 TAU	26 GEM	27 LEO	27 VIR	26 LIB	28 SAG
	29 LIB	28 SCO	29 SAG	30 AQU	29 PIS	30 TAU	29 GEM	28 CAN	29 VIR	29 LIB	28 SCO	30 CAP
			31 CAP		31 ARI			31 LEO			30 SAG	

2006

	JAN	FEB	MAR	APR	MAY	JUN	JUL	AUG	SEP	OCT	NOV	DEC
	1 AQU	1 ARI	1 ARI	1 GEM	1 CAN	2 VIR	2 LIB	1 SCO	2 CAP	1 AQU	2 ARI	1 TAU
	3 PIS	3 TAU	3 TAU	4 CAN	3 LEO	5 LIB	5 SCO	3 SAG	4 AQU	4 PIS	4 TAU	3 GEM
	5 ARI	6 GEM	5 GEM	6 LEO	6 VIR	7 SCO	7 SAG	6 CAP	6 PIS	6 ARI	6 GEM	6 CAN
	7 TAU	8 CAN	7 CAN	8 VIR	8 LIB	10 SAG	9 CAP	8 AQU	8 ARI	8 TAU	8 CAN	8 LEO
	9 GEM	10 LEO	10 LEO	11 LIB	11 SCO	12 CAP	11 AQU	10 PIS	10 TAU	10 GEM	10 LEO	10 VIR
	12 CAN	13 VIR	12 VIR	14 SCO	13 SAG	14 AQU	13 PIS	12 ARI	12 GEM	12 CAN	13 VIR	13 LIB
	14 LEO	16 LIB	15 LIB	16 SAG	15 CAP	16 PIS	15 ARI	14 TAU	14 CAN	14 LEO	15 LIB	15 SCO
	17 VIR	18 SCO	17 SCO	18 CAP	18 AQU	18 ARI	17 TAU	16 GEM	17 LEO	17 VIR	18 SCO	18 SAG
	19 LIB	20 SAG	20 SAG	20 AQU	20 PIS	20 TAU	20 GEM	18 CAN	19 VIR	19 LIB	20 SAG	20 CAP
	22 SCO	23 CAP	22 CAP	22 PIS	22 ARI	22 GEM	22 CAN	21 LEO	22 LIB	22 SCO	23 CAP	22 AQU
	24 SAG	25 AQU	24 AQU	25 ARI	24 TAU	25 CAN	24 LEO	23 VIR	24 SCO	24 SAG	25 AQU	24 PIS
	26 CAP	27 PIS	26 PIS	27 TAU	26 GEM	27 LEO	27 VIR	26 LIB	27 SAG	26 CAP	27 PIS	27 ARI
	28 AQU		28 ARI	29 GEM	28 CAN	29 VIR	29 LIB	28 SCO	29 CAP	29 AQU	29 ARI	29 TAU
	30 PIS		30 TAU		31 LEO			31 SAG		31 PIS		31 GEM

2007

	JAN	FEB	MAR	APR	MAY	JUN	JUL	AQU	SEP	OCT	NOV	DEC
	2 CAN	1 LEO	2 VIR	1 LIB	1 SCO	2 CAP	2 AQU	2 ARI	1 TAU	2 CAN	3 VIR	3 LIB
	4 LEO	3 VIR	5 LIB	3 SCO	3 SAG	4 AQU	4 PIS	4 TAU	3 GEM	4 LEO	5 LIB	5 SCO
	7 VIR	5 LIB	7 SCO	6 SAG	6 CAP	7 PIS	6 ARI	6 GEM	5 CAN	7 VIR	8 SCO	8 SAG
	9 LIB	8 SCO	10 SAG	8 CAP	8 AQU	9 ARI	8 TAU	9 CAN	7 LEO	9 LIB	10 SAG	10 CAP
	12 SCO	10 SAG	12 CAP	11 AQU	10 PIS	11 TAU	10 GEM	11 LEO	9 VIR	12 SCO	13 CAP	13 AQU
	14 SAG	13 CAP	14 AQU	13 PIS	12 ARI	13 GEM	12 CAN	13 VIR	12 LIB	14 SAG	15 AQU	15 PIS
	16 CAP	15 AQU	17 PIS	15 ARI	14 TAU	15 CAN	14 LEO	15 LIB	14 SCO	17 CAP	18 PIS	17 ARI
	19 AQU	17 PIS	19 ARI	17 TAU	16 GEM	17 LEO	17 VIR	18 SCO	17 SAG	19 AQU	20 ARI	19 TAU
	21 PIS	19 ARI	21 TAU	19 GEM	18 CAN	19 VIR	19 LIB	20 SAG	19 CAP	21 PIS	22 TAU	21 GEM
	23 ARI	21 TAU	23 GEM	21 CAN	21 LEO	22 LIB	22 SCO	23 CAP	22 AQU	23 ARI	24 GEM	23 CAN
	25 TAU	23 GEM	25 CAN	23 LEO	23 VIR	24 SCO	24 SAG	25 AQU	24 PIS	25 TAU	26 CAN	25 LEO
	27 GEM	25 CAN	27 LEO	26 VIR	25 LIB	27 SAG	27 CAP	27 PIS	26 ARI	27 GEM	28 LEO	27 VIR
	29 CAN	28 LEO	29 VIR	28 LIB	28 SCO	29 CAP	29 AQU	29 ARI	28 TAU	29 CAN	30 VIR	30 LIB
					31 SAG		31 PIS		30 GEM	31 LEO		

2008

	JAN	FEB	MAR	APR	MAY	JUN	JUL	AUG	SEP	OCT	NOV	DEC
	1 SCO	3 CAP	1 CAP	2 PIS	2 ARI	2 GEM	2 CAN	2 VIR	1 LIB	3 SAG	2 CAP	2 AQU
	4 SAG	5 AQU	3 AQU	4 ARI	4 TAU	4 CAN	4 LEO	4 LIB	3 SCO	5 CAP	4 AQU	4 PIS
	6 CAP	7 PIS	6 PIS	6 TAU	6 GEM	6 LEO	6 VIR	7 SCO	6 SAG	8 AQU	7 PIS	6 ARI
	9 AQU	10 ARI	8 ARI	8 GEM	8 CAN	8 VIR	8 LIB	9 SAG	8 CAP	10 PIS	9 ARI	9 TAU
	11 PIS	12 TAU	10 TAU	10 CAN	10 LEO	11 LIB	10 SCO	12 CAP	11 AQU	13 ARI	11 TAU	11 GEM
	13 ARI	14 GEM	12 GEM	13 LEO	12 VIR	13 SCO	13 SAG	14 AQU	13 PIS	15 TAU	13 GEM	13 CAN
	15 TAU	16 CAN	14 CAN	15 VIR	14 LIB	15 SAG	15 CAP	17 PIS	15 ARI	17 GEM	15 CAN	15 LEO
	18 GEM	18 LEO	16 LEO	17 LIB	17 SCO	18 CAP	18 AQU	19 ARI	17 TAU	19 CAN	17 LEO	17 VIR
	20 CAN	20 VIR	19 VIR	20 SCO	19 SAG	21 AQU	20 PIS	21 TAU	19 GEM	21 LEO	19 VIR	19 LIB
	22 LEO	23 LIB	21 LIB	22 SAG	22 CAP	23 PIS	23 ARI	23 GEM	21 CAN	23 VIR	22 LIB	21 SCO
	24 VIR	25 SCO	23 SCO	25 CAP	24 AQU	25 ARI	25 TAU	25 CAN	24 LEO	25 LIB	24 SCO	24 SAG
	26 LIB	28 SAG	26 SAG	27 AQU	27 PIS	28 TAU	27 GEM	27 LEO	26 VIR	28 SCO	27 SAG	26 CAP
	29 SCO		28 CAP	30 PIS	29 ARI	30 GEM	29 CAN	29 VIR	28 LIB	30 SAG	29 CAP	29 AQU
	31 SAG		31 AQU		31 TAU		31 LEO		30 SCO			31 PIS

2009

	JAN	FEB	MAR	APR	MAY	JUN	JUL	AUG	SEP	OCT	NOV	DEC
	3 ARI	1 TAU	3 GEM	1 CAN	2 VIR	1 LIB	3 SAG	2 CAP	3 PIS	3 ARI	1 TAU	1 GEM
	5 TAU	3 GEM	5 CAN	3 LEO	5 LIB	3 SCO	5 CAP	4 AQU	5 ARI	5 TAU	3 GEM	3 CAN
	7 GEM	5 CAN	7 LEO	5 VIR	7 SCO	6 SAG	8 AQU	7 PIS	8 TAU	7 GEM	6 CAN	5 LEO
	9 CAN	7 LEO	9 VIR	7 LIB	9 SAG	8 CAP	10 PIS	9 ARI	10 GEM	9 CAN	8 LEO	7 VIR
	11 LEO	10 VIR	11 LIB	10 SCO	12 CAP	11 AQU	13 ARI	11 TAU	12 CAN	12 LEO	10 VIR	9 LIB
	13 VIR	12 LIB	13 SCO	12 SAG	14 AQU	13 PIS	15 TAU	14 GEM	14 LEO	14 VIR	12 LIB	11 SCO
	15 LIB	14 SCO	16 SAG	15 CAP	17 PIS	16 ARI	17 GEM	16 CAN	16 VIR	16 LIB	14 SCO	14 SAG
	18 SCO	16 SAG	18 CAP	17 AQU	19 ARI	18 TAU	19 CAN	18 LEO	18 LIB	18 SCO	17 SAG	16 CAP
	20 SAG	19 CAP	21 AQU	20 PIS	21 TAU	20 GEM	21 LEO	20 VIR	20 SCO	20 SAG	19 CAP	19 AQU
	23 CAP	21 AQU	23 PIS	22 ARI	24 GEM	22 CAN	23 VIR	22 LIB	23 SAG	23 CAP	21 AQU	21 PIS
	25 AQU	24 PIS	26 ARI	24 TAU	26 CAN	24 LEO	26 LIB	24 SCO	25 CAP	25 AQU	24 PIS	24 ARI
	28 PIS	26 ARI	28 TAU	26 GEM	28 LEO	26 VIR	28 SCO	26 SAG	28 AQU	28 PIS	26 ARI	26 TAU
	30 ARI	28 TAU	30 GEM	28 CAN	30 VIR	28 LIB	30 SAG	29 CAP	30 PIS	30 ARI	29 TAU	28 GEM
				30 LEO		30 SCO		31 AQU				30 CAN

2010

	JAN	FEB	MAR	APR	MAY	JUN	JUL	AUG	SEP	OCT	NOV	DEC
	1 LEO	2 LIB	1 LIB	2 SAG	2 CAP	1 AQU	3 ARI	2 TAU	3 CAN	2 LEO	3 LIB	2 SCO
	3 VIR	4 SCO	3 SCO	4 CAP	4 AQU	3 PIS	5 TAU	4 GEM	5 LEO	4 VIR	5 SCO	4 SAG
	5 LIB	6 SAG	6 SAG	7 AQU	7 PIS	6 ARI	8 GEM	6 CAN	7 VIR	6 LIB	7 SAG	6 CAP
	8 SCO	9 CAP	8 CAP	9 PIS	9 ARI	8 TAU	10 CAN	8 LEO	9 LIB	8 SCO	9 CAP	9 AQU
	10 SAG	11 AQU	11 AQU	12 ARI	12 TAU	10 GEM	12 LEO	10 VIR	11 SCO	10 SAG	11 AQU	11 PIS
	12 CAP	14 PIS	13 PIS	14 TAU	14 GEM	12 CAN	14 VIR	12 LIB	13 SAG	12 CAP	14 PIS	14 ARI
	15 AQU	16 ARI	16 ARI	17 GEM	16 CAN	14 LEO	16 LIB	14 SCO	15 CAP	15 AQU	16 ARI	16 TAU
	18 PIS	19 TAU	18 TAU	19 CAN	18 LEO	17 VIR	18 SCO	17 SAG	18 AQU	17 PIS	19 TAU	18 GEM
	20 ARI	21 GEM	20 GEM	21 LEO	20 VIR	19 LIB	20 SAG	19 CAP	20 PIS	20 ARI	21 GEM	21 CAN
	22 TAU	23 CAN	23 CAN	23 VIR	22 LIB	21 SCO	23 CAP	21 AQU	23 ARI	22 TAU	24 CAN	23 LEO
	25 GEM	25 LEO	25 LEO	25 LIB	25 SCO	23 SAG	25 AQU	24 PIS	25 TAU	25 GEM	26 LEO	25 VIR
	27 CAN	27 VIR	27 VIR	27 SCO	27 SAG	25 CAP	28 PIS	26 ARI	28 GEM	27 CAN	28 VIR	27 LIB
	29 LEO		29 LIB	29 SAG	29 CAP	28 AQU	30 ARI	29 TAU	30 CAN	29 LEO	30 LIB	29 SCO
	31 VIR		31 SCO			30 PIS		31 GEM		31 VIR		31 SAG

2011

	JAN	FEB	MAR	APR	MAY	JUN	JUL	AUG	SEP	OCT	NOV	DEC
	3 CAP	1 AQU	1 AQU	2 ARI	2 TAU	3 CAN	2 LEO	1 VIR	1 SCO	3 CAP	1 AQU	1 PIS
	5 AQU	4 PIS	3 PIS	4 TAU	4 GEM	5 LEO	4 VIR	3 LIB	3 SAG	5 AQU	4 PIS	3 ARI
	7 PIS	6 ARI	6 ARI	7 GEM	6 CAN	7 VIR	6 LIB	5 SCO	5 CAP	7 PIS	6 ARI	6 TAU
	10 ARI	9 TAU	8 TAU	9 CAN	9 LEO	9 LIB	9 SCO	7 SAG	8 AQU	10 ARI	8 TAU	8 GEM
	12 TAU	11 GEM	11 GEM	11 LEO	11 VIR	11 SCO	11 SAG	9 CAP	10 PIS	12 TAU	11 GEM	11 CAN
	15 GEM	14 CAN	13 CAN	14 VIR	13 LIB	13 SAG	13 CAP	11 AQU	13 ARI	15 GEM	14 CAN	13 LEO
	17 CAN	16 LEO	15 LEO	16 LIB	15 SCO	16 CAP	16 AQU	14 PIS	15 TAU	17 CAN	16 LEO	15 VIR
	19 LEO	18 VIR	17 VIR	18 SCO	17 SAG	19 AQU	18 PIS	16 ARI	18 GEM	20 LEO	18 VIR	17 LIB
	21 VIR	20 LIB	19 LIB	20 SAG	20 CAP	21 PIS	20 ARI	19 TAU	20 CAN	22 VIR	20 LIB	20 SCO
	23 LIB	22 SCO	21 SCO	22 CAP	22 AQU	24 ARI	23 TAU	21 GEM	22 LEO	24 LIB	23 SCO	22 SAG
	25 SCO	24 SAG	23 SAG	24 AQU	24 PIS	26 TAU	25 GEM	24 CAN	24 VIR	26 SCO	25 SAG	24 CAP
	28 SAG	26 CAP	25 CAP	26 PIS	26 ARI	29 GEM	28 CAN	26 LEO	26 LIB	28 SAG	28 CAP	26 AQU
	30 CAP		28 AQU	29 ARI	29 TAU		30 LEO	28 VIR	28 SCO	30 CAP	30 AQU	28 PIS
			30 PIS		31 GEM			30 LIB	30 SAG			31 ARI

2012

JAN	FEB	MAR	APR	MAY	JUN	JUL	AUG	SEP	OCT	NOV	DEC
2 TAU	1 GEM	2 CAN	1 LEO	2 LIB	1 SCO	2 CAP	1 AQU	2 ARI	1 TAU	3 CAN	2 LEO
5 GEM	4 CAN	4 LEO	3 VIR	4 SCO	3 SAG	4 AQU	3 PIS	4 TAU	4 GEM	5 LEO	5 VIR
7 CAN	6 LEO	6 VIR	5 LIB	6 SAG	5 CAP	6 PIS	5 ARI	6 GEM	6 CAN	7 VIR	7 LIB
9 LEO	8 VIR	8 LIB	7 SCO	8 CAP	7 AQU	9 ARI	8 TAU	9 CAN	9 LEO	10 LIB	9 SCO
12 VIR	10 LIB	11 SCO	9 SAG	11 AQU	9 PIS	11 TAU	10 GEM	11 LEO	11 VIR	12 SCO	11 SAG
14 LIB	12 SCO	13 SAG	11 CAP	13 PIS	11 ARI	14 GEM	13 CAN	14 VIR	13 LIB	14 SAG	13 CAP
16 SCO	14 SAG	15 CAP	13 AQU	15 ARI	14 TAU	16 CAN	15 LEO	16 LIB	16 SCO	16 CAP	15 AQU
18 SAG	17 CAP	17 AQU	16 PIS	18 TAU	17 GEM	19 LEO	17 VIR	18 SCO	18 SCO	18 AQU	17 PIS
20 CAP	19 AQU	19 PIS	18 ARI	20 GEM	19 CAN	21 VIR	19 LIB	20 SAG	20 SAG	20 PIS	20 ARI
22 AQU	21 PIS	22 ARI	20 TAU	23 CAN	21 LEO	23 LIB	22 SCO	22 CAP	22 CAP	22 ARI	22 TAU
25 PIS	23 ARI	24 TAU	23 GEM	25 LEO	24 VIR	25 SCO	24 SAG	24 AQU	24 AQU	25 TAU	25 GEM
27 ARI	26 TAU	27 GEM	26 CAN	28 VIR	26 LIB	28 SAG	26 CAP	27 PIS	27 PIS	27 GEM	27 CAN
30 TAU	28 GEM	29 CAN	28 LEO	30 LIB	28 SCO	30 CAP	28 AQU	29 ARI	29 TAU	30 CAN	30 LEO
			30 VIR		30 SAG		30 PIS		31 GEM		

2013

JAN	FEB	MAR	APR	MAY	JUN	JUL	AUG	SEP	OCT	NOV	DEC
1 VIR	2 SCO	1 SCO	2 CAP	1 AQU	2 ARI	1 TAU	2 CAN	1 LEO	1 VIR	2 SCO	2 SAG
3 LIB	4 SAG	3 SAG	4 AQU	3 PIS	4 TAU	4 GEM	5 LEO	4 VIR	3 LIB	4 SAG	4 CAP
6 SCO	6 CAP	5 CAP	6 PIS	5 ARI	6 GEM	6 CAN	7 VIR	6 LIB	6 SCO	6 CAP	6 AQU
8 SAG	8 AQU	7 AQU	8 ARI	8 TAU	9 CAN	9 LEO	10 LIB	8 SCO	8 SAG	8 AQU	8 PIS
10 CAP	10 PIS	10 PIS	10 TAU	10 GEM	11 LEO	11 VIR	12 SCO	11 SAG	10 CAP	10 PIS	10 ARI
12 AQU	12 ARI	12 ARI	13 GEM	13 CAN	14 VIR	14 LIB	14 SAG	13 CAP	12 AQU	13 ARI	12 TAU
14 PIS	15 TAU	14 TAU	15 CAN	15 LEO	16 LIB	16 SCO	16 CAP	15 AQU	14 PIS	15 TAU	15 GEM
16 ARI	17 GEM	17 GEM	18 LEO	18 VIR	19 SCO	18 SAG	18 AQU	17 PIS	16 ARI	17 GEM	17 CAN
18 TAU	20 CAN	19 CAN	20 VIR	20 LIB	21 SAG	20 CAP	20 PIS	19 ARI	19 TAU	20 CAN	20 LEO
21 GEM	22 LEO	22 LEO	23 LIB	22 SCO	23 CAP	22 AQU	23 ARI	21 TAU	21 GEM	22 LEO	22 VIR
23 CAN	25 VIR	24 VIR	25 SCO	24 SAG	25 AQU	24 PIS	25 TAU	24 CAN	23 CAN	25 VIR	25 LIB
26 LEO	27 LIB	26 LIB	27 SAG	26 CAP	27 PIS	26 ARI	27 GEM	26 CAN	26 LEO	27 LIB	27 SCO
28 VIR		28 SCO	29 CAP	28 AQU	29 ARI	28 TAU	30 CAN	30 CAN	28 VIR	29 SCO	29 SAG
31 LIB		30 SAG		30 PIS		31 GEM			31 LIB		31 CAP

2014

JAN	FEB	MAR	APR	MAY	JUN	JUL	AUG	SEP	OCT	NOV	DEC
2 AQU	2 ARI	2 ARI	1 TAU	3 CAN	1 LEO	1 VIR	2 SCO	1 SAG	3 AQU	1 PIS	3 TAU
4 PIS	5 TAU	4 TAU	3 GEM	5 LEO	4 VIR	4 LIB	5 SAG	3 CAP	5 PIS	3 ARI	5 GEM
6 ARI	7 GEM	6 GEM	5 CAN	8 VIR	6 LIB	6 SCO	7 CAP	5 AQU	7 ARI	5 TAU	7 CAN
8 TAU	10 CAN	9 CAN	8 LEO	10 LIB	9 SCO	8 SAG	9 AQU	7 PIS	9 TAU	7 GEM	9 LEO
11 GEM	12 LEO	11 LEO	10 VIR	12 SCO	11 SAG	10 CAP	11 PIS	9 ARI	11 GEM	10 CAN	12 VIR
13 CAN	14 VIR	14 VIR	13 LIB	15 SAG	13 CAP	12 AQU	13 ARI	11 TAU	13 CAN	12 LEO	14 LIB
16 LEO	17 LIB	16 LIB	15 SCO	17 CAP	15 AQU	14 PIS	15 TAU	14 GEM	16 LEO	15 VIR	17 SCO
18 VIR	19 SCO	19 SCO	17 SAG	19 AQU	17 PIS	16 ARI	17 GEM	16 CAN	18 VIR	17 LIB	19 SAG
21 LIB	22 SAG	21 SAG	19 CAP	21 PIS	19 ARI	19 TAU	20 CAN	18 LEO	21 LIB	20 SCO	21 CAP
23 SCO	24 CAP	23 CAP	21 AQU	23 ARI	21 TAU	21 GEM	22 LEO	21 VIR	23 SCO	22 SAG	23 AQU
25 SAG	26 AQU	25 AQU	24 PIS	25 TAU	24 GEM	23 CAN	25 VIR	23 LIB	25 SAG	24 CAP	25 PIS
28 CAP	28 PIS	27 PIS	26 ARI	27 GEM	26 CAN	26 LEO	27 LIB	25 SCO	28 CAP	26 AQU	28 ARI
29 AQU		29 ARI	28 TAU	30 CAN	29 LEO	28 VIR	30 SCO	28 SAG	30 AQU	28 PIS	30 TAU
31 PIS			30 GEM			31 LIB		30 CAP		30 ARI	

2015

JAN	FEB	MAR	APR	MAY	JUN	JUL	AUG	SEP	OCT	NOV	DEC
1 GEM	2 LEO	1 LEO	3 LIB	2 SCO	1 SAG	1 CAP	1 PIS	2 TAU	1 GEM	2 LEO	2 VIR
3 CAN	5 VIR	4 VIR	5 SCO	5 SAG	3 CAP	3 AQU	3 ARI	4 GEM	3 CAN	4 VIR	4 LIB
6 LEO	7 LIB	6 LIB	8 SAG	7 CAP	6 AQU	5 PIS	5 TAU	6 CAN	6 LEO	7 LIB	7 SCO
8 VIR	10 SCO	9 SCO	10 CAP	9 AQU	8 PIS	7 ARI	8 GEM	8 LEO	8 VIR	9 SCO	9 SAG
11 LIB	12 SAG	11 SAG	12 AQU	11 PIS	10 ARI	9 TAU	10 CAN	11 VIR	11 LIB	12 SAG	12 CAP
13 SCO	14 CAP	14 CAP	14 PIS	14 ARI	12 TAU	11 GEM	12 LEO	13 LIB	13 SCO	14 CAP	14 AQU
16 SAG	16 AQU	16 AQU	16 ARI	16 TAU	14 GEM	14 CAN	15 VIR	16 SCO	16 SAG	17 AQU	16 PIS
18 CAP	18 PIS	18 PIS	18 TAU	18 GEM	16 CAN	16 LEO	17 LIB	18 SAG	18 CAP	19 PIS	18 ARI
20 AQU	20 ARI	20 ARI	20 GEM	20 CAN	19 LEO	18 VIR	20 SCO	21 CAP	20 AQU	21 ARI	20 TAU
22 PIS	22 TAU	22 TAU	22 CAN	22 LEO	21 VIR	21 LIB	22 SAG	23 AQU	23 PIS	23 TAU	22 GEM
24 ARI	24 GEM	24 GEM	25 LEO	25 VIR	24 LIB	23 SCO	24 CAP	25 PIS	25 ARI	25 GEM	25 CAN
26 TAU	27 CAN	26 CAN	27 VIR	27 LIB	26 SCO	26 SAG	27 AQU	27 ARI	27 TAU	27 CAN	27 LEO
28 GEM		29 LEO	30 LIB	30 SCO	28 SAG	28 CAP	29 PIS	29 TAU	29 GEM	29 LEO	29 VIR
31 CAN		31 VIR				30 AQU	31 ARI		31 CAN		

MOON CHARTS

2016

	JAN	FEB	MAR	APR	MAY	JUN	JUL	AUG	SEP	OCT	NOV	DEC
	1 LIB	2 SAG	3 CAP	1 AQU	1 PIS	1 TAU	1 GEM	1 LEO	2 LIB	2 SCO	1 SAG	1 CAP
	3 SCO	4 CAP	5 AQU	4 PIS	3 ARI	3 GEM	3 CAN	4 VIR	5 SCO	5 SAG	3 CAP	3 AQU
	6 SAG	7 AQU	7 PIS	6 ARI	5 TAU	5 CAN	5 LEO	6 LIB	7 SAG	7 CAP	6 AQU	5 PIS
	8 CAP	9 PIS	9 ARI	8 TAU	7 GEM	8 LEO	7 VIR	8 SCO	10 CAP	10 AQU	8 PIS	8 ARI
	10 AQU	11 ARI	11 TAU	10 GEM	9 CAN	10 VIR	10 LIB	11 SAG	12 AQU	12 PIS	10 ARI	10 TAU
	12 PIS	13 TAU	13 GEM	12 CAN	11 LEO	12 LIB	12 SCO	13 CAP	14 PIS	14 ARI	12 TAU	12 GEM
	14 ARI	15 GEM	15 CAN	14 LEO	14 VIR	15 SCO	15 SAG	16 AQU	16 ARI	16 TAU	14 GEM	14 CAN
	17 TAU	17 CAN	18 LEO	16 VIR	16 LIB	17 SAG	17 CAP	18 PIS	18 TAU	18 GEM	16 CAN	16 LEO
	19 GEM	19 LEO	20 VIR	19 LIB	19 SCO	20 CAP	19 AQU	20 ARI	21 GEM	20 CAN	18 LEO	18 VIR
	21 CAN	22 VIR	23 LIB	21 SCO	21 SAG	22 AQU	22 PIS	22 TAU	23 CAN	22 LEO	21 VIR	20 LIB
	23 LEO	24 LIB	25 SCO	24 SAG	24 CAP	24 PIS	24 ARI	24 GEM	25 LEO	24 VIR	23 LIB	23 SCO
	25 VIR	27 SCO	28 SAG	26 CAP	26 AQU	27 ARI	26 TAU	26 CAN	27 VIR	27 LIB	26 SCO	25 SAG
	28 LIB	29 SAG	30 CAP	29 AQU	28 PIS	29 TAU	28 GEM	28 LEO	30 LIB	29 SCO	28 SAG	28 CAP
	30 SCO				30 ARI		30 CAN	31 VIR				30 AQU

2017

	JAN	FEB	MAR	APR	MAY	JUN	JUL	AUG	SEP	OCT	NOV	DEC
	2 PIS	2 TAU	2 TAU	2 CAN	1 LEO	2 LIB	2 SCO	1 SAG	2 AQU	2 PIS	1 ARI	2 GEM
	4 ARI	4 GEM	4 GEM	4 LEO	4 VIR	5 SCO	5 SAG	3 CAP	5 PIS	4 ARI	3 TAU	4 CAN
	6 TAU	7 CAN	6 CAN	6 VIR	6 LIB	7 SAG	7 CAP	6 AQU	7 ARI	6 TAU	5 GEM	6 LEO
	8 GEM	9 LEO	8 LEO	9 LIB	9 SCO	10 CAP	10 AQU	8 PIS	9 TAU	9 GEM	7 CAN	8 VIR
	10 CAN	11 VIR	10 VIR	11 SCO	11 SAG	12 AQU	12 PIS	11 ARI	11 GEM	11 CAN	9 LEO	11 LIB
	12 LEO	13 LIB	13 LIB	14 SAG	14 CAP	15 PIS	14 ARI	13 TAU	13 CAN	13 LEO	11 VIR	13 SCO
	14 VIR	16 SCO	15 SCO	16 CAP	16 AQU	17 ARI	17 TAU	15 GEM	15 LEO	15 VIR	13 LIB	15 SAG
	17 LIB	18 SAG	17 SAG	19 AQU	18 PIS	19 TAU	19 GEM	17 CAN	17 VIR	17 LIB	16 SCO	18 CAP
	19 SCO	21 CAP	20 CAP	21 PIS	21 ARI	21 GEM	21 CAN	19 LEO	20 LIB	19 SCO	18 SAG	20 AQU
	22 SAG	23 AQU	22 AQU	23 ARI	23 TAU	23 CAN	23 LEO	21 VIR	22 SCO	22 SAG	21 CAP	23 PIS
	24 CAP	25 PIS	25 PIS	25 TAU	25 GEM	25 LEO	25 VIR	23 LIB	24 SAG	24 CAP	23 AQU	25 ARI
	27 AQU	27 ARI	27 ARI	27 GEM	27 CAN	27 VIR	27 LIB	26 SCO	27 CAP	27 AQU	26 PIS	28 TAU
	29 PIS		29 TAU	29 CAN	29 LEO		30 LIB	28 SAG	29 AQU	29 PIS	28 ARI	30 GEM
	31 ARI		31 GEM		31 VIR			31 CAP			30 TAU	

2018

	JAN	FEB	MAR	APR	MAY	JUN	JUL	AUG	SEP	OCT	NOV	DEC
	1 CAN	1 VIR	1 VIR	1 SCO	1 SAG	2 AQU	2 PIS	1 ARI	2 GEM	1 CAN	2 VIR	1 LIB
	3 LEO	3 LIB	3 LIB	4 SAG	3 CAP	5 PIS	4 ARI	3 TAU	4 CAN	3 LEO	4 LIB	3 SCO
	5 VIR	5 SCO	5 SCO	6 CAP	6 AQU	7 ARI	7 TAU	5 GEM	6 LEO	5 VIR	6 SCO	5 SAG
	7 LIB	8 SAG	7 SAG	9 AQU	8 PIS	9 TAU	9 GEM	7 CAN	8 VIR	7 LIB	8 SAG	8 CAP
	9 SCO	10 CAP	10 CAP	11 PIS	11 ARI	11 GEM	11 CAN	9 LEO	10 LIB	9 SCO	10 CAP	10 AQU
	12 SAG	13 AQU	12 AQU	13 ARI	13 TAU	14 CAN	13 LEO	11 VIR	12 SCO	12 SAG	13 AQU	13 PIS
	14 CAP	15 PIS	15 PIS	16 TAU	15 GEM	16 LEO	15 VIR	13 LIB	14 SAG	14 CAP	15 PIS	15 ARI
	17 AQU	18 ARI	17 ARI	18 GEM	17 CAN	18 VIR	17 LIB	16 SCO	17 CAP	17 AQU	18 ARI	18 TAU
	19 PIS	20 TAU	19 TAU	20 CAN	19 LEO	20 LIB	19 SCO	18 SAG	19 AQU	19 PIS	20 TAU	20 GEM
	22 ARI	22 GEM	22 GEM	22 LEO	21 VIR	22 SCO	22 SAG	20 CAP	22 PIS	22 ARI	22 GEM	22 CAN
	24 TAU	24 CAN	24 CAN	24 VIR	24 LIB	24 SAG	24 CAP	23 AQU	24 ARI	24 TAU	25 CAN	24 LEO
	26 GEM	26 LEO	26 LIB	26 LIB	26 SCO	27 CAP	27 AQU	25 PIS	26 TAU	26 GEM	27 LEO	26 VIR
	28 CAN		28 VIR	29 SCO	28 SAG	29 AQU	29 PIS	28 ARI	29 GEM	28 CAN	29 VIR	28 LIB
	30 LEO		30 LIB		31 CAP			30 TAU		30 LEO		30 SCO

2019

	JAN	FEB	MAR	APR	MAY	JUN	JUL	AUG	SEP	OCT	NOV	DEC
	2 SAG	3 AQU	2 AQU	1 PIS	1 ARI	2 GEM	1 CAN	2 VIR	2 SCO	2 SAG	3 AQU	3 PIS
	4 CAP	5 PIS	5 PIS	3 ARI	3 TAU	4 CAN	3 LEO	4 LIB	4 SAG	4 CAP	5 PIS	5 ARI
	7 AQU	8 ARI	7 ARI	6 TAU	5 GEM	6 LEO	5 VIR	6 SCO	7 CAP	6 AQU	8 ARI	8 TAU
	9 PIS	10 TAU	10 TAU	8 GEM	8 CAN	8 VIR	8 LIB	8 SAG	9 AQU	9 PIS	10 TAU	10 GEM
	12 ARI	13 GEM	12 GEM	10 CAN	10 LEO	10 LIB	10 SCO	10 CAP	12 PIS	11 ARI	13 GEM	12 CAN
	14 TAU	15 CAN	14 CAN	13 LEO	12 VIR	12 SCO	12 SAG	13 AQU	14 ARI	14 TAU	15 CAN	14 LEO
	16 GEM	17 LEO	16 LEO	15 VIR	14 LIB	15 SAG	14 CAP	15 PIS	17 TAU	16 GEM	17 LEO	17 VIR
	18 CAN	19 VIR	18 VIR	17 LIB	16 SCO	17 CAP	17 AQU	18 ARI	19 GEM	19 CAN	19 VIR	19 LIB
	20 LEO	21 LIB	20 LIB	19 SCO	18 SAG	19 AQU	19 PIS	20 TAU	21 CAN	21 LEO	21 LIB	21 SCO
	22 VIR	23 SCO	22 SCO	21 SAG	21 CAP	22 PIS	22 ARI	23 GEM	24 LEO	23 VIR	23 SCO	23 SAG
	24 LIB	25 SAG	25 SAG	23 CAP	23 AQU	24 ARI	24 TAU	25 CAN	26 VIR	25 LIB	26 SAG	25 CAP
	27 SCO	28 CAP	27 CAP	26 AQU	26 PIS	27 TAU	27 GEM	27 LEO	28 LIB	27 SCO	28 CAP	28 AQU
	29 SAG		29 AQU	28 PIS	28 ARI	29 GEM	29 CAN	29 VIR	30 SCO	29 SAG	30 AQU	30 PIS
	31 CAP				30 TAU		31 LEO	31 LIB		31 CAP		

2020

JAN	FEB	MAR	APR	MAY	JUN	JUL	AUG	SEP	OCT	NOV	DEC
1 ARI	3 GEM	1 GEM	2 LEO	2 VIR	2 SCO	1 SAG	2 AQU	1 PIS	3 TAU	2 GEM	1 CAN
4 TAU	5 CAN	3 CAN	4 VIR	4 LIB	4 SAG	3 CAP	4 PIS	3 ARI	5 GEM	4 CAN	4 LEO
6 GEM	7 LEO	6 LEO	6 LIB	6 SCO	6 CAP	6 AQU	7 ARI	6 TAU	8 CAN	7 LEO	6 VIR
9 CAN	9 VIR	8 VIR	8 SCO	8 SAG	8 AQU	8 PIS	9 TAU	8 GEM	10 LEO	9 VIR	8 LIB
11 LEO	11 LIB	10 LIB	10 SAG	10 CAP	11 PIS	11 ARI	12 GEM	11 CAN	12 VIR	11 LIB	10 SCO
13 VIR	13 SCO	12 SCO	12 CAP	12 AQU	13 ARI	13 TAU	14 CAN	13 LEO	15 LIB	13 SCO	12 SAG
15 LIB	15 SAG	14 SAG	15 AQU	14 PIS	16 TAU	16 GEM	17 LEO	15 VIR	17 SCO	15 SAG	14 CAP
17 SCO	18 CAP	16 CAP	17 PIS	17 ARI	18 GEM	18 CAN	19 VIR	17 LIB	18 SAG	17 CAP	17 AQU
19 SAG	20 AQU	18 AQU	20 ARI	19 TAU	21 CAN	20 LEO	21 LIB	19 SCO	21 CAP	19 AQU	19 PIS
22 CAP	23 PIS	21 PIS	22 TAU	22 GEM	23 LEO	22 VIR	23 SCO	21 SAG	23 AQU	21 PIS	21 ARI
24 AQU	25 ARI	23 ARI	25 GEM	24 CAN	25 VIR	24 LIB	25 SAG	23 CAP	25 PIS	24 ARI	24 TAU
26 PIS	28 TAU	26 TAU	27 CAN	27 LEO	27 LIB	26 SCO	27 CAP	26 AQU	28 ARI	26 TAU	26 GEM
29 ARI		28 GEM	29 LEO	29 VIR	29 SCO	29 SAG	29 AQU	28 PIS	30 TAU	29 GEM	29 CAN
31 TAU		31 CAN		31 LIB		31 CAP		30 ARI			31 LEO

2021

JAN	FEB	MAR	APR	MAY	JUN	JUL	AUG	SEP	OCT	NOV	DEC
2 VIR	1 LIB	2 SCO	1 SAG	2 AQU	1 PIS	3 TAU	2 GEM	1 CAN	3 VIR	1 LIB	1 SCO
5 LIB	3 SCO	4 SAG	3 CAP	4 PIS	3 ARI	5 GEM	4 CAN	3 LEO	5 LIB	3 SCO	3 SAG
7 SCO	5 SAG	6 CAP	5 AQU	6 ARI	6 TAU	8 CAN	7 LEO	5 VIR	7 SCO	5 SAG	5 CAP
9 SAG	7 CAP	9 AQU	7 PIS	9 TAU	8 GEM	10 LEO	9 VIR	7 LIB	9 SAG	7 CAP	7 AQU
11 CAP	9 AQU	11 PIS	9 ARI	12 GEM	11 CAN	13 VIR	11 LIB	9 SCO	11 CAP	9 AQU	9 PIS
13 AQU	12 PIS	13 ARI	12 TAU	14 CAN	13 LEO	15 LIB	13 SCO	11 SAG	13 AQU	12 PIS	11 ARI
15 PIS	14 ARI	16 TAU	15 GEM	17 LEO	15 VIR	17 SCO	15 SAG	13 CAP	15 PIS	14 ARI	14 TAU
18 ARI	16 TAU	18 GEM	17 CAN	19 VIR	18 LIB	19 SAG	18 CAP	16 AQU	18 ARI	16 TAU	16 GEM
20 TAU	19 GEM	21 CAN	20 LEO	21 LIB	20 SCO	21 CAP	20 AQU	18 PIS	20 TAU	19 GEM	19 CAN
23 GEM	21 CAN	23 LEO	22 VIR	23 SCO	22 SAG	23 AQU	22 PIS	20 ARI	23 GEM	21 CAN	21 LEO
25 CAN	24 LEO	25 VIR	24 LIB	25 SAG	24 CAP	25 PIS	24 ARI	23 TAU	25 CAN	24 LEO	24 VIR
27 LEO	26 VIR	28 LIB	26 SCO	27 CAP	26 AQU	28 ARI	26 TAU	25 GEM	28 LEO	26 VIR	26 LIB
30 VIR	28 LIB	30 SCO	28 SAG	29 AQU	28 PIS	30 TAU	29 GEM	28 CAN	30 VIR	29 LIB	28 SCO
			30 CAP		30 ARI			30 LEO			30 SAG

2022

JAN	FEB	MAR	APR	MAY	JUN	JUL	AUG	SEP	OCT	NOV	DEC
1 CAP	2 PIS	1 PIS	2 TAU	2 GEM	1 CAN	3 VIR	1 LIB	2 SAG	2 CAP	2 PIS	1 ARI
3 AQU	4 ARI	3 ARI	4 GEM	4 CAN	3 LEO	5 LIB	4 SCO	4 CAP	4 AQU	4 ARI	4 TAU
5 PIS	6 TAU	6 TAU	7 CAN	7 LEO	6 VIR	8 SCO	6 SAG	6 AQU	6 PIS	7 TAU	6 GEM
8 ARI	9 GEM	8 GEM	9 LEO	9 VIR	8 LIB	10 SAG	8 CAP	8 PIS	8 ARI	9 GEM	9 CAN
10 TAU	11 CAN	11 CAN	12 VIR	12 LIB	10 SCO	12 CAP	10 AQU	11 ARI	10 TAU	11 CAN	11 LEO
12 GEM	14 LEO	13 LEO	14 LIB	14 SCO	12 SAG	14 AQU	12 PIS	13 TAU	13 GEM	14 LEO	14 VIR
15 CAN	16 VIR	15 VIR	16 SCO	16 SAG	14 CAP	16 PIS	15 ARI	15 GEM	15 CAN	16 VIR	16 LIB
17 LEO	18 LIB	18 LIB	18 SAG	18 CAP	16 AQU	18 ARI	17 TAU	18 CAN	17 LEO	19 LIB	18 SCO
20 VIR	21 SCO	20 SCO	20 CAP	20 AQU	18 PIS	20 TAU	19 GEM	20 LEO	20 VIR	21 SCO	21 SAG
22 LIB	23 SAG	22 SAG	23 AQU	22 PIS	20 ARI	23 GEM	21 CAN	23 VIR	22 LIB	23 SAG	23 CAP
24 SCO	25 CAP	24 CAP	25 PIS	24 ARI	23 TAU	25 CAN	24 LEO	25 LIB	25 SCO	25 CAP	25 AQU
27 SAG	27 AQU	26 AQU	27 ARI	27 TAU	25 GEM	28 LEO	26 VIR	27 SCO	27 SAG	27 AQU	27 PIS
29 CAP		28 PIS	29 TAU	29 GEM	28 CAN	30 VIR	29 LIB	29 SAG	29 CAP	29 PIS	29 ARI
31 AQU		31 ARI			30 LEO		31 SCO		31 AQU		31 TAU

2023

JAN	FEB	MAR	APR	MAY	JUN	JUL	AUG	SEP	OCT	NOV	DEC
2 GEM	1 CAN	3 LEO	2 VIR	2 LIB	3 SAG	2 CAP	2 PIS	1 ARI	3 GEM	1 CAN	1 LEO
5 CAN	4 LEO	5 VIR	4 LIB	4 SCO	5 CAP	4 AQU	4 ARI	3 TAU	5 CAN	4 LEO	3 VIR
7 LEO	6 VIR	8 LIB	7 SCO	6 SAG	7 AQU	6 PIS	7 TAU	5 GEM	7 LEO	6 VIR	6 LIB
10 VIR	9 LIB	10 SCO	9 SAG	8 CAP	9 PIS	8 ARI	9 GEM	8 CAN	10 VIR	9 LIB	8 SCO
12 LIB	11 SCO	13 SAG	11 CAP	10 AQU	11 ARI	10 TAU	11 CAN	10 LEO	12 LIB	11 SCO	11 SAG
15 SCO	13 SAG	15 CAP	13 AQU	12 PIS	13 TAU	13 GEM	14 LEO	13 VIR	15 SCO	13 SAG	13 CAP
17 SAG	16 CAP	17 AQU	15 PIS	15 ARI	15 GEM	15 CAN	16 VIR	15 LIB	17 SAG	16 CAP	15 AQU
19 CAP	18 AQU	19 PIS	17 ARI	17 TAU	18 CAN	17 LEO	19 LIB	18 SCO	19 CAP	18 AQU	17 PIS
21 AQU	20 PIS	21 ARI	19 TAU	19 GEM	20 LEO	20 VIR	21 SCO	20 SAG	22 AQU	20 PIS	19 ARI
23 PIS	22 ARI	23 TAU	22 GEM	21 CAN	23 VIR	23 LIB	24 SAG	22 CAP	24 PIS	22 ARI	21 TAU
25 ARI	24 TAU	25 GEM	24 CAN	24 LEO	25 LIB	25 SCO	26 CAP	24 AQU	26 ARI	24 TAU	24 GEM
27 TAU	26 GEM	28 CAN	27 LEO	26 VIR	28 SCO	27 SAG	28 AQU	26 PIS	28 TAU	26 GEM	26 CAN
30 GEM	28 CAN	30 LEO	29 VIR	29 LIB	30 SAG	29 CAP	30 PIS	28 ARI	30 GEM	28 CAN	28 LEO
				31 SCO		31 AQU		30 TAU			31 VIR

197

2024

JAN	FEB	MAR	APR	MAY	JUN	JUL	AUG	SEP	OCT	NOV	DEC
2 LIB	1 SCO	2 SAG	3 AQU	2 PIS	3 TAU	2 GEM	3 LEO	1 VIR	1 LIB	3 SAG	2 CAP
5 SCO	4 SAG	4 CAP	5 PIS	5 GEM	5 GEM	4 CAN	5 VIR	4 LIB	4 SCO	5 CAP	4 AQU
7 SAG	6 CAP	6 AQU	7 ARI	7 CAN	7 CAN	6 LEO	8 LIB	7 SCO	6 SAG	7 AQU	7 PIS
9 CAP	8 AQU	8 PIS	9 TAU	8 GEM	9 LEO	9 VIR	10 SCO	9 SAG	9 CAP	9 PIS	9 ARI
11 AQU	10 PIS	10 ARI	11 GEM	10 CAN	12 VIR	11 LIB	13 SAG	11 CAP	11 AQU	12 ARI	11 TAU
13 PIS	12 ARI	12 TAU	13 CAN	13 LEO	14 LIB	14 SCO	15 CAP	14 AQU	13 PIS	14 TAU	13 GEM
15 ARI	14 TAU	14 GEM	15 LEO	15 VIR	17 SCO	16 SAG	17 AQU	16 PIS	15 ARI	16 GEM	15 CAN
18 TAU	16 GEM	17 CAN	18 VIR	18 LIB	19 SAG	19 CAP	19 PIS	18 ARI	17 TAU	18 CAN	17 LEO
20 GEM	18 CAN	19 LEO	20 LIB	20 SCO	21 CAP	21 AQU	21 ARI	20 TAU	20 GEM	20 LEO	20 VIR
22 CAN	21 LEO	22 VIR	23 SCO	23 SAG	23 AQU	23 PIS	23 TAU	22 GEM	21 CAN	22 VIR	22 LIB
25 LEO	23 VIR	24 LIB	25 SAG	25 CAP	26 PIS	25 ARI	25 GEM	24 CAN	24 LEO	25 LIB	25 SCO
27 VIR	26 LIB	27 SCO	28 CAP	27 AQU	28 ARI	27 TAU	28 CAN	26 LEO	26 VIR	27 SCO	27 SAG
30 LIB	28 SCO	29 SAG	30 AQU	29 PIS	30 TAU	29 GEM	30 LEO	29 VIR	28 LIB	30 SAG	29 CAP
		31 CAP		31 ARI		31 CAN			31 SCO		

2025

JAN	FEB	MAR	APR	MAY	JUN	JUL	AUG	SEP	OCT	NOV	DEC
1 AQU	1 ARI	1 ARI	1 GEM	1 CAN	1 VIR	1 LIB	3 SAG	1 CAP	1 AQU	2 ARI	1 TAU
3 PIS	3 TAU	3 TAU	3 CAN	3 LEO	4 LIB	4 SCO	5 CAP	4 AQU	3 PIS	4 TAU	3 GEM
5 ARI	6 GEM	5 GEM	5 LEO	5 VIR	6 SCO	6 SAG	7 AQU	6 PIS	5 ARI	6 GEM	5 CAN
7 TAU	8 CAN	7 CAN	8 VIR	8 LIB	9 SAG	9 CAP	9 PIS	8 ARI	8 TAU	8 CAN	7 LEO
9 GEM	10 LEO	9 LEO	10 LIB	10 SCO	11 CAP	11 AQU	12 ARI	10 TAU	10 GEM	10 LEO	10 VIR
11 CAN	12 VIR	12 VIR	13 SCO	13 SAG	14 AQU	13 PIS	14 TAU	12 GEM	12 CAN	12 VIR	12 LIB
14 LEO	15 LIB	14 LIB	15 SAG	15 CAP	16 PIS	15 ARI	16 GEM	14 CAN	14 LEO	15 LIB	14 SCO
16 VIR	17 SCO	17 SCO	18 CAP	18 AQU	18 ARI	18 TAU	18 CAN	17 LEO	16 VIR	17 SCO	17 SAG
18 LIB	20 SAG	19 SAG	20 AQU	20 PIS	20 TAU	20 GEM	20 LEO	19 VIR	18 LIB	20 SAG	19 CAP
21 SCO	22 CAP	22 CAP	23 PIS	22 ARI	22 GEM	22 CAN	23 VIR	21 LIB	21 SCO	22 CAP	22 AQU
23 SAG	25 AQU	24 AQU	25 ARI	24 TAU	24 CAN	24 LEO	25 LIB	24 SCO	23 SAG	25 AQU	24 PIS
26 CAP	27 PIS	26 PIS	27 TAU	26 GEM	27 LEO	26 VIR	27 SCO	26 SAG	26 CAP	27 PIS	27 ARI
28 AQU		28 ARI	29 GEM	28 CAN	29 VIR	29 LIB	30 SAG	29 CAP	28 AQU	29 ARI	29 TAU
30 PIS		30 TAU		30 LEO		31 SCO			31 PIS		31 GEM

2026

JAN	FEB	MAR	APR	MAY	JUN	JUL	AUG	SEP	OCT	NOV	DEC
2 CAN	2 VIR	2 VIR	3 SCO	3 SAG	1 CAP	1 AQU	2 ARI	1 TAU	2 CAN	3 VIR	2 LIB
4 LEO	5 LIB	4 LIB	5 SAG	5 CAP	4 AQU	4 PIS	4 TAU	3 GEM	4 LEO	5 LIB	4 SCO
6 VIR	7 SCO	6 SCO	8 CAP	8 AQU	6 PIS	6 ARI	7 GEM	5 CAN	6 VIR	7 SCO	7 SAG
8 LIB	10 SAG	9 SAG	10 AQU	10 PIS	9 ARI	8 TAU	9 CAN	7 LEO	9 LIB	9 SAG	9 CAP
11 SCO	12 CAP	11 CAP	13 PIS	12 ARI	11 TAU	10 GEM	11 LEO	9 VIR	11 SCO	12 CAP	12 AQU
13 SAG	15 AQU	14 AQU	15 ARI	14 TAU	13 GEM	12 CAN	13 VIR	11 LIB	13 SAG	15 AQU	14 PIS
16 CAP	17 PIS	16 PIS	17 TAU	16 GEM	15 CAN	14 LEO	15 LIB	14 SCO	16 CAP	17 PIS	17 ARI
18 AQU	19 ARI	18 ARI	19 GEM	18 CAN	17 LEO	16 VIR	17 SCO	16 SAG	18 AQU	20 ARI	19 TAU
21 PIS	21 TAU	21 TAU	21 CAN	20 LEO	19 VIR	18 LIB	20 SAG	18 CAP	21 PIS	22 TAU	21 GEM
23 ARI	23 GEM	23 GEM	23 LEO	23 VIR	21 LIB	20 SCO	22 CAP	21 AQU	23 ARI	24 GEM	23 CAN
25 TAU	26 CAN	25 CAN	25 VIR	25 LIB	24 SCO	23 SAG	25 AQU	23 PIS	25 TAU	26 CAN	25 LEO
27 GEM	28 LEO	27 LEO	28 LIB	27 SCO	26 SAG	26 CAP	27 PIS	26 ARI	27 GEM	28 LEO	27 VIR
29 CAN		29 VIR	30 SCO	30 SAG	29 CAP	28 AQU	29 ARI	28 TAU	29 CAN	30 VIR	29 LIB
31 LEO		31 LIB				31 PIS		30 GEM	31 LEO		

2027

JAN	FEB	MAR	APR	MAY	JUN	JUL	AUG	SEP	OCT	NOV	DEC
1 SCO	2 CAP	1 CAP	3 PIS	2 ARI	1 TAU	1 GEM	1 LEO	2 LIB	1 SCO	2 CAP	2 AQU
3 SAG	4 AQU	4 AQU	5 ARI	5 TAU	3 GEM	3 CAN	3 VIR	4 SCO	3 SAG	4 AQU	4 PIS
6 CAP	7 PIS	6 PIS	7 TAU	7 GEM	5 CAN	5 LEO	5 LIB	6 SAG	6 CAP	7 PIS	7 ARI
8 AQU	9 ARI	9 ARI	9 GEM	9 CAN	7 LEO	7 VIR	7 SCO	8 CAP	8 AQU	9 ARI	9 TAU
11 PIS	12 TAU	11 TAU	12 CAN	11 LEO	9 VIR	9 LIB	10 SAG	11 AQU	11 PIS	12 TAU	11 GEM
13 ARI	14 GEM	13 GEM	14 LEO	13 VIR	11 LIB	11 SCO	12 CAP	13 PIS	13 ARI	14 GEM	14 CAN
15 TAU	16 CAN	15 CAN	16 VIR	15 LIB	14 SCO	14 SAG	15 AQU	16 ARI	15 TAU	16 CAN	16 LEO
18 GEM	18 LEO	17 LEO	18 LIB	17 SCO	16 SAG	16 CAP	17 PIS	18 TAU	18 GEM	18 LEO	18 VIR
20 CAN	20 VIR	20 VIR	20 SCO	20 SAG	19 CAP	18 AQU	20 ARI	21 GEM	20 CAN	20 VIR	20 LIB
22 LEO	22 LIB	22 LIB	22 SAG	22 CAP	21 AQU	21 PIS	22 TAU	23 CAN	22 LEO	23 LIB	22 SCO
24 VIR	24 SCO	24 SCO	25 CAP	25 AQU	24 PIS	23 ARI	24 GEM	25 LEO	24 VIR	25 SCO	25 SAG
26 LIB	27 SAG	26 SAG	27 AQU	27 PIS	26 ARI	26 TAU	26 CAN	27 VIR	26 LIB	27 SAG	27 CAP
28 SCO		29 CAP	30 PIS	30 ARI	28 TAU	28 GEM	28 LEO	29 LIB	28 SCO	29 CAP	29 AQU
30 SAG		31 AQU				30 CAN	30 VIR		31 SAG		

2028

JAN	FEB	MAR	APR	MAY	JUN	JUL	AUG	SEP	OCT	NOV	DEC
1 PIS	2 TAU	3 GEM	1 CAN	1 LEO	1 LIB	3 SAG	1 CAP	2 PIS	2 ARI	1 TAU	1 GEM
3 ARI	4 GEM	5 CAN	3 LEO	3 VIR	3 SCO	5 CAP	4 AQU	5 ARI	5 TAU	3 GEM	3 CAN
6 TAU	6 CAN	7 LEO	5 VIR	5 LIB	5 SAG	7 AQU	6 PIS	7 TAU	7 GEM	6 CAN	5 LEO
8 GEM	9 LEO	9 VIR	7 LIB	7 SCO	8 CAP	10 PIS	9 ARI	9 GEM	9 CAN	8 LEO	7 VIR
10 CAN	11 VIR	11 LIB	9 SCO	9 SAG	10 AQU	12 ARI	11 TAU	12 CAN	12 LEO	10 VIR	9 LIB
12 LEO	13 LIB	13 SCO	12 SAG	11 CAP	12 PIS	15 TAU	13 GEM	14 LEO	14 VIR	12 LIB	11 SCO
14 VIR	15 SCO	15 SAG	14 CAP	14 AQU	15 ARI	17 GEM	16 CAN	16 VIR	16 LIB	14 SCO	14 SAG
16 LIB	17 SAG	17 CAP	16 AQU	16 PIS	17 TAU	19 CAN	18 LEO	18 LIB	18 SCO	16 SAG	16 CAP
18 SCO	19 CAP	20 AQU	19 PIS	19 ARI	20 GEM	21 LEO	20 VIR	20 SCO	20 SAG	18 CAP	18 AQU
21 SAG	22 AQU	22 PIS	21 ARI	21 TAU	22 CAN	23 VIR	22 LIB	22 SAG	22 CAP	21 AQU	20 PIS
23 CAP	24 PIS	25 ARI	24 TAU	23 GEM	24 LEO	25 LIB	24 SCO	25 CAP	24 AQU	23 PIS	23 ARI
25 AQU	27 ARI	27 TAU	26 GEM	26 CAN	26 VIR	28 SCO	26 SAG	27 AQU	27 PIS	26 ARI	25 TAU
28 PIS	29 TAU	30 GEM	28 CAN	28 LEO	28 LIB	30 SAG	28 CAP	30 PIS	29 ARI	28 TAU	28 GEM
30 ARI				30 VIR	30 SCO		31 AQU				30 CAN

2029

JAN	FEB	MAR	APR	MAY	JUN	JUL	AUG	SEP	OCT	NOV	DEC
1 LEO	2 LIB	1 LIB	2 SAG	1 CAP	2 PIS	2 ARI	1 TAU	2 CAN	2 LEO	3 LIB	2 SCO
4 VIR	4 SCO	3 SCO	4 CAP	4 AQU	5 ARI	5 TAU	3 GEM	4 LEO	4 VIR	5 SCO	4 SAG
6 LIB	6 SAG	5 SAG	6 AQU	6 PIS	7 TAU	7 GEM	6 CAN	6 VIR	6 LIB	7 SAG	6 CAP
8 SCO	8 CAP	8 CAP	9 PIS	8 ARI	10 GEM	9 CAN	8 LEO	9 LIB	8 SCO	9 CAP	8 AQU
10 SAG	11 AQU	10 AQU	11 ARI	11 TAU	12 CAN	12 LEO	10 VIR	11 SCO	10 SAG	11 AQU	10 PIS
12 CAP	13 PIS	12 PIS	14 TAU	13 GEM	14 LEO	14 VIR	12 LIB	13 SAG	12 CAP	13 PIS	13 ARI
14 AQU	16 ARI	15 ARI	16 GEM	16 CAN	17 VIR	16 LIB	14 SCO	15 CAP	14 AQU	15 ARI	15 TAU
17 PIS	18 TAU	17 TAU	19 CAN	18 LEO	19 LIB	18 SCO	16 SAG	17 AQU	17 PIS	18 TAU	18 GEM
19 ARI	21 GEM	20 GEM	21 LEO	20 VIR	21 SCO	21 SAG	19 CAP	20 PIS	19 ARI	21 GEM	20 CAN
22 TAU	23 CAN	22 CAN	23 VIR	23 LIB	23 SAG	23 CAP	21 AQU	22 ARI	22 TAU	23 CAN	23 LEO
24 GEM	25 LEO	25 LEO	25 LIB	25 SCO	25 CAP	25 AQU	23 PIS	24 TAU	24 GEM	25 LEO	25 VIR
27 CAN	27 VIR	27 VIR	27 SCO	27 SAG	27 AQU	27 PIS	26 ARI	27 GEM	27 CAN	27 VIR	27 LIB
29 LEO		29 LIB	29 SAG	29 CAP	30 PIS	29 ARI	28 TAU	30 CAN	29 LEO	30 LIB	29 SCO
31 VIR		31 SCO		31 AQU			31 GEM		31 VIR		31 SAG

2030

JAN	FEB	MAR	APR	MAY	JUN	JUL	AUG	SEP	OCT	NOV	DEC
2 CAP	1 AQU	3 PIS	1 ARI	1 TAU	2 CAN	2 LEO	1 VIR	1 SCO	1 SAG	1 AQU	1 PIS
5 AQU	3 PIS	5 ARI	4 TAU	3 GEM	5 LEO	4 VIR	3 LIB	3 SAG	3 CAP	3 PIS	3 ARI
7 PIS	5 ARI	7 TAU	6 GEM	6 CAN	7 VIR	7 LIB	5 SCO	5 CAP	5 AQU	6 ARI	5 TAU
9 ARI	8 TAU	10 GEM	9 CAN	8 LEO	9 LIB	9 SCO	7 SAG	7 AQU	7 PIS	8 TAU	8 GEM
12 TAU	10 GEM	12 CAN	11 LEO	11 VIR	11 SCO	11 SAG	9 CAP	10 PIS	9 ARI	10 GEM	10 CAN
14 GEM	13 CAN	15 LEO	13 VIR	13 LIB	13 SAG	13 CAP	11 AQU	12 ARI	12 TAU	13 CAN	13 LEO
17 CAN	15 LEO	17 VIR	16 LIB	15 SCO	15 CAP	15 AQU	13 PIS	14 TAU	14 GEM	16 LEO	15 VIR
19 LEO	18 VIR	19 LIB	18 SCO	17 SAG	17 AQU	17 PIS	16 ARI	17 GEM	17 CAN	18 VIR	18 LIB
21 VIR	20 LIB	21 SCO	20 SAG	19 CAP	19 PIS	19 ARI	18 TAU	19 CAN	19 LEO	20 LIB	20 SCO
23 LIB	22 SCO	23 SAG	22 CAP	21 AQU	22 ARI	22 TAU	21 GEM	22 LEO	22 VIR	22 SCO	22 SAG
26 SCO	24 SAG	25 CAP	24 AQU	23 PIS	24 TAU	24 GEM	23 CAN	24 VIR	24 LIB	24 SAG	24 CAP
28 SAG	26 CAP	27 AQU	26 PIS	26 ARI	27 GEM	27 CAN	25 LEO	26 LIB	26 SCO	26 CAP	26 AQU
30 CAP	28 AQU	30 PIS	28 ARI	28 TAU	29 CAN	29 LEO	28 VIR	28 SCO	28 SAG	28 AQU	28 PIS
				31 GEM			30 LIB		30 CAP		30 ARI

2031

JAN	FEB	MAR	APR	MAY	JUN	JUL	AUG	SEP	OCT	NOV	DEC
1 TAU	3 CAN	2 CAN	1 LEO	1 VIR	2 SCO	1 SAG	2 AQU	2 ARI	2 TAU	3 CAN	3 LEO
4 GEM	5 LEO	5 LEO	3 VIR	3 LIB	4 SAG	3 CAP	4 PIS	4 TAU	4 GEM	5 LEO	5 VIR
7 CAN	8 VIR	7 VIR	6 LIB	5 SCO	6 CAP	5 AQU	6 ARI	6 GEM	6 CAN	8 VIR	8 LIB
9 LEO	10 LIB	9 LIB	8 SCO	7 SAG	8 AQU	7 PIS	8 TAU	9 CAN	9 LEO	10 LIB	10 SCO
11 VIR	12 SCO	12 SCO	10 SAG	9 CAP	10 PIS	9 ARI	10 GEM	12 LEO	12 VIR	13 SCO	12 SAG
14 LIB	15 SAG	14 SAG	12 CAP	11 AQU	12 ARI	12 TAU	13 CAN	14 VIR	14 LIB	15 SAG	14 CAP
16 SCO	17 CAP	16 CAP	14 AQU	14 PIS	14 TAU	14 GEM	15 LEO	17 LIB	16 SCO	17 CAP	16 AQU
18 SAG	19 AQU	18 AQU	16 PIS	16 ARI	17 GEM	17 CAN	18 VIR	19 SCO	19 SAG	19 AQU	18 PIS
20 CAP	21 PIS	20 PIS	19 ARI	18 TAU	19 CAN	19 LEO	20 LIB	21 SAG	21 CAP	21 PIS	20 ARI
22 AQU	23 ARI	22 ARI	21 TAU	21 GEM	22 LEO	22 VIR	23 SCO	23 CAP	23 AQU	23 ARI	23 TAU
24 PIS	25 TAU	25 TAU	23 GEM	23 CAN	24 VIR	24 LIB	25 SAG	25 AQU	25 PIS	25 TAU	25 GEM
26 ARI	28 GEM	27 GEM	26 CAN	26 LEO	27 LIB	26 SCO	27 CAP	27 PIS	27 ARI	28 GEM	27 CAN
29 TAU		29 CAN	28 LEO	28 VIR	29 SCO	29 SAG	29 AQU	30 ARI	29 TAU	30 CAN	30 LEO
31 GEM				31 LIB		31 CAP	31 PIS		31 GEM		

JANUARY

JAN 1

Time	Sign
12:20 AM	LIBRA
2:55 AM	SCORPIO
5:25 AM	SAGITTARIUS
7:35 AM	CAPRICORN
9:15 AM	AQUARIUS
10:35 AM	PISCES
11:45 AM	ARIES
1:00 PM	TAURUS
2:35 PM	GEMINI
4:55 PM	CANCER
7:20 PM	LEO
9:55 PM	VIRGO

JAN 15

Time	Sign
1:55 AM	SCORPIO
4:25 AM	SAGITTARIUS
6:40 AM	CAPRICORN
8:10 AM	AQUARIUS
9:35 AM	PISCES
10:30 AM	ARIES
12:00 PM	TAURUS
1:40 PM	GEMINI
3:50 PM	CANCER
6:20 PM	LEO
8:55 PM	VIRGO
11:20 PM	LIBRA

FEBRUARY

FEB 1

Time	Sign
12:55 AM	SCORPIO
3:25 AM	SAGITTARIUS
5:40 AM	CAPRICORN
7:10 AM	AQUARIUS
8:35 AM	PISCES
9:45 AM	ARIES
11:00 AM	TAURUS
12:40 PM	GEMINI
2:55 PM	CANCER
5:15 PM	LEO
7:55 PM	VIRGO
10:20 PM	LIBRA

FEB 15

Time	Sign
12:05 AM	SCORPIO
2:25 AM	SAGITTARIUS
4:40 AM	CAPRICORN
6:15 AM	AQUARIUS
7:35 AM	PISCES
8:45 AM	ARIES
10:00 AM	TAURUS
11:35 AM	GEMINI
1:55 PM	CANCER
4:20 PM	LEO
6:55 PM	VIRGO
9:40 PM	LIBRA

MARCH

MAR 1

Time	Sign
1:20 AM	SAGITTARIUS
3:40 AM	CAPRICORN
5:15 AM	AQUARIUS
6:35 AM	PISCES
7:45 AM	ARIES
9:20 AM	TAURUS
10:40 AM	GEMINI
12:50 PM	CANCER
3:20 PM	LEO
5:55 PM	VIRGO
8:20 PM	LIBRA
10:50 PM	SCORPIO

MAR 15

Time	Sign
12:25 AM	SAGITTARIUS
2:40 AM	CAPRICORN
4:15 AM	AQUARIUS
5:35 AM	PISCES
6:45 AM	ARIES
8:00 AM	TAURUS
9:30 AM	GEMINI
11:50 AM	CANCER
2:50 PM	LEO
4:50 PM	VIRGO
7:20 PM	LIBRA
9:55 PM	SCORPIO

APRIL

APR 1

Time	Sign
1:40 AM	CAPRICORN
3:15 AM	AQUARIUS
4:35 AM	PISCES
5:50 AM	ARIES
7:05 AM	TAURUS
8:45 AM	GEMINI
10:50 AM	CANCER
1:15 PM	LEO
4:00 PM	VIRGO
6:15 PM	LIBRA
9:00 PM	SCORPIO
11:25 PM	SAGITTARIUS

APR 15

Time	Sign
12:20 AM	CAPRICORN
2:50 AM	AQUARIUS
3:35 AM	PISCES
4:45 AM	ARIES
6:00 AM	TAURUS
7:45 AM	GEMINI
9:55 AM	CANCER
12:20 PM	LEO
3:05 PM	VIRGO
5:20 PM	LIBRA
8:00 PM	SCORPIO
10:40 PM	SAGITTARIUS

MAY

MAY 1

Time	Sign
1:15 AM	AQUARIUS
2:35 AM	PISCES
3:50 AM	ARIES
5:00 AM	TAURUS
6:40 AM	GEMINI
8:55 AM	CANCER
11:20 AM	LEO
1:55 PM	VIRGO
4:20 PM	LIBRA
7:00 PM	SCORPIO
9:25 PM	SAGITTARIUS
11:40 PM	CAPRICORN

MAY 15

Time	Sign
2:15 AM	AQUARIUS
1:35 AM	PISCES
2:40 AM	ARIES
4:00 AM	TAURUS
5:35 AM	GEMINI
7:55 AM	CANCER
10:15 AM	LEO
12:55 PM	VIRGO
3:20 PM	LIBRA
5:55 PM	SCORPIO
8:20 PM	SAGITTARIUS
10:40 PM	CAPRICORN

JUNE

JUN 1

Time	Sign
12:35 AM	PISCES
1:45 AM	ARIES
3:00 AM	TAURUS
4:45 AM	GEMINI
6:55 AM	CANCER
9:20 AM	LEO
11:50 AM	VIRGO
2:20 PM	LIBRA
4:50 PM	SCORPIO
7:20 PM	SAGITTARIUS
9:40 PM	CAPRICORN
11:15 PM	AQUARIUS

JUN 15

Time	Sign
12:45 AM	ARIES
2:00 AM	TAURUS
3:45 AM	GEMINI
5:55 AM	CANCER
8:20 AM	LEO
10:55 AM	VIRGO
1:20 PM	LIBRA
3:55 PM	SCORPIO
6:20 PM	SAGITTARIUS
8:40 PM	CAPRICORN
10:10 PM	AQUARIUS
11:30 PM	PISCES

JULY

JUL 1

1:00 AM	TAURUS
2:40 AM	GEMINI
5:05 AM	CANCER
7:20 AM	LEO
9:55 AM	VIRGO
12:20 PM	LIBRA
3:00 PM	SCORPIO
5:25 PM	SAGITTARIUS
7:40 PM	CAPRICORN
9:15 PM	AQUARIUS
10:35 PM	PISCES
11:45 PM	ARIES

JUL 15

12:00 AM	TAURUS
1:30 AM	GEMINI
3:55 AM	CANCER
6:20 AM	LEO
8:55 AM	VIRGO
11:20 AM	LIBRA
1:55 PM	SCORPIO
4:20 PM	SAGITTARIUS
6:40 PM	CAPRICORN
8:15 PM	AQUARIUS
9:35 PM	PISCES
10:45 PM	ARIES

AUGUST

AUG 1

12:40 AM	GEMINI
2:55 AM	CANCER
5:20 AM	LEO
7:55 AM	VIRGO
10:20 AM	LIBRA
12:50 PM	SCORPIO
3:35 PM	SAGITTARIUS
5:40 PM	CAPRICORN
7:15 PM	AQUARIUS
8:35 PM	PISCES
9:50 PM	ARIES
11:00 PM	TAURUS

AUG 15

1:55 AM	CANCER
4:20 AM	LEO
6:55 AM	VIRGO
9:20 AM	LIBRA
11:55 AM	SCORPIO
2:25 PM	SAGITTARIUS
4:40 PM	CAPRICORN
6:10 PM	AQUARIUS
7:35 PM	PISCES
8:45 PM	ARIES
10:00 PM	TAURUS
11:35 PM	GEMINI

SEPTEMBER

SEP 1

1:05 AM	CANCER
3:20 AM	LEO
5:50 AM	VIRGO
8:20 AM	LIBRA
11:00 AM	SCORPIO
1:25 PM	SAGITTARIUS
3:40 PM	CAPRICORN
5:10 PM	AQUARIUS
6:35 PM	PISCES
7:45 PM	ARIES
8:55 PM	TAURUS
10:50 PM	GEMINI

SEP 15

12:00 AM	CANCER
2:25 AM	LEO
4:50 AM	VIRGO
7:15 AM	LIBRA
9:55 AM	SCORPIO
12:20 PM	SAGITTARIUS
2:40 PM	CAPRICORN
4:15 PM	AQUARIUS
5:35 PM	PISCES
6:45 PM	ARIES
8:00 PM	TAURUS
9:50 PM	GEMINI

OCTOBER

OCT 1

1:15 AM	LEO
4:05 AM	VIRGO
6:20 AM	LIBRA
8:50 AM	SCORPIO
11:25 AM	SAGITTARIUS
1:40 PM	CAPRICORN
3:15 PM	AQUARIUS
4:35 PM	PISCES
5:45 PM	ARIES
7:00 PM	TAURUS
8:50 PM	GEMINI
10:50 PM	CANCER

OCT 15

12:20 AM	LEO
2:50 AM	VIRGO
5:15 AM	LIBRA
7:50 AM	SCORPIO
10:25 AM	SAGITTARIUS
12:30 PM	CAPRICORN
2:10 PM	AQUARIUS
3:35 PM	PISCES
4:50 PM	ARIES
6:00 PM	TAURUS
7:35 PM	GEMINI
10:10 PM	CANCER

NOVEMBER

NOV 1

1:50 AM	VIRGO
4:15 AM	LIBRA
6:50 AM	SCORPIO
9:30 AM	SAGITTARIUS
11:35 AM	CAPRICORN
1:15 PM	AQUARIUS
2:30 PM	PISCES
3:35 PM	ARIES
5:10 PM	TAURUS
6:40 PM	GEMINI
9:05 PM	CANCER
11:20 PM	LEO

NOV 15

12:50 AM	VIRGO
3:20 AM	LIBRA
5:50 AM	SCORPIO
8:20 AM	SAGITTARIUS
10:40 AM	CAPRICORN
12:10 PM	AQUARIUS
1:35 PM	PISCES
2:45 PM	ARIES
4:00 PM	TAURUS
5:35 PM	GEMINI
8:05 PM	CANCER
10:20 PM	LEO

DECEMBER

DEC 1

12:00 AM	VIRGO
2:20 AM	LIBRA
4:50 AM	SCORPIO
7:25 AM	SAGITTARIUS
9:40 AM	CAPRICORN
11:15 AM	AQUARIUS
12:30 PM	PISCES
1:40 PM	ARIES
2:55 PM	TAURUS
4:35 PM	GEMINI
6:50 PM	CANCER
9:30 PM	LEO

DEC 15

1:20 AM	LIBRA
3:50 AM	SCORPIO
6:20 AM	SAGITTARIUS
8:40 AM	CAPRICORN
10:10 AM	AQUARIUS
11:35 AM	PISCES
12:40 PM	ARIES
2:00 PM	TAURUS
3:50 PM	GEMINI
5:50 PM	CANCER
8:30 PM	LEO
11:05 PM	VIRGO

ABOUT THE AUTHORS

AURORA TOWER (left) has been passionate about astrology all her life. She created independent studies in the history of astrology as an undergraduate at Brown University and has researched and studied various forms of astrology from Bali to India. She has contributed to or been featured in *Cosmopolitan*, *The New York Times*, *Lucky*, *ELLE*, *Town & Country*, and *The Huffington Post*, among others. She has also appeared on *Good Morning America* and ABC's *Nightline* to discuss topics related to astrology. She lives in Los Angeles and her sun sign is Gemini.

LAURA BROUNSTEIN (right) is the special projects director for *Cosmopolitan* and *Seventeen*, where she develops editorial partnerships and events like Cosmo's Fun Fearless Life conference. She also writes and edits for both magazines with a focus on women and power—and loves how astrology can tie into that. She frequently speaks publicly on these topics as well as social trends at national conferences like Her Campus's Her Conference event, and most recently, The Girls' Lounge in Davos, Switzerland. She lives in New York City and her sun sign is Libra.

INDEX

PHOTO CREDITS

Illustrations: © Naja Conrad Hansen, 16, 26, 36, 46, 56, 66, 76, 86, 96, 106, 116, 126; © Patrick George 142-143, 158-159; **Aries,** p. 14 (clockwise from top left): © Standret/Shutterstock, © Lenaer/ Shutterstock, © Samir Hussein/Getty Images, © Balazs Kovacs Images/Shutterstock, © Vitchanan Photography/Shutterstock, © Sean Pavone/Shutterstock, © Ovidiu Hrubaru/ Shutterstock, © Lenaer/Shutterstock; **Aries,** p. 15 (clockwise from top left): © Canadastock/ Shutterstock, © Kseniia Perminova/Shutterstock, © Balazs Kovacs Images/Shutterstock, © Kseniia Perminova/Shutterstock, © Sgranitz/ Getty im- ages, © LornaWu/Shutterstock, © Kseniia Perminova/Shutterstock, © Henry Monsour, © Miguel Villagran/Getty images; **Taurus,** p. 24 (clockwise from top left): © Caiaimage/Tom Merton/ Getty Images, © Henry Monsour, © Jimmy Yan/Shutterstock, © Victoria Fox/ Shutterstock, © Steve Granitz/Getty images, © 1000 Words/Shutterstock, © Alliance/ Shutterstock; **Taurus,** p. 25 (clockwise from top left): © Vizerskaya/Getty images, © iravgustin/ Shutterstock, © Mayer George/Shutterstock, © Nejron Photo/Shutterstock, © Your Inspiration/ Shutterstock, © Paul Matthew Photography/ Shutterstock, © Pandorabo/Shutterstock, © Silver Screen Collection/Getty images; **Gemini,** p. 34 (clockwise from top left): © Francesco Riccardo Iacomino/Getty Images, © Michael Ochs Archives/ Getty Images, © Willequet Manuel/Shutterstock, © Ann Haritonenko/Getty Images, © Vera Anderson/Getty Images, © Stefano Oppo/Getty Images, © Vvvita/Shutterstock, © Svitlana Sokolova/Shutterstock; **Gemini,** p. 35 (clockwise from top left): © Alex Grabchilev/ Evgeniya Bakanova/Getty Images, © Nina Malyna/ Shutterstock, © EpicStockMedia/Shutterstock, © Wundervisuals/Getty Images, © David Acosta Allely/Shutterstock, © JeniFoto/Shutterstock,

© Henry Monsour, © JM Travel Photography/ Shutterstock; **Cancer,** p. 44 (clockwise from top left): © Mbbirdy/Getty Images, © Aleksanda Nakic/iStockphoto, © Florida Stock/Shutterstock, © Kaponia Aliaksei/Shutterstock, © Michael Urban/Getty Images, © Tim Graham/Getty Images, © VT750/Shutterstock, © Evgeniya Porechenskaya/Shutterstock; **Cancer,** p. 45 (clockwise from top left): © Evgeniya Porechenskaya/Shutterstock, © Gregg DeGuire/ Getty Images, © Garsya/Shutterstock, © John Greim/Getty Images, © Syda Productions/ Shutterstock, © Aleshyn Andrei/Shutterstock, © CaiaImage/Getty Images, © Stefanie Hieb/Getty Images, © Ann Haritonenko/Shutterstock; **Leo,** p. 54 (clockwise from top left): © Keystone- France/Getty Images, © Perart/ Shutterstock, © Svyatoslava Vladzimirska/Shutterstock, © Caiaimage/Robert Daly/Getty Images, © Jrroman/ iStockphoto, © Ramona Heim/Shutterstock, © Svitlana Sokolova/Shutterstock, © Raquel Maria Carbonell Pagola/Getty Images; **Leo,** p. 55 (clock- wise from top left): © Pigprox/Shutterstock, © Claudia K/Shutterstock, © Diana Indiana/ Shutterstock, © Odd Andersen/Getty images, © Ann Haritonenko/Shutterstock, © Halay Alex/ Shutterstock, © Marka/Getty images, © Diana Indiana/Shutterstock, © Kevin Mazur/Getty im- ages **Virgo,** p. 65 (clockwise from top left): © Yarygin/Shutterstock, © Colin Anderson//Getty images, © Astronaut Images/Getty images, © Wolfilser/Shutterstock, © Svyatoslava Vladzimirsk/Shutterstock, © Al Bello/Getty Images, © Ayla Altintas/EyeEm/Getty Images; **Virgo,** p. 66 (clockwise from top left): © AFP// Getty Images, © Maksim Shirkov/Shutterstock, © Photobank.ch/Shutterstock, © Mtlapcevic/ Shutterstock, © Olga Kazakova/Shutterstock, © Indiey/Shutterstock, © Henry Monsour, © Frank Bienewald/Shutterstock; **Libra,** p. 74 (clockwise from top left): © Frank Bienewald/Getty Images, © ImagesbyTrista/iStockphoto, © Bonnin Studio/ Stocksy, © Bese/Shutterstock, © Andrea Raffin/ Shutterstock, © Javi Indy/Shutterstock, © Fanelie Rosier/ iStockphoto, © Mnowicki/Shutterstock; **Libra,** p. 75 (clockwise from top left): © Valeri Potapova/Shutterstock, © CoffeeAndMilk//iStock- photo, © Bellena/Shutterstock, © Henry Monsour, © Stefano Tinti/Shutterstock, © Andrekart Photography/Shutterstock, © Nature Art/ Shutterstock, © Featureflash/Shutterstock, © Tramont Ana/Shutterstock; **Scorpio,** p. 84 (clock- wise from top left): © Henry Monsour, © Bas Meelker/Shutterstock, © Oksanka007 / Shutterstock, © Subbotina Anna /Shutterstock, © Marchello74/Shutterstock, © Kevin Mazur/ Getty Images, © Svyatoslava Vladzimirska/ Shutterstock, © Greta Gabaglio/Shutterstock; **Scorpio,** p. 85 (clockwise from top left): © VitorF/ Shutterstock, © Shurmelyova /Shutterstock, © Westend61/Getty Images, © Fotoduki/ Shutterstock, © Elaine Nadiv/Shutterstock, © Paul Matthew Photography/Shutterstock, © In

Green/Shutterstock, © Sharland/Getty Images, © Alekleks/Shutterstock, **Sagittarius,** p. 94 (clock- wise from top left): © Seb Oliver/Getty Images, © Piskunov/Getty Images, © Christopher Polk /Getty Images, © FashionStock.com/Shutterstock, © Chase Dekker Wild-Life Image/Getty Images, © Henry Monsour, © YanLev/Shutterstock, **Sagittarius,** p. 95 (clockwise from top left): © Eyes Wide Open/Getty Images, © Halay Alex/ Shutterstock, © Matteo Colombo/Getty Images, © Coka/Shutterstock, © James Devaney/Getty Images, © Brian S/Shutterstock, © Ann Haritonenko/Shutterstock, © Saichol Chandee/ Shutterstock; **Capricorn,** p. 104 (clockwise from top left): © Guenter Fischer/Getty Images, © Yulia Kitsune/Shutterstock, © Ozgurdonmaz/Getty Images, ©Chris Jackson/Getty Images, © Marsil/ Shutterstock, © Igor Demchenkov/Shutterstock, © Stuart Murdoch / EyeEm/Getty Images, © Dmitry Tsvetkov/Shutterstock; **Capricorn,** p. 105 (clockwise from top left): © Joshua Haviv// Shutterstock, © Wrangler /Shutterstock, © Catherine McGann/Getty Images, © Alice- photo/Shutterstock, © Halay Alex/Shutterstock, © Anastasiya Domnitch/Shutterstock, © Urbans/ Shutterstock, © AS Inc/Shutterstock, © Nata Sha / Shutterstock; **Aquarius,** p. 114 (clockwise from top left): © Canadastock/Shutterstock, © AbElena/Shutterstock, © Halay Alex/Shutterstock, © Ann Haritonenko/Shutterstock, © AS Inc/ Shutterstock, © PeopleImage/Getty Images, © Slava296/Shutterstock, © Jason Merritt/Getty Images; **Aquarius,** p. 115 (clockwise from top left): © Eliks/Shutterstock, © PlusONE/Shutterstock, © Erik Isakson/Getty Images, © Vladitto/ Shutterstock, © Halay Ale/Shutterstock, © Max Krasnov/Shutterstock, © Fadel Senna/Getty Images, © Piotr Stryjewsk/Getty Images; **Pisces,** p. 124 (clockwise from top left): © Trinette Reed/ Getty Images, © Kiefer Pix/Shutterstock, © Lambada/Getty Images, © Mashakotcur/ Shutterstock, © Luxora/Shutterstock, © BigLike Images/Shutterstock, © Iordani/Shutterstock, © Joe Kohen/Getty Images; **Pisces,** p. 125 (clock- wise from top left): © Lola Tsvetaeva/Shutterstock, © Conee/iStockphoto, © MJTH/Shutterstock, © Shevtsovy/Shutterstock, © Foxys forest manu- facture/iStockphoto, © Peopleimages/Getty Images, © Mervas/Shutterstock, © Kevin Mazur/ Getty Images; **Modalities** (left to right/Getty images) p. 143: © David Livingston, © Jon Kopaloff, © Ari Perilstein; p. 148: © Jason LaVeris, © Han Myung-Gu; p. 149: © Albert L. Ortega, © Light Brigade/Bauer-Griffin; p. 152: © Mindy Small, © Walter McBride; p. 153: © Albert L. Ortega, © Tristan Fewings; p. 156: © Brendon Thorne, © Frazer Harrison; p. 157: © Chance Yeh, © NBC; p. 158: © Ray Tamarra, © Fred Hayes; p. 159: © Dan MacMedan, © George Pimentel; p. 162: © James Devaney, © Jeff Kravitz; p. 163: © Jon Kopaloff, © Jason Miller; p. 166: © Barry King, © Vera Anderson; p. 167: © Michael Tran, © Kevin Winter; **Author photo:** © Naomi Nishi

HEARSTBOOKS

An Imprint of Sterling Publishing Co., Inc.
1166 Avenue of the Americas
New York, NY 10036

ISBN 978-1-61837-213-0

Distributed in Canada by Sterling Publishing Co., Inc.
% Canadian Manda Group, 664 Annette Street
Toronto, Ontario, Canada M6S 2C8
Distributed in the United Kingdom by GMC Distribution Services
Castle Place, 166 High Street, Lewes, East Sussex, England BN7 1XU

For information about custom editions, special sales, and premium and corporate purchases, please contact Sterling Special Sales at 800-805-5489 or specialsales@sterlingpublishing.com.

Manufactured in China

2 4 6 8 10 9 7 5 3 1

www.sterlingpublishing.com

Cover and interior design by Kristen Male